The Explicit Body in Performance

The Explicit Body in Performance interrogates the avant-garde precedents and theoretical terrain that combined to produce feminist performance art. Among the many artists discussed are Carolee Schneeman, Karen Finley, Ana Mendieta, Sandra Bernhard, Annie Sprinkle, Robbie McCauley, Ann Magnuson, and Spiderwoman.

Rebecca Schneider tackles topics ranging across the 'post-porn modernist movement', New Right Censorship, commodity fetishism, perspectival vision, and primitivism. Employing diverse critical theories from Benjamin to Lacan, to postcolonial and queer theory, Schneider analyzes artistic and pop cultural depictions of the explicit body in late commodity capitalism.

Complemented by extensive photographic illustrations of the performative and artistic productions of postmodern feminist practitioners, *The Explicit Body in Performance* is a fascinating exploration of how these artists have wrestled with the representational structures of desire.

Rebecca Schneider lectures at Yale University is Visiting Assistant Professor of Drama at Dartmouth College. She is a contributing editor to *The Drama Review* and has published essays in a range of performance anthologies.

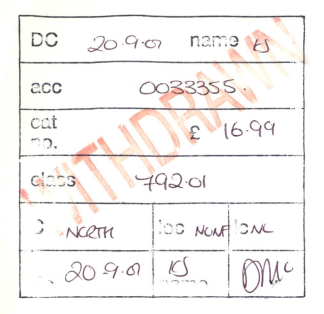

The Explicit Body in Performance

Rebecca Schneider

London and New York

First published 1997
by Routledge
11 New Fetter Lane, London EC4P 4EE

Simultaneously published in the USA and Canada
by Routledge
29 West 35th Street, New York, NY 10001

© 1997 Rebecca Schneider

Typeset in Garamond by Keystroke, Jacaranda Lodge, Wolverhampton

Printed and bound in Great Britain by Butler & Tanner, London and Frome

British Library Cataloguing in Publication Data
A catalogue record for this book is available from the British Library

Library of Congress Cataloging in Publication Data
A catalogue record for this book has been requested

ISBN 0–415–09025–3 (hbk)
ISBN 0–415–09026–1 (pbk)

for Joy, 1963

Contents

List of plates

Acknowledgments

There are many, many people who deserve my utmost gratitude. My family, my friends, my colleagues, my teachers, my students. I am particularly indebted to Richard Schechner for vision, respect, and encouragement. I am grateful to Peggy Phelan, chair of the Department of Performance Studies, New York University, for her guidance during the stages when this book was a dissertation. I am also indebted to the insight of Michael Taussig whose questions always raised more questions, providing considerable impact for the preliminary formulation of this work. Elin Diamond, Diana Taylor and Laurence Davies also deserve particular mention for unswerving collegial support. I am grateful to Carol Martin, Jose Munoz, May Joseph, and Barbara Kirschenblatt-Gimblett and also to the Faculty of Theater Studies at Yale and the Drama Department of Darmouth College; Ellen Donkin and Rhonda Blair of Hampshire College; and Jenny Spencer and Richard Burt of the University of Massachusetts. Acknowledgment goes, as well, to my students over the years at NYU, Yale, Dartmouth, and Hampshire, who sparked a great deal of my inquiry here.

Mariellen R. Sandford of *TDR* deserves acknowledgment for her consistent assistance and support in the early goings of my inquiry, as does Ann Daly. Without Mady Schutzman and Sally Charnow as compatriots in this effort, there would be no book. I also wish to thank my colleagues and friends who lended support – some earlier in the process, some later: Gabrielle Barnett, Jessica Payne, Shannon Jackson, Scott Westerfeld, Tony Speranza, Gary Maciag, Jon MacKenzie, Peter Tait, Gabrielle Cody and Bill Kavanagh. Nicole Ridgway deserves special note, as always, for her close readings of the manuscript, and for the strength of her friendship.

My editor, Talia Rodgers, cannot be thanked enough for her insight and encouragement. And her assistant, Sophie Powell, always made me feel right at home on the Internet.

Carolee Schneemann has been more than generous, making her home, her personal archives, and her friendship available to me throughout the research and writing process. Annie Sprinkle provided a sense of humor, which I hope comes through now and then in these pages. I would also like to thank Gloria Miguel, Muriel Miguel, and Lisa Mayo for their generosity of spirit, and their willingness to let me sit in on rehearsals.

My family, extended and near, have my utmost gratitude. Thanks go to my parents and AWA for equipment, fortitude, and perceptive analysis. To Laurel, Paul, Bethany, and Nathaniel Schneider, to Nina Bramhall, Cindy Davenport, and Katie-Louise Thomas for a variety of inputs and outputs during this long haul. Special thanks to Jody Scalise, and to Joe and Luke too, for love, faith, and all the rages of reciprocity. Finally, my daughter, Sarah Schneider Kavanagh, deserves my deepest thanks and love, for patience and understanding as well as for flashes of insight.

Introduction

For decades now on sunny Sundays after brunch, fur-clad uptowners and in-the-know suburbanites have clogged downtown Manhattan's West Broadway sidewalks. Eyeballing each other at galleries and grazing in expensive shops, these pomo *flaneurs* rub shoulders with black-leathered SoHo aesthetes, exchanging insignia of fashion. In 1985, a new breed of poster began to appear around and about downtown, especially near major SoHo art galleries. Strolling the avenue, a wandering eye might catch a boldfaced byline from one of these posters: ONLY FOUR COMMERCIAL GALLERIES IN NEW YORK SHOW BLACK WOMEN. ONLY ONE SHOWS MORE THAN ONE. In the late 1980s, art patrons might have stopped and thought before putting down money. As the posters gained in infamy, and were "written up" in such magazines as *Mirabella* (Carr 1992), shoppers might have inquired within – were these posters, by the Guerrilla Girls, for sale?

On one poster, a list of twenty galleries is followed by the words "THESE GALLERIES SHOW NO MORE THAN 10 PER CENT WOMEN ARTISTS OR NONE AT ALL." Other posters pose pointed questions: "DO WOMEN HAVE TO BE NAKED TO GET INTO THE MET MUSEUM?" This particular poster features a naked woman in a gorilla mask beside statistics on the Metropolitan Museum of Arts modern artists (more than 95 per cent male) and nudes (85 per cent female).

The group responsible for the posters is a feminist "gang" of artists who call themselves The Guerrilla Girls. These "girls," all working artists, appear in public wearing gorilla masks. They keep their identities secret to protect an anonymity which frees them to speak openly, without fear of reprisal, but also insures that notoriety cannot accrue to an individual career. Large and hairy, their masks have the look of generic department-store Halloween stock. While the masks render anonymity, they also render literal a certain symbolic paradigm. Not only do "gorilla" masks pun on "guerrilla" acts to create a kind of side-stepping, material translation, but the masks wield performative punch – they make explicit a social contract which has historically marked women and people of color as less evolved, more "primitive," than the implicitly higher primate, white Man. Alluding to primitivity, the gorilla masks appear to quote the racist primitivism at the heart of colonialism as well as the mimesis of all things "primitive" at the base of modern art. The conflation of the "primitive" mask with the masked identities of the female artists suggests a complex inter-relatedness between codings of race and gender, especially vis-à-vis the politics of representation and artistic authority.

Here, word play doubles as deeply serious body play, wrapped up with the ways words have played, with significant effect, upon bodies – bodies on the avenue, in the galleries, in the mirror, and framed as art. As the posters make abundantly clear, the appellations "female" or "black" are words which have historically overridden or amended the appellation "artist" when these words have been applied to the same person. Importantly, collapsing guerrilla and gorilla suggests a certain terror(ism) at the heart of hierarchical distinctions of difference, such as civilized/primitive or male/female. By collapsing the homo-phones across their own bodies in performative action, the artists render the symbolic literal. Their pun confuses the space between symbolic and literal reading, and in so doing it both plays with and questions dominant habits of comprehension. As Walter Benjamin noted in his essay "Task of the Translator," insistence on literal translation contains a "direct threat to comprehensibility" (1969:78). Rendering a word in translation (here translated across homophones) as if words were *materially* interchangeable underscores a literal versus symbolic meaning and unsettles habitual modes of sense making. Though wrapped in a laugh, Guerrilla Girls arguably provoke a threat in the form of critical inquiry into implicit structures of comprehensibility which have delineated terrains of art and validity of artists according to bodily signatures of gender and race. With all the force of literal translation, the posters, and their anonymous simian signatories, work to make those masked structures apparent.

This book is, in large part, about the explosive literality at the heart of much feminist performance art and performative actions. I have coined the phrase "explicit body" as a means of addressing the ways such work aims to explicate bodies in social relation. Interestingly, the words "explicit" and "explicate" stem from the Latin *explicare*, which means "to unfold." Unfolding the body, as if pulling back velvet curtains to expose a stage, the performance artists in this book peel back layers of signification that surround their bodies like ghosts at a grave. Peeling at signification, bringing ghosts to visibility, they are interested to expose not an originary, true, or redemptive body, but the sedimented layers of signification themselves.

A mass of orifices and appendages, details and tactile surfaces, the explicit body in representation is foremost a site of social markings, physical parts and gestural signatures of gender, race, class, age, sexuality – all of which bear ghosts of historical meaning, markings delineating social hierarchies of privilege and disprivilege. The body made explicit has become the *mise en scene* for a variety of feminist artists. I explore, here, the historical avant-garde precedents and the feminist theoretical/political terrain that combined to produce explicit body performance art, ranging from 1963 and Carolee Schneemann's *Eye/Body* to the early 1990s works of Annie Sprinkle, Karen Finley, Robbie McCauley, Ann Magnuson, Sandra Bernhard, Spiderwoman, and others. Challenging habitual modalities of vision which buttress socio-cultural assumptions about relations between subject and object, explicit body performance artists have deployed the material body to collide literal renderings against Symbolic Orders of meaning. Because the visceral, tactile body is the literal stage of this work, it is not surprising that much of the work discussed here trips across embattled boundaries between art and pornography – socio-political boundaries which this book attempts, in part, to explicate.

Researching thirty years of feminist explicit body performance from its early manifestations in the 1960s, I found a number of recurrent themes. First, much explicit body performance replays, across the body of the artist as stage, the historical drama of gender or race (and sometimes, brilliantly, gender and race). Second, these artists critically engage ways of seeing, specifically perspectivalism, which has inscribed women as given to be seen but not as given to see. Third, these artists often tug at the plumb lines marking bodies for gender, race, and class in order to expose their link with representational structures of desire in commodity capitalism. And fourth, feminist explicit body work talks back to precedent terms of avant-garde art transgression, raising questions about modernist "shock value" and the particular fascination with a "primitive," sexual, and excremental body. At base, the explicit body in much feminist work interrogates socio-cultural understandings of the "appropriate" and/or the appropriately transgressive – particularly who gets to mark what (in)appropriate where, and, who has the right to appropriate what where – keeping in mind the double meaning of the word "appropriate."

The body, explicitly presented, is of course nothing new to art practice, as I will explore in Chapter 1. But the issue of who has the right to author the explicit body in representation – or more to the point, who determines the *explication* of that body, what and how it *means* – has repeatedly been a matter of political and juridical concern. Thus the spectator who argues that prostitute/ performance artist Annie Sprinkle's quite humorous performance of porn imagery in "legit" art spaces is simply and only about the liberation of sexual exchange in the vein of "sex can be funny" or "sex can be fun" misses the deeper complexities and ironies which haunt and riddle such work. I aim to underscore and unpack the deeper complexities.

GHOST OF THE AVANT-GARDE

One of the complexities that riddles contemporary performance art is the status of transgression in art practice today. Inasmuch as postmodernity necessitates a distinction from modernity, cultural critics and postmodern theorists have made the claim that the avant-garde, and its "bad boy" hope in the political promise of transgression, died sometime in the 1960s. As the argument goes, late capitalism appropriates, incorporates, and consumes transgression into fashionable chic at such a rapid pace that the subversive impact of transgression has become impossible. As Philip Auslander put it after Hal Foster, there are no longer any cultural limits to transgress in the "seemingly limitless horizon of multinational capitalism" (1987:23; Foster 1985a:153). To meet the challenge of voracious appropriation, Foster articulated a hope in a postmodernism of "resistance" versus "transgression," a political art aimed not at busting outside of the tabooed bounds of normative culture, but rather aimed at questioning the bases and apparatus of normativity from within. Though Foster's analysis of the limits of transgression is important and compelling, I nevertheless find it telling (as have many before me) that the avant-garde and the option of "shock" that it championed should die just as women, artists of color, and gay and lesbian artists began to make critically incisive political art under their own gender-, race-, and preference-marked banners.

Basically, there is cause for suspicion. Hasn't it historically been the case that boys are given to transgress while girls are meant to resist? That boys are expected to transgress re-marks the tradition of bad-boy art as always already normative, and rewrites the modernist avant-garde as less transgressive than structurally institutional – which is part of Foster's point. But abandoning transgression might not be the issue so much as critically confronting the historical licensing of transgression in art practice. When women as active agents picked up the avant-garde tradition of transgressive shock, as they began to do with a certain *en masse* fervor in the 1960s, the terms of transgression necessarily shifted. Female transgression presented a structural impossibility – almost a double shock. After all, men transgress, women resist. Does the structural taboo on "transgressive femininity" (Leslie Jones 1992–3) relate in any way to the proclamation that transgression is necessarily failed, impossible, defunct – to the point of shutting down the avant-garde among generally male postmodern theorists who strive to re-mark their own present tactics as "resistant?"

At the very least, to suggest that nothing shocks anymore is certainly curious in an age of conservative right-wing anxiety over the "appropriate" cultural limits of aesthetic expression. Still, looked at from another angle, the abandonment of the avant-garde and the championing of "resistance" takes on an important political dimension. Conservatives are arguably nostalgic for modernist belief in the power of transgression, since transgression, or the inappropriate, certainly props the appropriate. If nothing can be considered transgressive, then nothing can be considered (in)appropriate. In their nostalgia for the (in)appropriate, the right wing make strange bedfellows with feminist, gay, and lesbian artists whom they see as providing contemporary transgression (see Phelan 1990, 1991). Looked at in this light, the politicized postmodern art world's claim that all transgression is defunct is in itself transgressive, disallowing the "transgression" upon which right wing agendas depend. And yet the timing of this claim is suspiciously gender-, race-, and preference-marked, coming at a moment when the terms of transgression, the agents of transgressive art, had radically shifted. The terrain is tangled indeed.

In an exploration of this tangle between avant-gardism and postmodernism, I look closely at one of the hot-spots of modernist shock in order to explore its postmodern transmogrifications. In Chapter 5 I take up the issue of "primitivism" in the modernist avant-garde, both as nostalgic site of loss and confrontational site of scandal. Citing the modernist imbrications of race and sex that combined in the cultural formulation of the "primitive," I explore the conflation of primitivism with bodily functions such as sex and excretion in the modernist avant-garde's appropriation of the primitive for shock value. It is my contention that conflations of "savagery" with physicality ghost contemporary explicit body works. But unlike the use of primitivism and shock in the modernist avant-garde, in contemporary feminist work it is the primitivized, or sexualized herself who (re)performs her primitivization. Thus feminist "savagery" is linked with, but distinct from, modernist bad-boy avant-gardes who sought to *employ* primitivity, to rediscover or cite savagery in their transgressive acts. It is possible to argue that a feminist explicit body artist cannot *employ* primitivism, as her body itself has been linked to the lure/threat of primitivity. She is already primitive, already transgressive. Given this, the primitivized herself deploys or re-plays her primitivization back across her body in a kind of double take, an effort to expose the cultural foundations of shock. As such, her work raises interesting questions about the contemporary social battle over the rights to transgression itself.

DESIRE AND THE SATIATE BODY

In much feminist explicit body performance art we can find, with the tools of feminist theory, an effort to make apparent the link between ways of seeing the body and ways of structuring desire according to the logic of commodity capitalism. This link is at the heart of this book. The image of the female body has, throughout the twentieth century, served as a symbol of desire in general. That desire might masquerade as "male," but it has recently been explored in its secret service, that is, its service to the general circulation of commodities in a dreamscape upon which late capitalism so intrinsically depends (see Irigaray 1985a:184; McClintock 1995:225). Desire is bought into, just as any tangible object is bought. Like a commodity, desire is produced. And like the commodities it facilitates, desire bears a secret akin to Marx's secret of commodities. The secret of circulating, insatiable desire is the labor that goes into its construction. Desire must appear as unmarked, as "human nature." But, like commodities themselves, it is nature designed, packaged, and sold – marketed, outfitted, and set upon a runway of dreams where it is also marked for gender as if by some great accident of God: desire is masculinized; the desired, feminized.

The ways in which desire in late capitalism is instituted and circulated as insatiable, promoting infinite accumulation, has placed the emblematic female body in a particular relation to impossibility – always just beyond reach, symbolizing that which can never quite be acquired, even for those possessing a body marked female. I have worked in these pages to link the emblematic inaccessibility of the woman-as-commodity-mascot with the legacies of perspectival ways of seeing which have erected the female body as Prime Signifier of the Vanishing Point – Dominatrix *and* Madonna of Loss. This effort was inspired by what appears in so much explicit body art as a ribald refusal to vanish, an excess linked to disruptions of normative "appropriate" vision. Such disruptions have marked these artists' works as politically volatile – threatening, perhaps, to a comprehensibility structured, like our society, around the insatiability of commodity exchange.

In general, I am fascinated by the ubiquitous and nostalgic paradigms of loss which riddle a society devoted to accumulation. Western civilization is in thrall to a "Real" we are acculturated to accept as forever beyond our grasp – keeping us reaching, keeping us spending. Platonic shadowscapes of illusion on cave walls have hardly disappeared. We still grasp for a truer reality beyond or behind the scenes as Plato's cave shadows become the flicker of representation across ad-scapes and TV screens. In my own strivings for some "true-real" I attempt to be more materialist than idealist, but I am hinged to a contradiction. I am drawn to the paradox, explicated by feminist theory, that the female body in representation has emblematized *both* the obsessive terrain of representational fantasy *and*, as empress/impress of the vanishing point, that which escapes or is beyond the representational field (de Lauretis 1987). Signifying desire, "she" is the obsessive emblem of representational fantasy – we see her body everywhere, selling a dream of a future real to a present posited always as "lack." Yet even as she is ubiquitously given to be seen, she simultaneously signifies a flirtatious impossibility of access, a paradoxical "reality" only of dream, of shadow, always beyond reach, always already lost.

Insatiable desire and paradigmatic lack are performative: the signs of desire and the drive of loss depend on bodies in exigency. Dramas of loss and insatiable desire are scripted across bodies, as images of men and women prop object relations driving commodity dreamscapes. Much explicit body performance art work aims to make explicit, to render literal, the symbolic foundations by which the thrall of loss and insatiability is exhibited in the space of the particular – across particular bodies engendered in social relation. The aim is not necessarily to erect a "True Woman," a "Real Woman," as much as to explicate the historical service of bodies to commodity dreamscapes and to wrestle with the effects of that service.

To render the symbolic literal is to disrupt and make apparent the fetishistic prerogatives of the symbol by which a thing, such as a body or a word, stands by convention for something else. To render literal is to collapse symbolic space, "leaving no room for the signified" (Kristeva 1986:214). It is to pose, borrowing Benjamin again and noting his allegiance to Bertolt Brecht, a "direct threat" to the naturalized social drama of "comprehensibility." To render literal is also to interrogate the notion that relations between sign and signified are fundamentally arbitrary. Denying the arbitrary, a notion at the very base of modernist and capitalist sensibilities of abstraction and meaning, invites a kind of hysteria, or a psychosis of the overly real – a psychosis historically linked to women.

In exploring the explicit body in performance I look at ways in which perspectival vision and commodity fetishism are played back across *the body as stage*. I argue for a critical (and ironically distantiated) "take" on the very distance between sign and signified, like the distance between viewer and viewed, in normative habits of comprehension. The performers in this study use their bodies as the stages across which they re-enact social dramas and traumas which have arbitrated cultural differentiations between truth and illusion, reality and dream, fact and fantasy, natural and unnatural, essential and constructed. The performers make apparent the ways in which bodies are stages for social theatrics, propping hosts of cultural assumptions, and their works suggest that these social theatrics might be differently scripted, differently dramatized, differently real-ized. Social dramas of foundational loss and dances of insatiable desire smack against explicitly literal bodily renderings which suggest the satiate and finite. Indeed, rendered literal, symbolic constructs can become volatile, and full of critical potential. As if enacting Barbara Kruger's art slogan "Your Gaze Hits the Side of My Face," much explicit body performance work suggests a confrontational satiability (both of pleasure and pain), and a refusal of the logic of infinite loss.

TWISTING THE MAP

I am concerned here not only with how, but perhaps more significantly with *why* some feminist performers choose to make the explicit body the means to their cultural criticism. Thus a significant amount of feminist and cultural critical theory is employed in exegesis, making my exploration of explicit body performance as deeply theoretical and discursive as it is descriptive. Indeed, in some ways this book takes a convoluted route, following the logic of the twister, in an effort to arrive at itself. A number of overlapping, even entangled angles combine to argue against each other.

I begin with "Binary terror and the explicit body." In this chapter I look at the particular link between commodities and women evident in the modernist art fascination with prostitution. Issues of boundary crossing between "porn" and "art" arise as the modernist thrall to the prostitute is replayed across the bodies of postmodern performance artists. In Chapter 2, "Logic of the twister, eye of the storm," I explore the structural impossibility of women as "real" within the representational premises of commodity capitalism – an impossibility recently championed by queer theory as potentially empowering. In these two chapters I consider works by Veronica Vera, Carolee Schneemann, Shigeko Kubota, Lynda Benglis, and Annie Sprinkle.

In Chapter 3, "Permission to see," I again explore Schneemann's work to unpack the legacies of visual perspectivalism relative to the "scene" of the body made explicit in contemporary feminist performance. Habits of perspectival vision have emblematically placed the female body at the vanishing point even as the primary scene or landscape of representation is feminized. Taking issue with those who claim that the twentieth century has seen the demise of perspectival ways of seeing, I argue that certain tenets of perspectival vision, particularly the removed, invisible viewer, are still very much at play even in so-called antiocular economies of vision. Throughout the first three chapters I suggest that explicit body performers employ second sight/site, a doubled vision, as they "look back" at visual perspective. Importantly, this looking back occurs both from the inside out and from the "space off" – that which is not admitted to the field of vision – simultaneously.

In "The secret's eye," Chapter 4, I work to link the legacy of perspectival vision's feminized vanishing point to commodity culture's emblematic placement of the female body as site and sign of insatiable desire. Feminist performance art interrogates the terms of insatiable desire by suggesting an in-your-face literality, a radical satiability that thwarts the consumptive mantra of infinite desire. Such works invite complicit, satiable reciprocity between viewer and viewed rather than the traditional perspectival one-way-street relationship by which masculinized producers are delineated from feminized consumers, just as the masculinized viewer is dislocated from the feminized viewed. Taking up the issue of the secret of commodities, and struggling to link that secret to economies of vision, I wrestle with the notion of a "secret's eye" and explore works by Karen Finley, Ann Magnuson, Sandra Bernhard and, again, Annie Sprinkle.

Chapter 5, "After us the savage goddess," wrestles with the historical Euro-American avant-garde which provides a complex backdrop for contemporary feminist postmodern performance practice. In this chapter I chart a troubled lineage from Jarry, to Dada, to Surrealism, to find contemporary feminist explicit body art in strained relationship to precedent. The vehicle for the route I take, and the leaps I make, is the modernist shock-property of the raced and gendered body marked "savage" in modernist paradigms of primitivism. It is extremely important to note, however, that many of the white artists in this study do not examine their whiteness in relation to the primitivity and sexuality they explicate – they do not make race explicit in their works. The imbrications of sex and race that are the legacies of modernist "shock" often remain implicit. While the female body's service to dreamscapes of symbolic phallic privilege are made explicit, and while the "savagery" of her transgressions reverberates with avant-garde confrontative primitivism, the whiteness of that body (in works by white artists) is often un(re)marked. It is my hope that reading the history of racially and sexually marked primitivism as ghosting the scene of explicit body work can provide a starting place for deeper analysis.

In Chapter 6, then, "Seeing the big show," I turn to a group of performers who do make whiteness visible relative to legacies of primitivism. Spiderwoman, a Native American performance troupe, explicates modernist primitivism and commodity fetishism across their literal bodies, replaying white fetishization of natives by playing whites playing natives. Spiderwoman does not deal with explicit sexuality as often as they deal with the legacies of primitivism in their work, in part because, as Richard Dyer notes, it is *white* women who have been positioned as the "apotheosis of desirability, all that a man could want, yet nothing that can be had, nor anything that a woman can be" (1988:64). Yet, in replaying white women across their own bodies (playing whites playing natives), they bring the centrality of race in that apotheosis to visibility. Doing battle with the cultural dictates of visibility and desire is a racially marked struggle as much as it is a sexually marked struggle. Robbie McCauley, an African American performance artist whose work I explore at the end of this chapter, drives this point home with raging clarity.

That the performers in this study who make primitivism most explicit are persons of color is not incidental. Dyer has noted the present structural impossibility by which white people only begin to "see whiteness where its difference from blackness is inescapable and at issue" (1988:46). This is a structural impossibility born of the blindspots surrounding social privilege. As many feminists of color have noted, it may be easier for white feminists to acknowledge their gender-marked disprivilege than to complicate their work by simultaneously doing battle with their race-marked privilege. While ramifications of class often come into the mix, especially in terms of sex work or domestic labor, the racialized landscapes of class and gender are too often disregarded. To overcome Dyer's structural impossibility, it is incumbent on white feminist performers to strive to make whiteness explicitly visible in their work, or better, to make it structural invisibility visible. Plays such as Caryl Churchill's *Cloud Nine* and Marquerite Duras's *India Song*, and performance pieces such as Sandra Bernhard's *Without You I'm Nothing* and Shannon Jackson's *White Noises* (1996), begin to accomplish this task. However, many of the explicit body artists explored in this book leave whiteness in the realm of the implicit. Given the historical imbrications of primitivism with the terrain of bodily function, the ways in which Spiderwoman, McCauley, and Bernhard make primitivism and its complicated bases in racial appropriation and feminization explicit across their bodies as stage become especially important to this book.

It remains to be noted that the critical analysis conducted here is my own performance. In the epilog of this book, "Returning from the dead," I return to a spot I could never have left – myself as viewer, complicit in an exchange across the bodies I read as "explicit." A theorist is generally granted status as disembodied or, in the trope of perspectival vision, distanced from that which she investigates, speaking for that which she reads. As I "perform" the analyses in this book, I do not intend to suggest that my interpretations here are the artists' own, nor even that my interpretations might fit these artists' intentions. As I hope my occasional engagements in personal narrative in these pages will illustrate, audience members are active participants in the reciprocity or complicity that is performative exchange – just as readers are active participants in text. As an audience member, then, I was part of the explicit body art I observed, implicated in the scenes I surveyed. For those performances I did not attend (those predating 1986), I am implicated in the performative scene of their documentation – historian as audience member once or twice removed. Meaning is a social affair, a matter of exchange, and – in line with the political purpose of feminist criticism – "meaning" can be a matter of change.

I once wrote that I wanted to pursue this project as if a tiger were at my tail. Little did I know that this tiger, with all its connotations of primitivity and wildness, would be at my back for so many years, through so many performances, and in the midst of so much productive inquiry in feminist theory. I initially wrote of the tiger because I wanted to preserve the urgency I felt in so much of the explicit body performance I witnessed, and the urgency I felt in myself as witness. I did not realize the degree to which this project would be an effort to turn to face the mythic beast of my own fears to, as Audre Lorde has written, "see whose face it wears" (1981b:101). This book is about the effort of turning, with the logic of the twister. But the ultimate aim of such turning is not to arrive, as T.S. Eliot hoped, to "know [ourselves] for the first time," but to keep on turning and turning and turning again, to take, always, a second look.

The performances I write about here are feminist, and the work I produce here is feminist, in so far as we can understand that embattled term to mean work with an agenda to provoke recognition of the historical, cultural, social, and political situation of those marked "woman." The terrain of my inquiry is representation because the battlefield of identity is inextricably wrapped up in the histories of the ways identities have been marked, imaged, reproduced in the realm of cultural imagery. Thus, it should be noted from the outset that when I write about women I am not writing about some essentialized category transcendent of history, transcendent of representation. Rather, I am writing about women as born of and entangled in history, entangled in representation. So too when I write about race, I am most often writing about "primitivism," or the historical legacy of the ways people of color have been marked as less advanced, less civilized, than men of European descent. I am writing about "race" as entangled in a cultural binary of "black/white" – a binary that is, like the delimiting and heterosexist binary of "men/women," absurd given the spectrum of color, the spectrum of sexualities, and the spectrum of class distinctions such a binary often serves to disavow. Thus, it can be argued that I am not writing about race at all, or women at all, but am in fact writing about those categories as haunting – the historical legacies of bodily markings as social insignia which ghost and riddle the living, those of us still bearing bodies, still trying to turn.

1 Binary terror and the body made explicit

"My body is a temple."

The declaration rings of 1960s and 1970s cultural feminist attempts to resurrect the Goddess and celebrate female biology. But in 1989 "My body is a temple" appeared in large bold type on a promo flyer featuring a photograph of a nude black man performing oral sex with Veronica Vera, a white "porn queen" who had recently become a "performance artist." In Plate 1.1 we see the man's broad and muscular backside, his head bent to his task. With her black-lace corseted front to the camera, Vera's is the only face we see, but her expression is so stock, so standard, that it is only readable relative to the iconic lexicon of pornography. It is the stock porn-pleasure face, the semi-comatose, open-mouthed, lax-tongued expression signifying "X-rated." Nothing out of the porn-ordinary at all. Yet, despite the stock quality of the pose, Vera's promotion was not conventional porn promotion.

The photograph, titled *Marty and Veronica*, is a 1982 Robert Mapplethorpe. Vera's use of the photo in her 1989 promo flier made the most of the Helms/Mapplethorpe funding controversy exploding in the art world at the end of the 1980s.[1] A new label heralded the not-so-tongue-in-cheek politics of the porn Vera was wielding, and that label was the three-letter word "art," giving a twist of up-scale validity to the four-letter "porn." Avant-garde art venues began presenting work such as Vera's in the mid-1980s, among them Franklin Furnace Gallery, The Kitchen, and the New Museum in Manhattan (Fuchs 1989). At the same time that the appellation "art" appeared to bequeath "porn" a dubious validity, the outright and blatant quoting of porn in the art space threatened the tenets of that very validity – a project entirely in keeping with modernist avant-garde anti-art agendas spanning the twentieth century. Discretionary boundaries defining supposedly discrete centers – porn and art – were laid on top of each other, resulting in an interrogation not only of form and content, but of function and frame. In much of this work – especially work wielding the label "feminist" – it is the pornographized object, the woman in front of the camera, who is reincarnated as artist.

Since the early 1960s women have been involved in performance art and have worked to "liberate" the body marked female from the confines of patriarchal delimitation. In the later 1980s and early 1990s, the clash of the rubrics "porn"

Plate 1.1 Robert Mapplethorpe, 1982, *Marty and Veronica* with Veronica Vera.
© 1982 The Estate of Robert Mapplethorpe.

and "art" manipulated by artists such as Vera, Scarlot O, Carol Leigh (a.k.a. Scarlot Harlot), and Annie Sprinkle would complicate the already embattled debates about the terms of that liberation.[2] One of the earliest instances of porn artists working in art spaces was a "feminist" exploration sponsored by Franklin Furnace Gallery in January 1984 titled *Deep Inside Porn Stars*. The project was presented as the culminating performance in a month-long exhibit and performance series titled "The Second Coming," organized by the woman's art collective Carnival Knowledge. *Deep Inside Porn Stars* was advertised as a show in which porn stars would recreate on stage "what goes on at the on-going support group meetings between seven celebrated sex stars." Changing clothes in the course of their re-enactment, the seven stars transformed "from glamour girls to 'regular girls'" (Sprinkle 1991:102–3). The terms of this porn/art exchange were clearly outlined in the Furnace program notes. Sprinkle and Gloria Leonard conceived the idea and presented the show as "a unique opportunity to be aligned with other feminist artists, usually considered arch-adversaries of the adult entertainment movement." For their part, Furnace published the statement: "We welcome this moment when women, regardless of calling, can respectfully stand together."

Common to the flavor of this exchange was the statement made by Carol Leigh: "I'm not ashamed. I'm proud. I'm proud . . . that I'm not ashamed" (Delacoste and Alexander 1987:182). This early feminist collaboration across the porn and art divide was, in essence, a kind of consciousness-raising effort, reminiscent of late 1960s consciousness-raising groups which were extremely influential, as Moira Roth has argued, in the development of early feminist performance art in general (1983:16–17). But within five years, much porn/art performance exchange would abandon neat explanations and careful distinctions between "regular" and "glamour" girls, and even, as in Sprinkle's 1991 video *Linda Les and Annie: The First Female-to-Male Transsexual Love Story*, distinctions delimiting "girl" at all.

Works at the boundaries of porn and art raised, anew, old questions about the social functions masked by the implicit "high" of fundable art and "low" of porn, questions which simultaneously interrogated the social functions of sexual economies such as gender, and in Vera's particular flyer, race. In the later 1980s, such questions became increasingly complex and lost the careful tone of *Deep Inside Porn Stars*. In the example of Vera's use of *Marty and Veronica*, we read that Vera's body is a temple, a sacred place, yet clearly the iconography of that sacrality is the iconography of pornography, socially marked as sacrilegious, base, and profane. Thus, to the degree that the artist's object – her own body – fits the stock porn format, or works within the standard lexicon of porn significances, sacrality doubles as its own social underbelly, the realm of the base, the familiar, standardized, and class-marked taboo of porn.

Vivian Patraka has written of the terror unleashed in the collapse of binary distinctions – or "binary terror" as she calls it (1992:163). The terror that accompanies the dissolution of a binary habit of sense-making and self-fashioning is directly proportionate to the social safety insured in the maintenance of such apparatus of sense. The rigidity of our social binaries – male/female, white/black, civilized/primitive, art/porn – are sacred to our Western cultural ways of knowing, and theorists have long pointed to the necessity of interrogating such foundational distinctions to discover precisely how they bolster the social network as a whole, precisely what they uphold and what they exclude. Indeed, the interrogation of binaries – the "forcefield" of antinomies between subject and object[3] – is arguably the general project of dialectical materialism, especially of the Frankfurt School variety. Interrogation of dialectical distinctions for the purposes of understanding social networks is a method of inquiry linked to the modernist avant-garde methodological collapse of such distinctions, or strategic binary explosion, more in the vein of theorists of the French Collège de Sociologie. Collège founder Georges Bataille, whose work, as well as that of the Frankfurt School's Walter Benjamin, surface repeatedly in this study, was fascinated with binary terror. Interested in the combustive moment of violent interaction that occurs when "two necessary and incompatible positions impossibly meet," Bataille did not see a transformation or resolution of the socially matrixed forcefield of dialectics, nor, unlike contemporary feminists, was he intent on crafting political change (Stoekl 1985:xxiii). But Bataille's combustion of binaries ignited insight born of terror, like the insight which for Benjamin "flashes up in a moment of danger" exposing the deeper nervous net-workings of our social dialectics (Benjamin 1969:225). Such moments of danger were sought by Antonin Artaud as well, and similarly provoked by binary explosion, specifically the collapse of socially coded distinctions between mind and matter.[4] The danger inherent in binary explosion – the fear unleashed in close interrogation of our distinctions – is manipulated with political purpose in contemporary feminist performative interrogations of social symbolic constructs made explicit across literal bodies.

Binary terror is provoked when the word "art" is flashed over the image "porn." In fact, a host of distinctions is threatened, as if linked to one another in a circle of dominoes making up the Symbolic Order. Most obvious is the distinction between form and content – a distinction questioned throughout Mapple-thorpe's oeuvre. Unpacking that distinction in the case of *Marty and Veronica/My Body is a Temple*, the obvious question arises as to whether the formal mastery of Mapplethorpe's photography allows a viewer to ignore the blatant confrontation of its contents. The contents of the Vera/"Marty"/Mapplethorpe collaboration confront the category of art precisely because they make absolutely no deviation from porn standard. To admit that Mapplethorpe's content itself is in any way aesthetic would be to admit pornography, lock, stock and barrel, into the art museum. But, does privileging the formal aspects of Mapplethorpe's photogra-phy allow us to dismiss the contents together with their explicit confrontation? Can we separate form from content here, when the blatancy of Mapplethorpe's content is so obviously integral to his manipulation, indeed his interrogation, of form?

The argument that Mapplethorpe was a master of classical form won Dennis Barrie his acquittal when on trial for obscenity after mounting Mapplethorpe's *Perfect Moment* exhibition at his Cincinnati gallery in 1990. In effect, the court found that Mapplethorpe's mastery of formal properties – and importantly the symmetry of *classical* formal properties – excused, even eclipsed, the supposed obscene confrontation of his contents (Phelan 1993:45–7). Yet the necessity of a "decision" regarding the dialectical tension between form and content makes Mapplethorpe's manipulation of this dialectic apparent. That Mapplethorpe's work had to be "decided" lends credence to the notion that framing itself is ultimately that which denotes artistic value, a notion that dates back at least to Duchamp, and that framing is less an aesthetic concern than a social, political, and ultimately legal concern. Any image framed in an art museum or an art history textbook is "decided" art, historically buttressed by the language of form *over* content, while the same image appearing as a fold-out in *Bazoombas* or *Hot Pussy* is, by virtue of the content-oriented venue, porn. Thus it is not the contents within the frames but the decided nature of the frames themselves that "artify" or "pornographize." The apparent transgression of venue relative to content was precisely what caused the general Mapplethorpe uproar in the first place. The Western cultural tradition of ascendancy of form over content was reinscribed in a decision which, ironically, both instituted and eclipsed porn content within an art frame.

As Barrie's case had to be decided relative to appropriateness of venue, it was the critical art commentary that could be extracted from Mapplethorpe's work in formalist art historical banter that ultimately decided his case in the direction of "art." Antecedent to appropriate framing, then, is the application of art historical commentary. It might follow from this that the application of art historical commentary provides a frame around the frame, as it were, and that such commentary is where art has always and only existed, and, further, that the process of decision-making relative to the social sanctioning of art has been an arena for broader social, political, and legal commentary upon the socially, culturally, and politically appropriate.[5]

The Vera/Mapplethorpe piece and the collapse of the space between porn and art which their collaboration invites provokes Patraka's notion of binary terror – a terror that results in the necessity of "decision." In Mapplethorpe's picture and in Vera's modeling for and then re-framing of that picture within a doubled and/or collapsed context of porn *and* art, the classical symmetry of Mapplethorpe's formal arrangement interacts with the unruly content of Vera's porn-standard – that standard itself a matter of symbolic form (the black teddy and high heels, the porn pose, the seamed stockings, and lax-mouth expression). Indeed, as Barrie's case exemplifies, Mapplethorpe's classical symmetry of form beckons a viewer to place his photograph alongside other "formally correct" canonical entries across the history of Western art. And yet it is this very placing beside that becomes confrontative precisely because Mapplethorpe's content, rife with contemporary taboos of class, race, and subcultural references, can be seen to comment on social and political histories eclipsed from formalist approaches to art.

Mapplethorpe's classical formality creates a deliberate ghosting – his work quotes and thus is ghosted by art-canonical precedent of classical form. But the content, too, can be said to be ghosted, and not only by the lexicon of formal porn imagery. When placed within the formalized trajectory of the art canon, the explicitly "inappropriate" contents can be read relative to historically "appropriate" contents, raising provocative questions. Looking to art-canonical precedence, Vera's explicit reference to herself as a templed goddess places her in company with other holy women enshrined in art. Some of them are the high holy prostitutes of modernism, from Olympia to Nana. As in such modernist works, the obvious and even clichéd transgression of the space between whore and virgin, low and high, is in full swing.

In the border crossing between whore and virgin in *My Body is a Temple*, however, Vera's porn-specific body works less simply to transgress a high ideal with low content than to interrogate the formal terms of the distinction between high and low – terms indelibly linked to the explicitly marked body in formalized social distinctions between the appropriate and inappropriate.[6] That is, it is possible to "read" Mapplethorpe's photo of *Marty and Veronica* as an exposition of the tension between the appropriate and inappropriate as explicitly marked by race, gender, and class. In the photograph, it is not the black man's penis (that mytho-cultural locus of white male fear and envy) that prompts the white woman's mimesis of pleasure[7] – it is, rather, his equally invisible tongue. Yet Vera's lax-mouthed expression seems to suggest that his unseen tongue is working – dare we read *speaking*? Consider aesthetic precedence: With the aesthetic distance and supposed disinterestedness afforded the symbol, the white dove stand-in for the Holy Father repeatedly penetrates and impregnates the Virgin Mother through her unsuspecting *ear* in paintings canonized in the halls of art museums around the Western world. In Vera's "art," however, a black man speaks into the cunt of the consenting prostitute/artist/ model – not in the same frame, please! Not beside each other, please! Maintaining the contexts of art and porn as separate and distinct categories can keep the force of their relationship under-cover, discrete. However, when porn imagery bleeds out of its social sanctioning as appropriate underground, into the "light-of-day" of art, the content of its formalized taboos (especially as they stick to the standardized lexical imagery of the sex industry) has the potential to become incendiary social commentary. Such works are arguably less invested in transgression for transgression's sake than in explication of the terms of transgression as they "talk back" to the formal apparatus of sacrality, unveiling secrets in aesthetic symbolism by literalizing that which such symbolism excludes, secret(e)ing that which such symbolism secrets. This literalization, manipulated most often across the explicit body, triggers issues of the state, the family, gender, and race.

Art contexts have traditionally been considered the domain of symbolic form and thus afforded an aesthetic distance of "disinterestedness." Pornography threatens the myth of disinterestedness, flooding the field with a ribald literality marked by porn's immediate and "interested" aim toward sexual or visceral effect. In the tangle of issues implied in works which challenge art with porn, the collapse of the symbolic into the literal, and the literal into the symbolic, is fundamental. This collapse doubles as the collapse of obscenity into sacrality and sacrality into obscenity, which provokes, in turn, a host of subsequent binary terrors, making apparent the depth of Helmsian anxiety over policing the social pact which marks porn porn and art art.

Coming out of the porn industry, or "coming out" as porn queens in art spaces, Veronica Vera and Annie Sprinkle call themselves post-porn modernists. Vera and Sprinkle cross from porn into art. In 1985 Sprinkle appeared as a porn queen in *The Prometheus Project*, a "legit" avant-garde theater piece directed by Richard Schechner at the Performing Garage in Manhattan, an avant-garde venue Schechner founded in the 1960s. She appeared as a "show within a show," as well as the character Io, doing one of the show-and-tell acts she performed regularly on 42nd Street – to the consternation of several art-world critics (Rabkin *et al.* 1986; see also Fuchs 1989:42–7). Still, in this work, Sprinkle was appearing under the validating authorship of the art-established Schechner, a fact that would change when her one-woman show, *Post Porn Modernism* moved from the Harmony Club to the Kitchen in 1988.

As Sprinkle and Vera and others crossed from porn to art, several women crossed from the art and performance side of the tracks into the porn world, toting their "artist" identities with them. In September 1992 performance artist/TV personality Sandra Bernhard appeared as a bunny for *Playboy*. Bernhard's images appeared virtually without deviation from bunny standard – she was naked, her white skin painted in gold as if she belonged in Fort Knox, attended by a bevy of bunnies, stroked by macho men, and so on. Nevertheless, the cynical irony that attends Bernhard's persona and her identity as an artist invited (whether it was achieved or not) an alternative reading to her bunnydom along the lines of "the joke's on you." In the late 1980s Linda Montano, trained at San Francisco Art Institute, crossed from art to porn with the same sense of escapade she employed in crossing from "art" to "life" in the 1970s (see Montano 1981). In 1987, with the help of Sprinkle and Vera, Montano was transformed from an artist and ex-nun into a "pin-up girl" at Montano's "Summer Saint Camp" as part of her Seven Years of Living Art project (see Plate 1.2). Montano published images and text on her new art/porn boundary crossing in a "legit" publication, appearing as a porn queen dubbed "Mother Superior" in *The Drama Review* (Montano 1989). Similarly, Ann Magnuson, a performance artist and character on the ABC series *Anything But Love*, published her picture as a pin-up girl even as she was starring in her one-woman show *You Could Be Home Now* at New York's Public Theater in October 1992. Magnuson appeared as a pin up in the trendy *Paper Magazine*, "New York's Only Guide With Style," under the heading "The Revenge of the Vargas Pinup Girl," (Plate 1.3) redoubling on Madonna's pop/porn boundary confusion with the joke: "I have a Sex Book, too."

From Sprinkle to Magnuson, Vera to Montano – from both sides of the art/porn divide – such artists can be said to perform their work upon the body as stage. These artists wield identity politics as a manipulable *mise en scène* of physical properties in a kind of visceral cultural analysis that, riddled with irony, often hits in the troubled space between send-up humor and searing critique. But the issues raised by interrogating the boundaries of art and porn are not separate from more general "body issues" faced by women artists not overtly involved in, or not explicitly quoting, the sex industry. Whether porn icon-ography is invoked in women's work or not, any overt manipulation of the gendered/colored/classed body against dominant codes delimiting those bodies raises the issue of the social regulation of the appropriate and the inappropriate. Arguably, any body bearing female markings is automatically shadowed by the history of that body's signification, its delimitation as a signifier of sexuality – either explicitly (literally) in porn, or implicitly (symbolically) in art and popular representation.

The broadly based sexualization of the female form is perhaps most blatantly illustrated across the oeuvre of photographer Cindy Sherman. Sherman's relent-lessly failed attempts to find and quote across her own body an image of white

Plate 1.2 Linda Montano as sex-goddess/saint. This is a page from the scrapbook "Our Week at Sister Rosita's Summer Saint Camp" as it appeared on the cover of *The Drama Review* 33, no. 1, 1989. Photo by Jennifer Blick.

woman from popular and art iconography that does not evoke a cultural narrative of "femininity" illustrates, often painfully, the structural complicities between cultural understandings of "white womanhood" and ideologies of vision in representation.[8] In her early work, Sherman photographed herself – the artist – in familiar poses and scenes marked "female," directly quoting film stills. In her later work, Sherman's "take" on this popular imagery becomes progressively more disturbing and, in her 1992 "Sex Pictures" (Sherman 1993), explicitly illustrative of the tenuous boundary between art and pornography.

The term "explicit body" aims at foregrounding some of the issues inherent in crossing tracks of cultural distinctions, such as those between art and porn, but also those between male and female, black and white, or subject and object. Binary terrorism – or strategic implosion of binaried distinctions – impacts "the body" directly as it occurs in the fraught space between subject and object that

Plate 1.3 Ann Magnuson, *The Revenge of the Vargas Pinup Girl*, as it appeared in *Paper Magazine*, October 1992, with one modification. There were no pasties in *Paper Magazine*. Magnuson regretted the lack of pasties and asked that they be applied for any subsequent publication. Photo by Len Prince.

demarcates one body from another. Obviously, race is *not* a matter of black and white, but includes a vast spectrum not only of colors but of complex ethnicities and cultural traditions. So, too, men and women come in a panoply of preferences, experiences, and even bodily markings which threaten a strict understanding of the binary division when examined in particular. Nevertheless, we live with a dominant culture which organizes race and gender by binaried "appropriates." Binary terrorism assaults the generalizations of such symbolic constructs by privileging the cacophony inherent in unruly particulars. Social symbolism organizes bodies by markings, relegating them male body, female body, colored body, white body, and so on, and the weight of historical social significances ascribed to bodily markings has literal impact upon *particular* bodies bearing those marks. Making any body explicit *as socially marked*, and foregrounding the historical, political, cultural, and economic issues involved in its marking, is a strategy at the base of many contemporary feminist explicit body works. Manipulating the body itself as *mise en scène*, such artists make *their own bodies* explicit as the stage, canvas, or screen across which social agendas of privilege and disprivilege have been manipulated.

That feminist performance artists use the explicit body as strategy is not to say that the body explicitly depicted is anything new to art history. Scratching even lightly at the surface of distinctions between art and porn reveals countless examples of physical explicitness and seemingly obscene content in canonically "decided" art (see Finch 1992). Bodily parts have been displayed for millennia in the art canon as well as in avant-garde provocation. The distinction between "art" and "pornography" at the Greco-Roman roots of Western civilization is nonexistent. Even after the repressive triumph of Christianity in the Middle Ages, explicitly sexual physicality found expression as art. Indeed, as Lynn Hunt notes in *The Invention of Pornography: Obscenity and the Origins of Modernity*, pornography did not constitute a wholly separate and distinct category of written and visual representation before the early nineteenth century, and then it only emerged relative to its regulation, which is to say, relative to mass reproduction and the crisis of mass availability, especially to "lower classes and women" (1993:9, 12). The word pornography, which first appeared in the Oxford English Dictionary in 1857, referred originally to writing about prostitution. Nineteenth-century regulation of pornography was clearly associated with the democratization of culture and the perceived need to police the borders between public (masculine) domain and private (feminine) domain – the need, that is, to regulate social, political, and economic distinctions between genders, races, and classes.

Thus, historically, the demarcation between art and porn has not been concerned with the explicit sexual body itself, but rather with its agency, which is to say with *who gets to make what explicit where and for whom*. More directed toward the control of the frame around the explicit gendered body than the presentation of the body itself – as "obscene" material and work "about prostitution" continued to be labeled "art" and enshrined in museums – the issue of distinction and control concerned who, or what interest group, was allowed to author or frame and ultimately *explicate* the terrain of "the body" and appropriate bodily parts. As noted in the Introduction, the words explicit and explicate stem from the Latin *explicare*, which means "to unfold." Who, the issue seems to be, gets to control the unfolding of bodily signifiers?

RE-VAMPING THE GHOSTS OF MODERNISM

An invocation of ghosts may seem oddly placed in a book on c
explicit body performance art. Ghosts, after all, are explicitly
signifiers. But they are also particularly postmodern entities. Within
the modernist myth of originality, every act, public and private, is ghosted
by precedence. Form is ruin, ghosted by content, and content is ghosted by the
historical trajectory of its forms. A swastika is not a contentless form and nor is
a human body in any imaginable stretch of technological or surgical trans-
mogrification. If modernism was, as Adorno has stated, in thrall to the "category
of the new,"[9] postmodernism positions itself relative to this thrall. Modernist
tropes double back upon themselves, becoming "post" in an after-modernism in
which anything recognized as "new" is recognized, in being "new," as old. In the
postmodern paradigm, the old paradoxically erupts on the scene as the true new
even as it ricochets back into temporal position again as outmoded. Postmodern
artworks garner their postmodernity in their ghost dancing, their playful
mimicry of precedence, positioning themselves relative to an extant, continually
eruptive field of precursory modernist imagery and modernist obsession. In
artworks with a conscious political agenda – such as feminist works – this
playful, ping-pong mimesis is also political strategy (see Diamond 1989 and
1990/91).

Modern construction and inscription of the female body, and more insidiously
the "reality effects" occasioned by those inscriptions, ghost contemporary
feminist counter-constructions.[10] Even in combat boots feminine form is
hounded by the historical legacy of sex discrimination in everyday social practice,
by the history and control of woman's "appropriate" imaging, and by the effects
which that appropriation (the Modern Woman, the Cult of True Womanhood,
the House Wife) has had upon women's lives. The raging '90s impulse to herald
identity as performative rather than fixed, natural, essential, or foundational is an
impulse that must at all times acknowledge the historical backdrop of its own
project – that certain markings of identity bear the historical weight of privilege
and others the historical weight of disprivilege (Butler 1990b). Performative
insignia of identity – marked masculine or feminine, white or black, straight
or gay, upper or lower class – cannot be separated from the historical ramifications ghosting those insignia. The policing of "appropriate" identities relative
to "appropriate" bodies or properties, indeed the designation of psyches as
contained and defined by bodily matter, has fueled the long-burning furnace
of Western self-fashioning (see Brennan 1993:10, 79–117). If the very real
historical effects of identity construction are ignored or dismissed in favor of
performativity for its own sake, the critical promise in exploring performative
acts risks tumbling into an "anything goes" of mix-'n'-match gender codes
without political drive. After all, to discover the degree to which gender codings
are performative rather than "natural" does not in and of itself alter the show. To
be "just acting" doesn't necessarily mean anything to Desdemona if the climax
continues to result in her death (see Blau 1990:161). The degree to which the

"real" is a ruse of performance does not alter the mechanism by which such ruses bring everyday realities into their effects. Put yet another way: while the "real" may always be performative, or constructed, that construction and its reconstruction and its re-reconstruction exist in a battlefield ghosted by that construction's historical effectivity – its reality effects.

The notion of "performance," when attentive to the reality effects of performativity, bears well the complexities of complicity. Performance implies always an audience/performer or ritual participant relationship – a reciprocity, a practice in the constructions of cultural reality relative to its effects. As such the study of performance and the trope of performativity have become integral to a cultural critical analysis which wants to explore the dynamic two-way street, the "space between" self and others, subjects and objects, masters and slaves, or any system of social signification.

Michel Foucault made evident the ways in which power and knowledge are inherently discursive formations and the ways in which discursive formations are *events*, with impact on bodies in time and space (1976, 1980b). Thus bodies, and the social organization of bodies, are immediately implicated in any scene or site of knowledge. Sitting before an "object" of study, the question becomes one of how to apprehend – with the double connotation that word bears of both "know" and "fear" – that object a second time, that is, after/in/aware of the history of objectification, which is always already a history of bodies in social practice. Particularly because the social status of women has been so closely aligned with her general cultural representation as sex, her status as object given to be seen, this question of how to apprehend the space between masculinized subject (given to know) and feminized object (given to be known) has prompted feminist inquiry into the dynamics of Western cultural ways of knowing traditionally wrapped up with visuality, with vision set forth as proprietary, transcendent of tactility, omnisciently disinterested, and essentially separate from the object which it apprehends.[11] The question becomes: how can we see otherwise, without replicating the dynamics of indifferent visuality as if for the first time in a kind of Nietzschean Eternal Return of the Same? How do we see for a second time?

Interestingly, Webster's Ninth Collegiate Dictionary definition for "second sight" is reminiscent of the general irrational, antifoundational attributes ascribed to the second sex: "The power of seeing beyond the visible; intuitive, visionary, or prophetic power." Like "woman's intuition," second sight is a feminized domain. Seeing beyond the visible is, of course, oxymoronic, as is the materialist impulse to see sight, to show the show. And yet this impulse toward the oxymoronic might fit the scene of "woman" with some precision, for women are culturally positioned as inherently oxymoronic in the sense that, after Teresa de Lauretis, woman is unrepresentable except as representation (de Lauretis 1987:20). As has been amply pointed out in feminist texts as academic as Peggy Phelan's *Unmarked* or as popular as Deborah Tannen's "Markers" in the *New York Times Magazine*, there is no way a woman can escape the historical ramifications of that representation unless she passes from visibility as woman, passing as a man.[12] As "woman," she is a preceded by her own markings, standing in relation to her body in history as if beside herself.

Theater artists and theorists, inspired in large part by Bertolt Brecht, have noted that this very "standing beside herself," when exacerbated, underlined, or made explicit creates room for the critical analysis upon which feminism is insistent. Such theorists have seen promise in de Lauretis's "unrepresent-able except as representation," arguing that re-presentation *of* representation is precisely what needs to happen, and further, that the theater – a venue of masquerade even more than film because the tension between "real" and "represented" is at all times observable in the present moment of the actor's body *on stage* – is precisely the venue for such a critical analysis of gender. As Alisa Solomon argues, "On stage . . . 'woman' may be *re*presented, but at the same time a living, breathing woman can be *pre*sented and it's possible for her to comment on the character or image she represents, that is, to make those quotation marks around 'woman' visible. In semiotic terms, she can widen the distance between signified and signifier, by calling attention to that gap . . . Thus she breaks the illusion that spectators are being shown what is natural" (Solomon forthcoming:15).

While "widening the distance between sign and signified" may indeed call attention to the illusion of the natural, I argue here that explicit body performers call attention to that illusion by collapsing the distance between sign and signified – making "the gap," as Solomon calls it, apparent by provoking its implosion across the visceral space of their own bodies. The collapse of sign and signified onto the literal space of the body employs a binary terrorism that similarly makes evident and interrogates the social ramifications of the gap. Still, whether she widens or collapses the distance between sign and signified, any performer who insists upon wielding her alienation effect *as a "woman,"* will be ghosted by the paradoxical historical inscription of that very appellation as always relative to representation.

Whatever promise is located in the theater, or in performativity generally, is a promise that remains ghosted by the historical inscription of woman as inherently oxymoronic – unrepresentable except as representation. Standing beside herself, ghosted by her historical delimitations, the challenge for feminists in theater is to wrestle with those ghosts in a way that brings the dynamics of such ghosting to light. That is, the effort should not be to banish ghosts to find some pure, unghosted originary – some true woman that exists without quotation marks – but rather to summon the ghosts, to bring them out of the shadows and into the scene where they always already exist, to make them apparent *as players.* The effort to denaturalize gender must be coupled with the project of historicizing the shadows, explicating or making explicit the haunting effects of naturalization.

Summoning ghosts, we find that one of the hallmarks of modernism was the rise of realist depictions of "lowlife" subjects in the frame of high art. The social and political upheavals of the mid-nineteenth century generated an aesthetics which rejected Romantic modes of idealization in art and literature in the effort to depict and project a notion of concrete contemporary "reality." Desire for democracy in the arts opened up a new range of subjects, previously considered unworthy of representation. With a particularly modernist twist, an artist could reinscribe the "low" through mimetic representation while remaining at an aesthetic and quasi-scientific vantage point which actually buttressed the "high" of that artist's perspective and, by extension, the perspective of his art- and science-appreciating audience. Especially with the rise of science-inspired naturalism, but also via science-inspired modernist formalisms,[13] lowlife could be appropriately brought into the frame and under the gaze of those who purveyed and those who owned art. As the subjects of modern "masters," lowlife (prostitutes, criminals, savages) could be framed – the socially inappropriate could be appropriated under the auspices and ultimate explications of a master's eye.

The prostitute's body became emblematic of such border crossing between high and low. Widely imaged across modernist canvases and texts, the prostitute, like the racially marked "primitive," became a quintessential object of modernist fascination.[14] As Baudelaire illustrated and as Christine Buci-Glucksmann has explicated, the prostitute can be read as an allegory for modernity itself (1987). As a woman, the prostitute straddled the border between the appropriate (she is a human female) and the inappropriate (she is a whore), ideal and material. In this way the ambivalence of the prostitute is arguably linked to the ambivalence of the primitive or colonial subject who was both appropriate (human) and inappropriate (not-quite human) (Bhabha 1984). For Walter Benjamin, theoriz- ing modernism, the prostitute presented a prime dialectical image because of the ambivalence inherent in her status as both "commodity and seller" in one (1973:171). Benjamin cited modernist fascination with the prostitute as stemming from the general concern over the place of art in commodity capitalism. Relative to that concern, the prostitute appeared to embody a paradox: as both commodity and seller she embodied a bizarre and potentially terroristic collapse of active and passive, subject and object, into a single entity. We might extend that concern farther to explore prostitution as both emblematic of and threatening to some of the operative tenets of commodity capitalism. The prostitute is not only commodity and seller, but laborer – outing the "coagulated" human labor "concealed" in the commodity (Marx 1977:142, 149). In the commodity of the prostitue labor is undisguised, appearing rather as the labor *of* disguise. As laborer *and* commodity *and* seller, the secret bleeds, the mystical properties of the commodity dreamscape are exposed – labor-value is made overtly apparent in the commodity object/subject of the whore. In Susan Buck-Morss's words, carved through Benjamin out of Marx's *Capital*:

> The prostitute is the ur-form of the wage laborer, selling herself in order to survive. Prostitution is indeed an objective emblem of capitalism, a hieroglyph of the true nature of social reality in the sense that the Egyptian hieroglyphs were viewed by the Renaissance – and in Marx's sense as well: "Value trans- forms . . . every product of labor into a social hieroglyph. People then try to

decode the meaning of the hieroglyph in order to get behind the secret of their own social product. . . ." The image of the whore reveals this secret like a rebus. Whereas every trace of the wage laborer who produced the commodity is extinguished when it is torn out of context by its exhibition on display, in the prostitute, both moments remain visible.

(1989:184)

In modernist painting, the prostitute's inappropriate image served the realist agenda. As the opposite of ideal, yet looking like the ideal, she was appropriated to signify both the end of romantic idealism and the site of nostalgia for its loss. In Manet's 1863 paintings *Le Dejeuner sur l'herbe* and *Olympia*, the prostitute became the strained site of tension, she was a paradox containing both the historical beauty of the ideal and a contemporary reality marked as corrupt (Clark 1985, and Sayre 1989:67–8).

Manet's *Olympia* (Plate 1.4) caused a scandal when it was unveiled in 1863. The painting was proclaimed indecent not because of nudity or sexual display, but rather because of the nude's seeming self-possession. Manet had painted a courtesan, or in modern parlance a prostitute, laying on a couch much like the courtesan in Titian's famous *The Venus of Urbino*. Indeed the painting appeared to mock Titian's classic. Unlike Titian's courtesan, Manet's naked Olympia "looked back" at her audience not with seductive pleasure but with a pride that resembled disdain. Olympia's expression seemed to deny her availability to the viewer. The subservience of her status was challenged by her defiant sense of self, as if she were reveling with narcissistic pleasure in her show, her "elegant artificiality," her mimetic appropriation of the ideal (Nochlin 1971:203).

Georges Bataille has argued that modern art began with Manet because Manet's subjects defied their traditional contexts. Manet began what Bataille saw as modernism's destruction of paintings' pretexts, a destruction here carried out across the body of woman. In the case of *Olympia*, the social pretext of prostitution was challenged as the courtesan both indicated and denied the conventional reading of her position as entirely subservient, destroying the over-arching validity of that conventional reading. Seemingly self-possessed, Olympia challenged the pretext that she exists only to be possessed by the owner/viewer/consumer of her image. In Bataille's words: "The picture obliterates the text, and the meaning of the picture is not in the text behind it but in the obliteration of that text" (1983:62).

And yet it is worth noting that regardless of both pretext and anti-pretext, regardless of gaze and supposed counter-gaze, the frame of "art" remained intact. Olympia's disdainful glance existed under Manet's authorizing signature, and under the more invisible signature of those who determined membership in the category of decided, "great," or canonical art. Of course, the scandal died down, and ultimately the painting became accepted as a realist classic: a high art depiction of realist "contemporaneity," lowlife pride in the form of a defiant gaze framed by an authorizing gaze – perspective countered and re-contained by perspective, locked at a standstill. Though it may seem like a nagging point, the imaged prostitute herself had no agency in the debate over her seeming defiance.

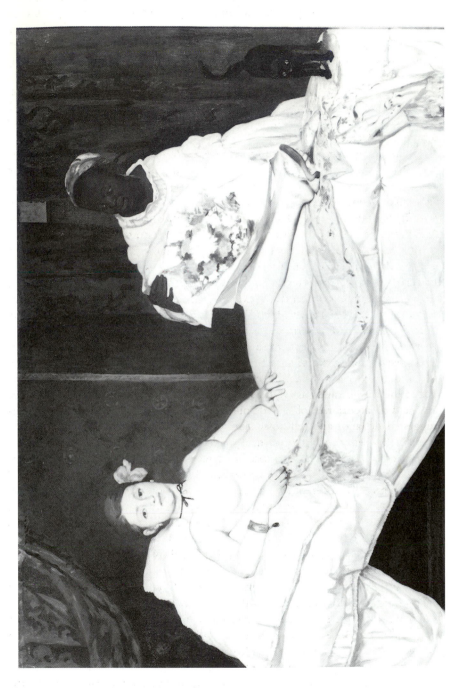

Plate 1.4 Eduard Manet, 1863, *L'Olympia*. Courtesy of the Musée d'Orsay.

The argument was relative to the manipulation of a representational icon, the passive terrain of the scopic field did not *herself* revolt but was appropriated by an artist whose agency as artist was not in question. Regardless of the destruction of her "pretext" imagined by "her" gaze, she remained iconic, reproduced, available for interpretation, open for discourse and relative to the authorizing signatures she ultimately enhanced. No matter how defiantly Manet may be argued to have rendered her gaze, it is almost absurd to point out that neither "Olympia" nor the model Victorine Meurent who posed as Olympia with supposed self-possession could co-sign the painting or wield even an ounce of art-historical agency.[15]

Olympia's seeming disdain simply signaled realist artists' newfound "objectivity" toward the scopic field more than it signaled a fundamentally new position for the woman given to be seen – so often, in realist works, a prostitute. In some important ways, Olympia's ostensible challenge to the viewer was undermined within the painting itself. Following Sander Gilman's reading of the painting, Manet's placement of the black serving woman in *Olympia* is key. The servant can be read relative to pretexts of contemporary racisms and sexisms as underscoring the dangerous "primitive" nature of uncontrolled female sexuality – a pretext Manet did not attempt to destroy. Reading the black woman according to popular dictates of Victorian attitudes toward race, class, and sex, the servant becomes an iconic stand-in for Olympia's own sexuality (Gilman 1985:228). Functioning as a displacement of the white woman's sex, the servant holds a vulvic white floral bouquet. Even as Olympia appears to defy pretexts, her sex is offered for the gaze through the body of her servant – open, in full bloom, and immanently available. At the foot of the bed is a small black cat, staring out at the viewer much as Olympia stares, a "promiscuous beast" rendered here as "natural accessories of the demi-monde" (Nochlin 1971:203). Olympia's suggested defiance and self-possession thus become deeply suspect in that the scene of her sexuality is displaced beyond her person onto the symbolic bodies of a black servant and a black cat. Importantly, the black woman is compliant in relation to Olympia's seeming defiance. Her eyes rest, like the imagined viewer's, on Olympia's body, making the black servant a simultaneous and complex stand-in for the viewer's gaze, repossessing Olympia's sex for the viewer. Wrapped in the symbolic rebound of primitivism and sexism, her sex is not hers to manipulate. We can posit the question: what if the gaze of the black woman were also rendered as self-possessed and defiant? What pretexts might such a doubled defiance have destroyed?

The placement of the black serving woman in Olympia speaks to the different positioning of white women and women of color relative to the dictates of desire and visibility. White women are ambivalent signs, split between the binaried poles of potential virgin and potential fallen whore, whereas black women historically have been socially decided, as Gilman notes – never virginal, never pure, but signifying, as in *Olympia*, the always already fallen site of primitive, animal sexuality.[16] Thus, in seeking to control and contain their sex, in the effort to become a "lady," or even in defiantly flaunting their sex as a "defiant" whore, white women would be caught in an effort to control, contain, defy, or manipulate an inherent primitivism. Because the "primitive" is scripted according to hierarchies of race, women wrestling with sexuality would historically have been wrapped up in racist paradigms of symbolic displacement. Manet's manipulation of the symbolic displacements in *Olympia* serve to recapitulate Olympia's seeming defiance, bringing the prostitute back to the viewer as comprehensible. The situation is redolent with racism. White women who might have sought to control their own sex would have been caught up in seeking to control their displacements – to render invisible or to manipulate the signs of their symbolic fallen doubles: persons of color.

If, as we explore in the next chapter, white women are emblematic of the vanishing point of vision, ambivalently both that which is represented and that which escapes representation, black women have been positioned as always already vanished. In Manet's painting, Olympia's body represents the scopic field, the given to be seen, and as such she symbolically contains the vanishing point of perspective. The black woman is the stand-in, the double, for the vanishing point of Olympia's own genitalia. The black woman, then, does not *contain* the vanishing point (the female genitalia) with all its attendant dangers, she is herself the vanishing point, making the white woman's sex (the vulvic white flower bouquet she offers Olympia and the viewer) available for the gaze. Thus, as Manet has rendered her, the servant does not contain but completely embodies the vanishing point, symbolically vanished yet guiding the gaze of a presumed white male viewer who is himself dislocated from the scene, standing on the other side of Olympia at the unseen peep hole, peering in.

BESIDE HERSELF: POSTMODERN ARTISTS AND MODERN WHORES

Olympia's would-be defiance is altogether different from postmodern works which do not attempt to represent the low within a frame of high art, but actually attempt to wrestle with the frame itself, crossing the border between high and low at the level of the frame. Something very different is afoot when a work does not symbolically depict a subject of social degradation, but actually *is* that degradation, terrorizing the sacrosanct divide between the symbolic and the literal. Concerned about the place of an artist in a burgeoning market economy, Baudelaire, in *Fusées*, answered his own question "What is art?" with one word: "Prostitution" (1945). He also romanticized and identified with savage "Apaches," low class "rag pickers," and "lesbians" (see Benjamin 1973). Yet Baudelaire's suggestion that the artist prostitutes himself when making art as a commodity remained metaphorical. Baudelaire did not become a literal whore any more than he became a lesbian. Nor did he really cross class, no matter what state of abjection he courted as a "bohemian" artist (see Seigel 1986). Artistic slumming could suggest a border crossing – a flirtation or metaphoric identification with the "low." But metaphoric gesturing toward the whorehouse is one thing. It is quite another thing when an actual prostitute attempts to claim the place of the artist in the museum, or, for that matter, when a woman does so – especially a woman unwilling to abandon the passion associated with forthright sexual agency, or what is inscribed in terms of masculine virtue as virility.[17]

When the whore attempts to cross the border as artist versus artist's object, the sacred divide between porn and art is thrown immediately into relief. When Olympia defies the validating signature of the male artist and steps out of his frame to authorize her own framing, perhaps stretching out live in the museum or gallery and claiming space as art *and* artist, she not only directly challenges the terms of demarcation between high and low, but unearths the gendered dynamics in that relation. The sexually active woman as both (low) object *and* (high) artist straddles and challenges a deeply ingrained gender divide in which active, or overt, or "virile" female sexuality is conceived as inherently animalistic, primitive, and perverse.

Because female sexuality is socially, culturally, politically, and economically debased in patriarchal society – even while seemingly worshipped aesthetically – it is antithetical to the positively ascribed "virility" of an artist. In 1917 Duchamp could "create" a woman – Rrose Sélavy – as the alter-ego of his artist self, sometimes signing his Readymades with her name. Readily made by Duchamp's performative action, gender (which means, ultimately, the female gender in the way that race, in white society, means "black") was arguably de-naturalized and rendered performative (Amelia Jones 1993). But while Duchamp could cross between artist and woman with bravado and a bad-boy aplomb that bordered on grace, it was something different for *women*, those bearing the literal markings of woman in their physical bodies, to cross as artists. If Rrose Sélavy was Duchamp's alter-ego, the 1960s saw a bold rush of refusal on the part of feminist artists to allow female embodiment to be "alter" – to be opposed to artistic identity – and works began to appear which incorporated and emphasized the explicit body of the female *artist* in the art work.

In 1963, exactly 100 years after *Olympia*,[18] Carolee Schneemann stretched out nude in an art installation she had built called *Mink Paws' Turret*. She titled the series of photographs taken of her entry into her art *Eye/Body*. With this move she had become both artist and object, both eye and body at once. She was the artist *and* the nude. She was Olympia *and* Manet – a move which gave a certain agency and artistic authority to the defiant pride of those delimited as "low." We will examine *Eye/Body* in more depth below, but it is important to note another work here which followed on the heels of *Eye/Body*. In 1964, Schneemann performed a live version of Manet's *Olympia* in an installation by sculptor Robert Morris titled *Site* (Plate 1.5). In this piece, Schneemann the artist lay on Olympia's couch (here a simple wooden board), dressed like Olympia in nothing but a black neck choker, while Morris dismantled and moved a series of wooden planks he had assembled around her. Schneemann and Morris literalized the "framing" of Olympia, and granted the art object status as artist in a defiant move that questioned the fundamental tenets of aesthetic authority – counter-mimicking Manet's mimicry of Titian. Interestingly, however, the black serving woman of Manet's *Olympia* had simply vanished. She was nowhere in *Site*.

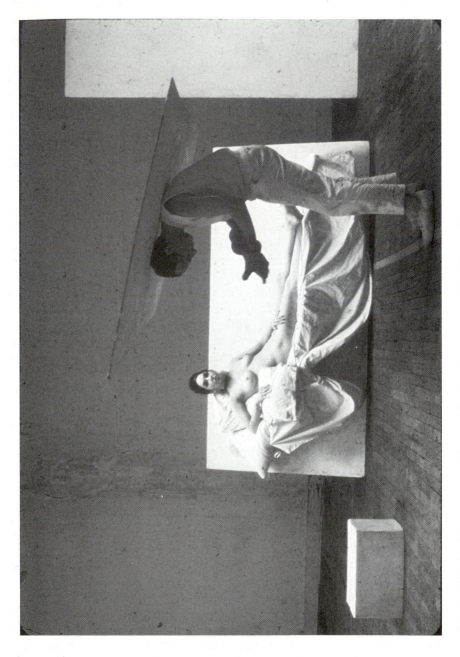

Plate 1.5 Carolee Schneemann and Robert Morris during a rehearsal for *Site*, 1964. Photo by Hans Numuth, courtesy Carolee Schneemann.

In 1965 Morris wrote that "The objects I used [in *Site*] held no inherent interest for me but were means for dealing with specific problems." For Morris, those "problems" were ones of space and time without political implication (1965:169). Schneemann, however, had agreed to participate in the project because the "object" held inherent political interest linked to feminism, as the object was, inexorably, her own body (see Sayre 1989:67–73). The emphasis on the structure was for Morris an anti-romantic way of emphasizing the labor of construction, while for Schneemann the anti-romanticism was inherent in the "labored" construction of femininity. If we grant Schneemann agency as artist, the sexual politics of *Olympia* were made explicit by Schneemann's replaying of the prostitute across her own body as artist while a male artist built and dismantled and rebuilt a structure around her to locate her scene under his authority. With hindsight, however, Schneemann has said that she felt immobilized by *Site*, and that the project succumbed to Morris's apolitical "framing" in which she felt re-fixed.[19]

The erasure of the black female body in *Site* was also deeply problematic. Without a black body to distinguish it, whiteness in white culture appears to be invisible (a white body is not read as marked by race), and because the black serving woman was vanished, Schneemann's whiteness, in her claiming agency, appeared unmarked. As already standing in for the vanishing point in Manet's painting, the re-vanishing or double-vanishing of the black servant in *Site* was not remarked, and any agency Schneemann may be read to have claimed would have been claimed across the black woman's explicit erasure. Difficult questions arise as to white women's strategic replaying of the sexualized body for purposes of remarking, reclaiming agency. By what counter-erasures are white women's agencies repossessed?

The inability to deal with race, or the blatant ignoring of race as an issue within feminism, was rampant in the 1960s, 1970s, and 1980s. It is still an issue today. But no one critiqued Morris and Schneemann at the time for their omission. Rather, Schneemann was in trouble for reasons linked to the oxymoronic notion of "female agency" she championed. Because she made her body the literal site of so much of her art, and because she underscored her sexuality as a creative force in her work, Schneemann was often dismissed as self-indulgent and narcissistic by the art establishment. But she was not alone. Other women, many influenced by Schneemann, had begun to make similar work confronting the sacrosanct boundaries separating female sexuality and artistic authority (Lippard 1976:122). The roots of feminist performance art, which would flourish in the 1970s, took obstinate hold and many boundaries, closely linked to the socially demarcated margins separating artist/woman, high/low, subject/object, began to leak and bleed together under the banner of political purpose.

A close look at Schneemann's early career provides an entry into issues at the heart of contemporary feminist performance art of the explicit body. In much of her early work, Schneemann experimented with "flesh as material" and imagined a nervous system of bodies in interaction with interchangeable bodily parts, all in the service of sexual freedom and sexual pleasure. Indeed, today these works seem like Edenic precursors to the incisions of a post-Lapsarian performative feminism: within twenty-five years of *Eye/Body*, explicit body work would include such feminist artists as Orlan who, in the 1990s, takes her own "flesh as material" as she undergoes a series of plastic surgery operations to rearrange her bodily "parts" to conform, with ironic mimicry, to women depicted in canonical art (Rose 1993).

EYE/BODY: CAROLEE SCHNEEMANN BESIDE HERSELF

Fresh out of graduate school as a painter, Schneemann arrived in New York City in 1961 and became almost immediately involved in performative Happenings. She was inspired by her participation in Claus Oldenburg's *Store* several months after her arrival, but cites her first performance-art piece as having taken place before she even hit the city scene. Schneemann created *Labyrinth* in Sidney, Illinois, in the summer of 1960. A natural disaster – a twister – had ripped through her town and toppled her favorite tree. The artist marked the fallen tree and flooded-out rock walls as an "environment" and invited friends and fellow artists to "encounter" the ruins, asking them to make contact with mud, water, high grass, and branches as she watched through a window (Schneemann 1979:7).

As a graduate student in painting at the University of Illinois, Schneemann had read Artaud's *Theatre and Its Double*. She developed a taste for concretizing versus abstracting, literalizing versus symbolizing as a way of inciting a visceral immediacy of address. It was a taste that would carry across her entire career. The tumultuous combination of Artaud with Virginia Woolf, Wilhelm Reich, Simone de Beauvoir, and Cezanne activated in the young painter a drive for "sensate involvement" in her work, both on the part of artist and on the part of spectator. At first, her emphasis on tactility was directly related to the modernist hope in the redemptive power of things *as themselves* – the idea of the revenge of an object in the face of its arbitrary tutelage to its sign. Her early work thus took the form of "concretions" – material artworks which highlighted tactile sensations in sharp edges, shards, and fragments. In her early work, sensate involvement hovered without clear political articulation around notions of active objects, the object's gesture, and eyes which touch.

In New York in 1961, Schneemann became involved in the Fluxus movement as well as Happenings. With Dick Higgins she formed a brief and contentious association called "Happenings-Fluxus." This association began in 1962 with an evening for the Living Theater in which Schneemann offered a piece entitled "Environment for Sound and Motions" with performers Philip Corner, LaMonte Young, Malcolm Goldstein, James Tenney, and Yvonne Rainer, among others. In this piece, performers made out lists of possible actions, positions, and interactions with props, with each other, and with the audience. Each performer carried out the actions with a different rhythm and cadence. The Happening was thus an encounter between these cadences, rhythms, and a variety of objects, gestures, and sounds (see Kirby 1965, Sandford 1995). Following this performance, Schneemann was invited to join with Yvonne Rainer and a group of dancers in collaborative experimentation that would become the Judson Dance Theater (Rainer 1974; Banes 1983). Schneemann's first event with this group took place at Judson Church in January 1963 and was titled *Newspaper Event*. In this improvisational piece Schneemann began to develop her interest in the material body as both a personal-particular environment and as a social environment "in conjunction with others." She imagined a plasticity, a kind of nervous system of bodies in interaction, in which bodily parts could be interchanged:

> I was thinking of an organism interchanging its parts (phagocyte). I noted five principles; 1) the primary experience of the body as your own environment. 2) the body within the actual, particular environment. 3) the materials of that environment – soft, responsive, tactile, active, malleable (paper . . . paper). 4) the active environment of one another. 5) the visual structure of the bodies and materials defining the space.
>
> (Schneemann 1979:33)

After *Newspaper Event* came *Chromelodeon* and *Lateral Splay*, both at Judson. In the course of these pieces, Schneemann's interest in flesh as material began to be provoked by her experience as a female artist in the male-dominated movements of Fluxus and Happenings, pushing her to explore the ways in which material flesh existed in bodies which could not be divorced from the histories of their socio-cultural signification. This preoccupation with a specific tactility – the materiality of flesh and the object-status of the female body relative to its socio-cultural delimitations – generated a turning point, a politicizing point, a feminist turn in her work. It was *Eye/Body*, (Plate 1.6) begun in 1962 and performed in December 1963 in her own loft, that moved Schneemann across her own threshold. She stepped directly into her environment, entering and becoming her own work.

Walking into Schneemann's New York loft in 1963 one walked into her work – entering art, penetrating it with a sensate body. Of course, this physical entry into art was happening quite a lot in the late '50s and throughout the '60s as the boundaries of aesthetic mediums found themselves bleeding together into "environmental" and "intermedia" expression.[20] But Schneemann's was among the very first American installations to incorporate the artist's own body as primary visual and visceral terrain. When she transformed her loft into a "kinetic environment," Schneemann placed her own body into the environmental frame of her art, performing a series of actions in prescient anticipation of the veritable explosion of body art in the later '60s and '70s. The environment consisted of 4 × 9 foot panels, broken glass and shards of mirrors, photographs, lights, and motorized umbrellas. Schneemann stepped into her work, and, in what she called a "kind of shamanic ritual," she incorporated her naked body into her construction by painting, greasing, and chalking herself. Historians have suggested that *Eye/Body* and Schneemann's subsequent kinetic theater production *Meat Joy* (performed in 1964 in Paris, London, and New York) "charted

Plate 1.6 Carolee Schneemann, *Eye/Body*, 1963. Photo by Erro, courtesy of Carolee Schneemann.

a new direction," and even "anticipated not only the so-called 1960s sexual revolution, but feminism" (Stiles 1993:98, n80; Lippard 1976:122). But in the 1960s Schneemann felt acutely that her work was dismissed as "self-indulgent exhibitionism, intended only to stimulate men" (Schneemann 1990:25).

Importantly, much of her impulse to include her body, explicitly, in her work came from the fact that when Schneemann began constructing the installation in 1962 the artist was fed up with feeling that her gender inhibited her consideration as a serious contributor to the art world. Beyond the dance-identified circles of Judson Church, she felt she had partial status, and was personally troubled by the suspicion that she was included only as a "cunt mascot" in the heavily male cliques of Fluxus and Happenings.[21] Her response to this feeling

– covering her naked body in paint, grease, chalk, ropes, and plastic, and incorporating it directly into her work – was to address her mascot-dom directly. *Eye/Body* established her artist's body as "visual territory," as if to declare: If I am a token, then I'll be a token to reckon with. But the work also suggested a complex theoretical terrain of perspectival vision on the flip. *Eye/Body* suggested embodied vision, a bodily eye – sighted eyes – artist's eyes – not only in the seer, but in the body of the seen.

In *Eye/Body* Schneemann was not only image but image-maker,[22] and it is this overt doubling across the explicit terrain of engenderment which marks *Eye/Body* as historically significant for feminist performance art. Though there are possible important correlatives that can be resurrected from history – such as, as some suggest, the proto-performance of nineteenth-century hysterics[23] – in *Eye/Body* Schneemann manipulated both her own live female body and her artist's agency without finding herself institutionalized as mentally ill. Instead, she found herself excommunicated from the "Art Stud Club." George Maciunus, father of Fluxus, declared her work too "messy" for inclusion.[24]

In 1976, thirteen years after *Eye/Body*, Lucy Lippard addressed the continuing broad dismissal of women's art work: "Men can use beautiful, sexy women as neutral objects or surfaces, but when women use their own faces and bodies, they are immediately accused of narcissism." Lippard suggested that work such as Schneemann's employed "defiant narcissism" and cited Lynda Benglis's work as a prime example. In 1974 Benglis printed a full-color advertisement in *Artforum* in which she appeared as a greased nude in sunglasses, belligerently sprouting a gigantic dildo. The editors of *Artforum* accompanied Benglis's photograph with an irate letter on how her ad was "an object of extreme vulgarity . . . brutalizing ourselves and . . . our readers," about which Lippard wrote:

> The uproar that this image created proved conclusively that there are still things women may not do . . . No such clamor arose in 1970 when Vito Acconci burned hair from his chest, "pulling at it, making it supple, flexible – an attempt to develop a female breast," then tucked his penis between his legs to "extend the sex change," and finally "acquired a female form" by having a woman kneel behind him with his penis "disappearing" in her mouth. Nor was there any hullabaloo when Scott Burton promenaded 14th Street in drag . . . or when William Wegman made his amusing trompe l'oeil "breast" piece.
>
> (1976:104, 125, 127)

Nudity was not the problem. Sexual display was not the problem. *The agency of the body displayed, the author-ity of the agent* – that was the problem with women's work.

The live nude was widely used in Happenings as an object, and often as an "active" object, or an object with choice within the improvisational field of an artist's conception. But Schneemann was using the live nude as more than an active object. Whether she ultimately wished it, the object of her body was unavoidably also *herself* – the nude *as* the artist, not just as the artist's (active) object. That the active, creating force of the artist should manifest as *explicitly female* meant that Schneemann's "actions" were loaded with contradiction in a culture which aligned active with masculine and passive with feminine.[25] As mentioned above, Duchamp's masquerade of the feminine fitted the construct-edness, the "made," the authored quality of art. To *put on* a female profile fitted the pattern of the artist making the object – the object being the feminine, passive principle, that which is put on or put off. In *Eye/Body*, on the contrary, the clean lines between constructed and constructor, finder and found, subject and object, artist and art, mind and body, were blurred. That which tradition-ally did the constructing, the "male principle," was in this case conspicuously, explicitly, and unapologetically "female." The female here was not simply a Duchampian guise, or better, not *only* a guise, but somehow both guise *and* essence. Schneemann could not simply drop the guise of "woman" to appear as essentially a man, an artist – nor did she want to. The constructed and the essential were here inexorably tangled in a very "messy" embrace.

It is useful to consider carefully the dynamics of essentialism in explicit body works by women. Theorist Diana Fuss has explored the political transgression inherent in the feminist employment of essentialism. Linking Lacan and Irigaray, Fuss writes:

> Irigaray's reading of Aristotle's understanding of essence reminds me of Lacan's distinction between *being* and *having* the phallus: a woman does not *possess* the phallus, she *is* the Phallus. Similarly, we can say that, in Aristotelian logic, a woman does not *have* an essence, she *is* Essence. Therefore to give "woman" essence is to undo Western phallomorphism and to offer women entry into subjecthood . . . A woman who lays claim to an essence of her own undoes the conventional binarisms of essence/accident, form/matter, and actuality/potentiality.
>
> (1989:71)

As Fuss is keenly aware, the claiming of essence *at all* fell appropriately under materialist poststructuralist attack, and the issue of essence became an embattled one for feminists. The poststructuralist project to interrogate the political ground of subjectivity (the essentialist bases of *any* authority) ran full force against the feminist project to claim subjectivity and authority. The post-structural project to "resist" all essentialized subjectivity and the feminist project to transgress by claiming a female essence, generated a certain "stall," or impasse, in feminist inquiry (Case 1990:7–13). But that impasse has lately led to the philosophical positioning of "both at once" – feminists who bear an Irigarayan "double gesture," paradoxically essentialist and constructivist at once. Like a Brechtian "not, but" this feminist "both/and" makes room for critical inquiry, political agency, and discursive mobility. This double agency was arguably present as "messiness" in Schneemann's work even in the early 1960s.

Schneemann's essentialism was most obvious in her goddess imagery – snakes placed across her body in *Eye/Body* were allusions to the Goddess. But that essentialism was tinged with declarations of her own agency – her status as constructor, artist, active creator. She upset feminists on both sides of the essentialist/materialist divide. Rigidly essentialist feminists, such as the Heresies collective in the 1960s, chastised Schneemann for debasing the Goddess with what they read as sexual narcissism in her work. Twenty years later, strictly materialist feminists similarly dismissed Schneemann's work, reading any gestures toward goddess-identified sacrality as always already nostalgic and therefore naively apolitical (see Dolan 1988:83).

But if the both/and tangle of the constructed and the essential generated a "messy" embrace, Schneemann intended this mess. She wanted her body to remain erotic, sexual, both "desired *and* desiring," while underscoring it as clearly volitional as well: "marked, written over in a text of stroke and gesture discovered by my creative female will." In 1979 she explicated her essentialist insistence on *female* will as strategic:

> I write "my creative female will" because for years my most audacious works were viewed as if someone else inhabiting me had created them – they were considered "masculine" when seen as aggressive, bold. As if I were inhabited by a stray male principle; which would be an interesting possibility – except in the early sixties this notion was used to blot out, denigrate, deflect the coherence, necessity and personal integrity of what I made and how it was made.
>
> (1979:52)

Schneemann was making it as hard as possible to attribute her active creation to a "stray male principle." The male/female binarism was thus confused. Was the artist making or finding the object or was the object making the artist? In the 1960s many chose to believe that indeed the object was making the artist – that is, that it was only the conventional appeal of Schneemann's curvaceous and long-legged dimensions that got her any attention at all. Found Object by Great Male Artist might be acceptable, but Found Artist by Great Female Object? Thus Schneemann's efforts to expose and explode her "cunt-mascotdom" were often predictably dismissed as narcissistic exhibitionism, disavowed as simply her effort to ride into the scene on the strength of her object appeal.

In 1963 *Eye/Body* existed in something of a vacuum. According to Schneemann:

> I had no reviews because I was taking people one by one through [*Mink Paws' Turret*, an exhibit in her loft in which *Eye/Body* occurred]. I was inviting people over to the studio to look at it. I had open house usually once a month, and everybody trooped through. And that was the way to be connected to what was happening to the other artists and critics and people traveling in and out from Europe. I took the photo series [of *Eye/Body*] to Alan Solomon who was about to be director of the Jewish Museum and making it very vital and wild and I remember that he said, "If you want to paint, paint. If you want to run around naked, you don't belong in the art

world." People were always shocking me with closed reactions. I knew I was onto something, but I didn't know what exactly – I just knew this was really significant. A few other artist's knew it too, without having any theoretical base for it.

(Schneemann 1992)

That other artists "knew it too" is abundantly clear with historical hindsight. Schneemann was not alone. Female Fluxus artists and early cultural feminists began to use their bodies explicitly in their work, exploring, among other things, the paradox of being artist and object at once – Fluxus artists such as Yoko Ono, Shigeko Kubota, and Charlotte Moorman, and cultural feminists such as Hannah Wilke and Martha Wilson to name but a few. Generally these women's works were, in Yoko Ono's words, "rejected as animalistic" by male colleagues in the male-dominated art establishment (Stiles 1993:77). When Shigeko Kubota performed her *Vagina Painting* (Plate 1.7) at the Perpetual Fluxfest in New York City in 1965 she squatted on the floor and painted on a paper with a brush that extended from her vagina. Her male colleagues hated the piece (Stiles 1993), despite the fact that Yves Klein's 1960 use of nude women as "living brushes" in 1959 had been widely celebrated. Woman as artist's brush, woman fetishized as phallus was acceptable, even chic. But woman *with* brush was in some way woman *with* phallus and thus unnatural, monstrous, threatening, primitive – certainly not artistic. Women artists making actions when "the actors were all men" demanded a certain transvestitism that not all were prepared to employ.[26] Some, like Kubota, Ono, and Schneemann, wanted to remain women and wield the brush, that is be both female and artist. Such works were, as David James wrote of Schneemann's 1964/65 film *Fuses*, "hardly able to be seen" and, as I have already mentioned, were often dismissed with denigration, accusations of narcissism, sexual innuendo, and mockery (James 1989:317–21).

Despite the pressure of establishment dismissal, the thirty years between the early 1960s and the early 1990s have seen an accumulation and exaggeration of method on the part of feminist artists resisting the invisible barricades which had, for so long, kept women marginalized as subject seeing, central as object seen – marginalized as artist producing, central as art produced. These efforts have been made not by politely knocking on the closed doors of museums, galleries, and performance spaces, but by women creating, ultimately, an insistent scene of their own – sidestepping "Art Stud Club" requirements for inclusion. Though the representation of women artists in mainstream venues is still relatively scant, as Guerrilla Girl posters make clear, what can ironically be called "women's work" is not, today, readily dismissible. This is due in large part to the fact that women artists in the 1960s, and with great momentum in the 1970s, combined their art with a blatant feminist activism. Some works explicitly addressed the problematic dynamics of being a woman and an artist (Langer 1988). Some works provoked the wrath of the status quo by exploring taboo subjects such as menstruation,[27] the male body through a "female gaze,"

Plate 1.7 Shigeko Kubota performing her *Vagina Painting* at Perpetual Fluxfest, New York City, 1965. Photo by George Maciunus.

or active female sexual drive imagined as something other than monstrous and something other than phallobsessive. The body of the artist was implicated in the body of the artist's work in particularly personal – which was to say political – ways.

Of course, the medium of performance and the notion of an artist's actions (if not explicitly the artist's body) were increasingly celebrated by the art world in general. This celebration was notable in particular increase after Jackson Pollock's mid-1950s emphasis on the "action" of his brush and the flight of his paint through air, but is traceable in performative avant-garde lineage back through Duchamp, Dada, and the Futurists. In contrast to the general emphasis on purely "concrete" actions, however, the works of women could not be approached as if embodied actions transcended social prejudices of gender, race, and class – as if the base and elemental body with which artists, with rapid increase, had become particularly enthralled were not riddled in their materiality with less concrete socio-political significances.

Works by men which did employ the political overtones of the explicit body – such as Paik's 1962 *Young Penis Symphony*, in which ten young men, hidden from the audience behind a large sheet of paper, stuck their penises through the paper one at a time – were subject to very different responses than explicit body works created by women. Paik's piece might have "poked" fun at the spectacle of phallic size and power, but his display remained, under his authorizing signature, in good humor. In contrast, Martha Edleheit has said of her early 1970s paintings of male nudes with penises which "droop" that even her "neutral" eye bothered men "who are not used to being treated so indifferently, or only literally . . . a straightforwardly presented penis much disturbs them too: mere viewing is a kind of judgment" (Holder 1988:14). While it might be possible to argue that Paik's piece *was* in good humor and works like Edleheit's neutral "droop" or Louis Bourgeois's *Fillete*, a two-foot-long penis done in moist-looking malleable latex and hung from a meat hook, were not, it is also possible to argue that "good humor" was extended to male artists and their utilizations of the body far more generously than to female artists.

Another example, also concerning Paik, better illustrates the situation: Charlotte Moorman was arrested, tried, and found guilty for indecent exposure during her 1967 performance of Paik's 1966 *Opera Sextronique* in which she exposed her breasts. Paik, however, was found not guilty as the judge deemed it impossible to create "pornographic music." Moorman had to spend the night in a cell with women arrested for prostitution among other crimes. These women tried to pull Moorman's hair out when she explained her "misconduct" to them (Dubin 1992:126). As Kristine Stiles writes, "Paik and Moorman's actions are extraordinary demonstrations of the role the body plays in structuring not only the meaning and presence of objects, but the juridical and institutional practices that control, manage, and litigate that body" (1993:84).

For the woman artist authoring work, the problem was immense. The explicit body itself was not the problem – there had been "exposure" in art for centuries – but the lines by which the explicit body was explicated, by which it was framed, displayed, and, even more importantly, "authored," had been very well policed, by juridical and avant-garde establishments alike. As Schneemann wrote of *Eye/Body* and its general dismissal:

> In 1963 to use my body as an extension of my painting-constructions was to challenge and threaten the psychic territorial power lines by which women were admitted to the Art Stud Club so long as they behaved *enough* like the men, did work clearly in the traditions and pathways hacked out by the men.
>
> (1979:52)

In the 1960s embodied works by women could not be easily digested into the territorial "bad boy" oeuvre of the avant-garde. Their authorizing signatures were suspect. And very often these works bore autobiographical or at the very least "personal" overtones which challenged the formalism at the base of so much avant-garde practice, pointing to socially and politically contexted experience of form versus abstracted formal principles, a fact which had enormous influence on the broader 1970s generation of feminist performance art.

The 1970s was a decade art critic and historian Moira Roth has called "The Amazing Decade" of women's art. Feminist performance art burgeoned on the West Coast around Judy Chicago and Womanhouse and in New York among women who had been either excommunicated, like Schneemann, from the "Art Studs Club," or who were entering the scene with their "consciousnesses" already raised (see Roth 1983). By the 1980s, artists falling under the rubric "female" commanded greater recognition. Interestingly, this recognition grew in direct proportion to the challenging of the stronghold of formalism in the arts, a challenge forwarded by the innovations of feminist painters, photographers, film-makers, and performers such as Sherrie Levine, Cindy Sherman, Laurie Anderson, Yvonne Rainer, Linda Montano, Nancy Spero, Jenny Holzer, Barbara Kruger, and Louise Lawler, and promoted by editors such as Ingrid Sischy of *Artforum* and curators such as Marcia Tucker of the New Museum and Martha Wilson of Franklin Furnace in New York. As women artists became more difficult to ignore, feminist theory and practice gained in complexity, and as theory and practice gained in complexity, women artists became more difficult to ignore. If the 1970s feminists had, in an effort to establish a feminist voice and a feminist stronghold, largely been seeking a "true" or positive or essential image of "woman," by the mid-1980s artists were able to declare that the "woman" they sought was a cultural construct, a strategic moment, and could move to the more materialist notion that identity is produced through the machinations of representation. Intersecting with poststructuralist theories in a powerfully burgeoning amalgam of French and Anglo-American feminisms, artists in the mid-1980s could better deal with the messy terrain between the essential and the constructed, aiming with a firm theoretical base beyond "essential" woman to analyze how and why meaning and its engenderment is produced. This shifting of emphasis away from essentialized female nature toward a radical interrogation of both engenderment and nature motivated and gained motivation from the general politicization of aesthetics at the backbone of critical postmodernist inquiry.

Feminist critiques of essentialism can thus be said to have grown out of essentialist feminist critiques, as one generation grows out of another. With obvious inheritance from their cultural or essentialist feminist predecessors, the body remained a performative site for a generation of materialist explicit body performers, but the terms of the drama had shifted from, broadly speaking, invocation of empowered female imagery to parodies played out across bodily parts in which identity became a manipulable *mise en scène* of physical accouterment and "self" became something as shifty as costuming or plastic surgery. One of the dramas played out across the explicit body became, increasingly in the later 1980s and early 1990s, a drama at the juridical and institutional intersection of porn and art. The issue of the "appropriate" venue for the explicit body became most clearly an issue not only of who bears the right to wield the explicit body in the frame of art – Manet or Olympia? – but, as suggested earlier, who bears the rights to explicate the socio-historical significances of that body and that frame.

2 Logic of the twister, eye of the storm

I was to walk with the storm and hold my power, and get my answers to life and things in storms. The symbol of lightning was painted on my back. This was to be mine forever.

Zora Neale Hurston, on her initiation into voodoo (1969:192)

The sleepwalkers are coming awake, and for the first time this awakening has a collective reality; it is no longer such a lonely thing to open one's eyes. Re-vision – the act of looking back, of seeing with fresh eyes, of entering an old text from a new critical direction – is for women more than a chapter in cultural history; it is an act of survival.

Adrienne Rich (1979:35)

Storm's a comin'
  a blowin' for you and for me.

Linda Mussmann (1987)

Feminist endeavor has long labored in the effort to wake sleepwalkers – to incite active subjects where patriarchal worldviews had calcified passive objects. Writers forming the backbone of twentieth-century Western feminist philosophy, such as Virginia Woolf and Simone de Beauvoir, worked to bring about an Other perspective, the view from the looking glass as it were, to invest the object's occluded eye with the fraught and sometimes multiple "I" of a newly born subject. Ironically, however, the attempt to "re-vise," to open the eyes of objectified woman to some kind of woman-identified counter-sight, some counter-subjectivity, became, even as it began to succeed, entangled in the post-colonial problematics of humanist identity. Even as "woman" struggled to emerge, the structural impossibility of her arrival on the scene as a "subject" became only more apparent – her emergence necessarily called into question the humanist category of unitary subjectivity and threatened the uniocular perspectivalism that props that subjectivity. As Woolf and de Beauvoir were both aware, the problem was paradoxical: when Others became Selves, Selves, historically founded on the distinction from said Others, became impossible. Thus, at the threshold of identity, the doorway appeared illusory, a cardboard cut-out from a Hollywood Western. At the threshold of this illusion, the impossible amalgam "woman self" threatened to expose the politics, to show the show in the rickety boundary between Self and Other. In a sense, then, "woman" became only more clearly the riddle she had been inscribed to be.

Needless to say, the broad poststructural collapse of identity into its own illusions presented, at the close of the 1980s, a renewal of this paradox for endeavors marked feminist. Notions like Adrienne Rich's – that waking from sleepwalking could mean the "survival" of women – began to ring hollow. Should "woman" really survive? Was there anything really to rescue, falling as "woman" does under the category of "mankind"? The question ran parallel to postcolonial inquiry. Should colonial categories survive? Should persons continue to be understood by categories such as colonizer and colonized, master and slave? Does maintenance of such categories maintain historical privileges delineated by said categories? Or, just as the colonized are no longer colonial subjects but post-colonials, should we declare ourselves postgender and approach the conditions of our gender distinctions as a historical situation with present-day repercussions but without present-day investment? Should we allow distinctions such as "man" and "woman" to become historical mythemes, outmoded ways of knowing? Should we look instead at the ways our bodies and identities have historically been marked relative to socio-political agendas, loosening ourselves from the ultimate jurisprudence of those markings?

Though survival came under question, Adrienne Rich's metaphor of sleep-walking remained pertinent. Late 1980s and early 1990s materialist feminists began to employ the dream metaphor in a more Benjaminian sense. Waking from the dreamscape of modern identity came to mean awakening not "out" of the dream and into "reality," but more precisely waking "into" the dream – awakening to the fact that we dream, that our social reality, our Symbolic Order, is affected, even constituted, by our social dreamscapes.[1] Thus we acknowledge the collective dream-properties of the Symbolic Order and simultaneously recognize those dreamscapes as bearing reality effects. Waking up to a dream and to dream effects means that the utopian notions of "escape" and "survival" have to be reconsidered. Dream effects do not automatically dissipate upon waking. Identity effects, bodily markings, historical legacies repeat as noisome ghosts of collective memory, marking and re-marking the wake-walker within the social dreamscape.[2]

Though we grapple with the reality effects of patriarchy's gender-dreams in everyday life – though a woman in the '90s makes some 72 cents to a man's dollar – "woman," "man," and even "gender" are no longer solid rocks on which to pose one's identity politics. If the door beckoning us to try to achieve subjectivity, selfhood, active and substantive identity – the door, that is, to full inclusion in "mankind" – has been recognized as the dream or mirage historically veiling the imperial privilege of propertied white men, then the suggestion from 1990s gay and lesbian, postcolonial, and feminist quarters shifted from the attempt to enter the room marked subject, to the effort to get said subjects to "come out" from behind the veils of subjectivity. Thus the growing theoretical and practical strategy has been to wield the veil or guise of subjectivity against itself, to engage in the performative, enact identity as mirage, as decoy, as strategy – exaggerate, parody, expose, and finally abandon unitary notions of identity altogether. Indeed, the impasse at the threshold of identity dreams has begun to generate inspired inquiries into the engenderment of our illusions and the performative bases of "nature." The impasse itself becomes passage, and "passing" or "posing" its operative trope in an emergent line of theoretical inquiry marked "queer."

The queer unsettles the norm – or asks the norm to "come out" from behind the veil of its dreamscaped secretions. When the familiar is made strange, when the norm is recognized as queer (or when the queer can become the norm), then "gender" as a foundational way of knowing loses a good deal of its exchange value. The current uproar about "family values" and "loss of morality" has a good deal to do with fear, and a good deal to do with concern for the functioning of a capitalist "free market" – a market which has depended on a gendered divide between production and consumption, the maintenance of a conceptual space for commodity exchange through the marking of work-based production spheres as masculine and domestic/leisure consumption spheres as feminine. Without gender, or more to the point, without compulsory heterosexuality as a foundational base delimiting "men" and "women," distingiushing "production" and "consumption," what becomes of sense-making? When we embrace the full implications of Luce Irigaray's insight into gender and capital in *This Sex Which is Not One* (1985a), how do we retain even our most fundamental habits of engenderment, of meaning, of exchange?[3] Without gender what happens to knowledge? To the law? To capital? To capitalist laws of knowledge?

A certain social terror accompanies this storm. Theater director Linda Mussmann employed the twister as an allegory in her 1987 play *If Kansas Goes* to point to binary terrorism – the terror that accompanies the dismemberment of our comfortable distinctions, the unsettling of sense:

> She watched it growing blacker and blacker.
> The leaves on the elms turned underside-up.
> She watched things tumble across the plains.
> The dust and the objects too light to hold their own
> rolled across the horizon.
> Yes the storm was a comin'
> The air pressure was rising and breathing became more difficult
> as she watched the dark and the light argue
> Was this day or was this night?
> The two negotiated . . .
> first one then the other.
> light to dark
> dark to light
> one then the other
> and then both at once . . .

And was I ready to meet my maker?
I thought.
Not yet
and yet . . .

(Mussmann 1987; see also Schneider 1988/89)

Storms, of course, are passing things. But Mussmann chooses to ride rather than survive, and Zora Neale Hurston, in the counter-colonial logic of Haitian voodoo (Dayan 1991), claims the storm as her source of power. From the logic of the storm, stasis or the status quo might be the passing thing. Riding with the storm is to see stasis as passing. And passing is, perhaps, the stuff of stasis: the norm "passes," after all, as that which is settled, passing for the fixed, the natural, as that to which we think we must return, twisted as we are in its embrace.

IMPASSE: UNNATURAL ACTS

1993. I watch a woman on a bed in a video.

Scratch, glitch, break.

Glitches and scratches, breaks and doubled images tell me "art" or "avant-garde" or any number of referents which locate me historically, aesthetically, and to a certain extent politically in the scene of viewing – a woman on a bed. Dips and bends and waves in the video image separate this woman on this bed from other women on other beds – beds in popular culture, beds which open themselves across the wide screens of the American Cinema of the Twin Duplex variety. Or perhaps the doubled images by which the bed appears to slide in and out of itself, to double over on its lovers, to swerve and slip beyond its own materiality – perhaps these liberties from stasis serve to separate me, the viewer, from other viewers before other beds in other, less seemingly self-concerned, or self-aware venues. I wonder about this as I watch the woman on the bed, or at least I run the video back across my mind, thinking about the doubling slips and slides and thinking about, watching for, "a way" to write the scene of performance artist Carolee Schneemann on the bed of her own video, in the frame of "art," getting laid.

Getting laid.

Slip. Slide.

Like so many other women on so many other beds, this woman makes love. We are accustomed to popular culture, well versed in mainstream "appropriate" depictions of "appropriate" desire (man has woman). Precedent leaves us practiced at reading the woman's body as the site of the sex that takes place. How can we not be versed in the patriarchal, heterosexual imperative which drives our mainstream narrative structures and by which we read that She signifies sex while He has sex? We know, in other words, that she is the sex that he has. But here I come to a twist in the narrative, a glitch in the image. The video is Schneemann's 1991 *Vesper's Stampede to My Holy Mouth*, and Schneemann's cat, Vesper, is Schneemann's lover.

Schneemann's cats had appeared in earlier films, most notably her early *Fuses* (1964/65), a film which documented Schneemann's explicit lovemaking with her human male partner James Tenney. *Fuses* featured Kitch, a gray kitty who watched Schneemann's erotic/art escapades with Tenney from a dignified remove. Unlike Kitch, however, Vesper no longer watches Schneemann's lovemaking from a distance. Indeed the distance has dramatically collapsed. In *Vesper's Stampede*, the male lover has disappeared and the artist's lover has become, explicitly, the artist's cat. Of course, bestiality is no stranger to art or popular culture – after all, Disney's *Beauty and the Beast* was also released in 1991 – but Schneemann's beast, kissed, refrains from popping into a blond, biceps-beridden prince. No symbolic leaps here, no metaphoric stand-ins, but the twist and slap of the literal: her pussy remains, resolutely, her pussy.

On my screen, Schneemann kisses and, yes, is kissed by a cat, licked by a cat, touched by a cat which, I can see, sticks its tongue in her mouth to pleasure her as they roll on the bed. Video effects by videographer Victoria Vesna, and Schneemann's thirty-year history as performance artist and film-maker, serve to assure me that on the one hand this piece is intended as "art." On the other hand, I am coaxed by the voice-over to believe that there are no kitty food tricks here, that this is something "real," something documentary, something intimate and exposed between true loves. As in *Fuses*, Schneemann reaches for the everyday, the sense of passionate and quotidian intimacy as it repeats across familiar bodies. *Fuses*, documenting Schneemann's lovemaking with her human male partner, underscored a kind of vibrant erotic ease between mates – one might say a "natural" passion (augmented by the fact that heterosexual intercourse is naturalized in this culture). *Vesper's Stampede* puts forward that same quotidian passion and similarly strives toward a notion of "nature" – but here that "nature" confronts social convention, almost in direct proportion to the gentle quotidian flow of the voice-over. Bestiality is defined in Webster's Ninth Collegiate Dictionary as "sexual relations between a human being and a lower animal," and to be bestial is to "lack in intelligence or reason," or to be "marked by base or inhuman instincts or desires." Rubbing against the grain of convention, woman and man are replaced by woman and cat. As opposed to the historical fetishization of woman *as* desire in a heterosexual paradigm (she *is* his desire), Schneemann, involved with her cat, becomes overtly "marked" by her own "base" desires, – she *has* desires and they are base (see Plate 2.1).

Human heterosexual sexuality is licensed and promoted by society through representation and law, veiling that sexuality in the cloak of "natural" as if sexual mores and practices were not always already socially and culturally discursive. Bestiality, however, is deeply marked socially, related historically to other socially contested practices, such as homosexual sex or cross-racial sex, under the general rubric "Crimes Against Nature." In *Vesper's Stampede to My Holy Mouth*, and in a series of photographs titled *Infinity Kisses*, Schneemann's criminality (which she dubs, like Vera's temple reference, "holy") is presented as banally quotidian. The criminal accrues to Schneemann's actions only because she tenderly rolls it along, resisting an aggrandizing bullhorn which might proclaim her sexual

Plate 2.1 A selection of photographs from Carolee Schneemann's *Infinity Kisses* series, 1991. Courtesy of Carolee Schneemann.

relations "shocking and transgressive." Schneemann does not claim transgression, rather she claims quotidian normativity – and that claim of quotidian becomes, ironically, her transgression. Sidestepping the historical bravado behind many transgressive avant-garde actions,[4] Schneemann combines her roots in 1960s Fluxus art and Judson Church performance with her 1960s and 1970s cultural feminist autobiographical impulse (the personal as political) to let her bestial documentations slip into the yawning profanity of the everyday. As casually as she might floss her teeth, insert her tampon, look in her mirror – she accepts Vesper's kisses. The camera shifts from straightforward footage to the slip and slide of editing techniques as the video artwork, too, slaps against the steady documentary tone of the voice-over.

Questions stimulated by kitty kisses ricochet easily off the backdrop of current feminist theory. Feminists of the materialist school have heralded gender a "basically innovative affair," examining the social and political underpinnings of gender construction in hopes of busting if not entirely out of "womanhood," then certainly out of the rigidity of its epistemological delimitations (Butler 1990a:282). Because it is obvious in Schneemann's bestial provocation that kitty's precise gender (is Vesper male or female?) is neither apparent nor important to the video, the work implies a bypass of gendering altogether *vis-à-vis* sexuality. Perhaps such art-bestiality is a multiplication of sexualities as much as an interruption of gender codes, that is, a multiplication of possibilities in the hope-filled vein of Derrida's "incalculable choreographies" (Derrida and MacDonald 1982:76). Or perhaps, more provocatively, by flagrantly denying gender, bestiality in fact points to the tyranny of gender's "norms," making them apparent for critique. Perhaps both. After all, humans are habitually marked as "animal" or "primitive" based on markings of race and class, inevitably tangling the explicitly marked body in representation with the historical trajectory of socially instituted hierarchies of humanity.[5]

Over a sound collage of cat purrs, Schneemann speaks straightforwardly of the traditional symbolic conflation of women with cats – the "promiscuous beast" in Manet's *Olympia*. She cites the torture and murder of cats together with the "witches" that cared for them, and the history of cats as women's "familiars" and sexual partners. As the image in the frame doubles and twists upon itself, Schneemann speaks tenderly of her relations with Vesper and Vesper's immediate predecessor, Cluny, in the intimate details of their everyday love lives. "Interspecies erotic imagery," Schneemann has said with an artist's confidence. But in another tone of voice: "My cat Cluny was the first and the best" – somewhat wistfully, with a smile.[6]

What does "shock value" mean, if anything, in today's twitching, shell-shocked field of postmodern intentions? Is there yet some punch in the modernist drive toward montage – the scratch/glitch schism between the familiar and the strange through which the great white hope of critical inquiry had envisioned itself flashing, seeping, coming? What is the significance of the fact that in *Vesper's Stampede*, as in much art/life performance art, any shock that accrues to Schneemann's bestiality accrues as much to the banal frame of her autobiographical "real" life as to the "unnatural" act she performs in that quotidian space? That is, the schism, the shock, and ultimately the critical punch in Schneemann's work rests not simply in her provocation of the "unnatural," but in her exploration of cultural distinctions *between* natural and unnatural as she confounds those distinctions across the stage of her quotidian sexuality – her own body, in her own bed, every day. Here, as across almost all thirty years of her work, Schneemann makes of herself a kind of living human montage – a walking, breathing, sensate allegorical dilemma – as she stubbornly retains a sensuous sense of Nature while at the same time embracing Nature's myriad self-shattering crimes. She is, in a sense, a double agent: both a cultural feminist Earth Mother/Goddess and, simultaneously, a disaster at the cultural heart of our concepts of Nature – again, a natural disaster. Her work causes cultural assumptions about the natural and unnatural to ricochet against their own projections, off the screen of her own body, the scene of her art, the seen of her everyday life, into a kind of critical relief.

What is particularly important here is that the seemingly paradoxical positioning between the natural and the criminal is a split particularly familiar to the social engenderment of "woman." In her study of the history of witchcraft and its strategic revitalization in cultural feminism, Sylvia Bovenschen points with no uncertain irony to the traditional perception of the "unnatural" state of witchery as inherently imbedded in the "nature" of female sexuality, which is to say paradoxically that female nature contains within it an inherent crime against nature (1978:86). Marilyn Frye has written on how this natural/unnatural conundrum conspires to erase women as sentient, "real" beings of substance and authority. Speaking of lesbians rather than witches Frye writes:

> The fact that these relations are characterized as unnatural is revealing. For what is unnatural is contrary to the laws of nature, or contrary to the nature of the substance of the entity in question. But what is contrary to the laws of nature cannot happen: that is what it means to call these laws the laws of nature. And I cannot do what is contrary to my nature, for if I could do it, it would be in my nature to do it. To call something "unnatural" is to say it cannot be. This definition defines sapphists, that is lesbians, as naturally impossible as well as logically impossible.
>
> (1983: 159)

Frye goes on to illustrate how this erasure is in fact the case for all women, saying "women, in general, are not countenanced by the phallocratic scheme, are not real: there are no women" (1983:162).

The effect of inscribing women as "other" with a nature which cancels nature is to exile women to the paradoxical realm of a reality which is always already fantastical, a really unreal – or, a reality which cancels a woman's status as "real" in favor of her service to performativity, masquerade, representation. This is the situation explicated by Lacan in his analysis of women's foreclosure from the Symbolic only to return "in the Real of the symptom" – the symptomatic realm of representation.[7] The abundance of women in representation is simply, then, an abundance of the dictum of woman as representation, rather than a link to any woman existing independently of or prior to that representation. Constructed as a natural unnatural, an unreal real, woman has existence relative only to her representation: her representation both precedes and succeeds her, she is always chasing after it. What the whirlwind of such analysis lays bare, then, is that ultimately even "she herself" stands for her own representation – a particular woman stands beside herself, representative of the way womanhood has been represented (as a successful or failed, compliant or belligerent copy).[8] Frye's contention that "there are no women" is revised by Deborah Tannen to catch woman in relation to her representation: "there [are] no unmarked women" (1993:54). And, as we will soon see, we might translate "unmarked" to suit the particular demands of the capitalist dreamscape: there are no private women.

The body marked female has signified the feminized realm of representation, and the obsessive representation of woman in terms of desirability has served to inscribe the agency of the representer as masculine. Frye points out that in order to buttress women's delimitation to the representational realm, "women" have been structurally blinded. In Frye's words, the "phallocratic scheme [can]not admit women as authors of perception, as seers" (1983:165). Such an admittance would give "women" agency as producers. Blindness is a marker of woman's relegation to the scopic field, but more, it is a marker of her historical relegation to the private sphere of consumption rather than the public sphere of production. Developing capitalism entrenched women within the domain of private life, relegating her to the role of consumer, a delimitation which gendered the sphere of production as male, "man-made," civilized, and progressive. Marked and marketed as consumers, women have historically been denied access to the executive means of production, as notions of "abundance" shifted from maternal to paternal paradigms of productivity (Lears 1994:17–39). Her role as nonproducer kept the domain of the private, leisure-marked home separate and distinct from the public, work-marked domain, generating and maintaining a conceptual space for commodity exchange. The feminine became consumptive. Yet she stood, ironically, as the abundantly public insignia of white male rights to "private" property, indeed his right to self-possession (see Robinson 1996). It is this situation which creates a paradox in the notion of a private woman, a self-possessed woman. Self-possession, both of consumer and commodity, seemed to defy the dictates of the desire-driven market which she served, standing, as she did, as the *public* insignia of the *private* realm, the consumptive vehicle of masculine private property.

As consumers who did not produce products – or were not Producers even when they were workers – so too women were represented but did not produce representation – or had to struggle inordinately for acknowledgement when they did. As consumer *and* emblematic insignia of commodity status, she was given to consume herself. She signified the visual terrain of representation, marking it with consumptive desire, but she was rarely acknowledged as an image-maker, she did not "see." This blinding arguably enabled a stream of desire marked as an insatiable and limitless one-way street in which the consumer was feminized, inscribed with lack (a lack which could propel exchange), always chasing after her own image as if chasing after her own denied vision.[9] Women of color were not only blinded, but, as Anne McClintock notes in an analysis of advertising and colonialism, generally vanished, rendered invisible in the desire-marked terrain of representation by which white women and colonial men of color were feminized through "exhibition value." The "voyeuristic panorama of surplus as spectacle" adopted white women as fetishes of the (fetishizing) logic of commodities, propping the market and signifying, paradoxically, *both* insatiability/inaccessibility *and* white man's privileged access, his "market worth" (McClintock 1995:208, 219, 225). In seeking to possess her and her emblematic consumptiveness (consider the high model's anorectic vacancy), he acquires not satisfaction but the social insignia of insatiability – inaccessibility itself. He "owns" or "controls" or is "wedded to" consumption itself, the inaccessible emblem, the driving force of market fever. He *has* consumption – she *is* consumption.

TWISTER: LOOKING INTO LOOKING OUT

Contemporary feminist performance artists present their own bodies beside or relative to the history of reading the body marked female, the body rendered consumptive in representation. In this sense, the contemporary explicit body performer consciously and explicitly stands beside herself in that she grapples overtly with the history of her body's explication, wrestling with the ghosts of that explication. Given this "standing beside," or "side-stepping" to borrow from Elin Diamond (1989:68), feminist artists can be understood to present their bodies as dialectical images.

"Dialectical image" is a phrase coined by Walter Benjamin to refer to an object or constellation of objects which tell the secret – which reveal or expose the traces of their false promises, their secret(ed) service to the dreamscapes of capitalism. Dialectical images are objects which show the show, which make it apparent that they are not entirely that which they have been given to represent – the way cracks in face paint or runs in mascara might show the material in tension with the constructed ideal. Like secrets bared, dialectical images evidence commodity dreamscapes as bearing secrets, as propped by masquerade. For Benjamin, prostitutes present prime dialectical images. As "commodity and seller in one," prostitutes show the show of their commodification and cannot completely pass as that which they purport to be. Dialectical images such as prostitutes (Benjamin also cites used or outmoded commodities) can talk or gesture back to the entire social enterprise which secret(e)s them. For Benjamin, reading dialectical images for the secrets they tell and the memories they hold provides a counter-history to modernity's myriad promises. Objects accumulating in the cracks of dreams, in the promises of "progress," can be read back against pervasive myths of nature, value, and social order.

Dialectical images provoke a viewer/reader to think again – to take a second look. It is somehow in the flickering undecidability between the viewing subject's reading and the object's cracks (exposing masquerade) that dialectical images threaten to work. The challenge in engaging dialectical images seems to lie somewhere between – a space at once exceedingly private, full of located and personal particulars of reading, and radically public, full of socially inscribed dreamscapes, pretexts for reading. The crack of this space between the personal particular and the socially inscribed is a fraught space. It is a space feminist performance artists, and cultural critical theorists writing on performativity have been approaching as deeply imbricated in the social dynamics of the marked body.

Into this fraught space I found myself repeatedly placing a specific contemporary performance artist, pornographer and prostitute Annie Sprinkle, as one places a question mark. In my mind, Sprinkle also sat at the threshold of the "both/and," the messy impasse between essentialist and constructivist critiques of gender. Sprinkle's work became, for me, problematically emblematic of the tense stand-off between the literal, material body and her complex ghosting, the symbolic body of "woman."

I had been running the Sprinkle performance of *Post Porn Modernism* I had seen at The Kitchen in Manhattan in 1990 across my memory in a kind of eternal return. I kept replaying the image of Sprinkle's spectators standing in the line that bridged the magic gulf between the stage and the house, waiting to accept Sprinkle's invitation to shine flashlights through the speculum she had inserted into her vagina. Sprinkle called this scene a "Public Cervix Announcement." As she labored in the awkward project of inserting the speculum – bent over herself, easing it in – she joked and smiled at her audience, explaining that any spectator who wished could come to the edge of the stage to See the Big Show (see Plate 2.2). She had already held up a hand-drawn diagram, explicating the female parts in anatomical proportion, describing their function and placement like an excessively compliant Sex Education nurse of Junior High School fantasies. Now she sat spread-eagled at the edge of the stage, speculum inserted, with an attendant or two (sometimes male, sometimes female) ready to pass out flashlights to brave audience members.

Spectators had to choose either to join the line of spectators leading up to the stage to peer through the speculum one by one, or to remain in their seats watching other spectators spectating Sprinkle's cervix. Spectators who chose to stand in line would find themselves rubbing shoulders with all kinds of expectations. Sprinkle's shows in art venues generally draw a mixed crowd: porn fans as well as art-world connoisseurs, sprinkled with a batch of New Age sex positivists. Distinctions have the opportunity to blur. Interestingly, porn *aficionados* often came to The Kitchen armed with large zoom-lens cameras, ready to step right up and snap their private shots, an action welcomed by Sprinkle as "OK" and even "fun." Avant-garde seekers came expecting the shock or the rush of this encounter – the "slumming" so familiar to the cutting edge. New Agers waited for the holy masturbation scene, in which Annie croons and masturbates in the name of self-transformation and accepting love. But whether one chose to remain seated, or joined in the line of expectations, everyone had the opportunity to observe their own choices.

Plate 2.2 Annie Sprinkle inserting a speculum during a 1989 performance of *Post Porn Modernism*. Photo by Les Barany, courtesy of Annie Sprinkle.

For many in attendance, those choices became fraught with unexpected complexities. Theater director and academic Richard Schechner told me that on the night in 1990 when he attended Sprinkle's show at The Kitchen, he chose to stay in his seat. Schechner himself had mounted such sexually open avant-garde pieces as *Dionysus in 69* with the Performance Group, and had even cast Sprinkle in his *Prometheus Project* in 1985 (having "discovered" her Nurse Sprinkle show on 42nd Street when he took a graduate class in performance studies on a field trip to Times Square),[10] but because of the complex repercussions involved in choosing to look, he found himself remaining in his seat. "I chose not to look. That was an interesting choice for me. I was curious. But I was also with [female companions] and feared that my looking would be construed as 'being sexually excited' – and why not? – but I did not want to suffer the outcome of that 'accusation.'" Still, the choice not to look was as interesting and fraught as the choice to look. From their seats, spectators viewed the cervix from another angle: the wide-angled view of the cervix as show. Indeed the cervix itself was hardly any more of a show than the showing was a show, and this concatenation of display left no spot in the theater uninvolved – complicity was broadly based.

The first time I attended *Post Porn Modernism*, I was the only one of my companions (two women) who decided to join the line. Standing in line, however, I felt a mounting sense of confusion about my choice. How was I to focus my particular gaze? Who was I when I looked? And how would my looking be any different from the man with the large camera several spots in front of me who blurted out in a state of excitement: "It looks just like the head of my penis!"? These questions were not answered as I was ushered before Sprinkle and handed a flashlight. Neither were these questions answered when I saw Sprinkle smiling down at me from the stage like some kind of priest with a wafer in hand, beckoning me to "take, look." Neither were they answered when I saw the round pink cervix peeking back at me. Nor when I returned to my seat. Nor, really, to this day. Rather, the questions remain, in all their visceral tactility, the most fascinating aspect of the performance.

All of us at The Kitchen who chose to look stood in line for the theatrical "moment" when, at the site of the cervix, the name of art would slap against the name of porn across the stage within the stage, the proscenium of the prostitute's body. That this step would occur through the focusing device of gynecology invoking, that is, the scientific gaze of medical discourse, was replete with ironies. Unfolding the scene again and again across my memory, however, it grew in proportion and came to multiply into the tangle of questions that eventually formed the basis of this book. Playing the scene back, I found myself encountering Sprinkle's cervix as a theoretical third eye, like a gaze from the blind spot, meeting the spectator's – my – gaze. I imagined that gaze as a kind of counter-gaze which instantly doubled back over a field of modernist obsessions. I thought about Bataille's horror and fascination with the envaginated eyeball in his *Story of the Eye*, about Freud's inscription of the female genitals as "blinding" in "The Uncanny," and about Walter Benjamin's efforts to "invest" an object or the objectified with its own gaze, as if it might not already possess such capabilities of its own. Passing such remarkable modernists across the path of my inquiry I tried, in my mind's eye, to hold on to the tactile and viscous pinkness of Annie's cervical eyeball, peering out, effulgent, from the socket of her vagina. I thought about my own eye meeting this cervical gaze as well as my own eye seen seeing by Annie's other eyes, the ones in her head, watching me watch her and perhaps even catching the glint of her own cervix reflected in my retina. I thought of the smile she shot me. Did I smile back?

And then, in the midst of theories about third eyes and cervical gazes, there was the troubling reverberation of personal memory. The visceral experience of standing at the edge of the stage reminded me of standing at the edge of another stage – the stage in church – preparing to kneel with congregation members before the altar to accept Christ's Body into my own mouth. For me, this memory bore the slap of the literal when doubled with Sprinkle's more immediate bodily offering, and swept me away from academic discourse to face the more dangerous head winds of personal narrative.

My father was a Methodist minister. I am his oldest child. Protestants can take communion at any age, and so, as a minister's daughter, I began to practice communion very early, lining up at the altar to hear the voice of the father speaking with the Voice of the Father saying "take, eat, this is my body, which I give for you." When I was very young, I could not have fully distinguished between literal father and symbolic father. The literal father offered the Symbolic Father for consumption, and consumption signified repentance and forgiveness. When I grew older and understood that my literal father was not the Symbolic Father, I also came to understand, with "Father, Son, and Holy Ghost," that as a daughter I could never be a father, never a son – and was suspicious of the third, disembodied category as truly inclusive. So, even as I came to understand the distinction between literal and symbolic, I was solidly reminded of their link: that literal fathers and literal sons were as linked to the Symbolic as a gaze is to the side of a face.

Scratch, glitch

Literally speaking, it was a storm – a hurricane – that interrupted my repetitive rethinking of these encounters. I was far from The Kitchen, off the coast of Massachusetts, but still entranced, caught, by the lingering after-image of Sprinkle's performance and the theoretical and personal questions that followed in its wake, when I found myself in the midst of a "natural disaster." The storm disrupted my inquiry and dispersed the Sprinkle spectators and church congregation members that, like porn fans and art patrons, had lined up side by side in my mind. I had come, in any case, to an impasse.

If I had been looking for Annie's cervix somehow to look back at me, with some kind of female gaze, I was caught. The notion of a "returned" gaze or an object's eye seemed always to be reacting to an initializing challenge, always servicing a scene marked by the self-perpetuating and ultimately boring tango-hold of patriarchal objectification, always complicit in a drama of dominance or submission. The impulse to find an "object's eye," like a "female gaze," seemed fraught with the impulse to create yet another de-objectified subject, caught in the binaried dance between subject and object that had set the Western stage for the shadow play of gender in the first place. The object's eye, visioned, must tell a more complicated story than newly born subjecthood.

The tempest, at the point of impasse, offered more than a good reason to break.

Break.

I stepped outside the house onto the porch. Taking the enormous push of the wind as some kind of invitation and sensing the rush of first fear, I misrecognized myself as vital, witty enough to survive, ready. Never mind that the windows had been creaking as though possessed by spirits of the shipwrecked drowned. Never mind that there was something close to my own flesh color in the spiky tentacles of tree interiors twisted into sudden exposure. I stepped off the porch and onto the wide field of the yard. I was alive and infinitely capable – whipped by the rush, defying the elements, balancing on the edge of destruction.

I found my body flat on its face in an instant. Hit by a blast that must have jumped round the corner of the house, I was thrown well off the spot I'd been bravely, or naively, romancing. I crawled back to the porch, then into the house. Shaken by the infinitude of my own naiveté, I watched the rest of the unrest from the inside, through windows preoccupied with the whispered potential of instant explosion, sudden death. I watched trees twist off their own trunks, almost gracefully, and come dramatically down as if in a bow of submission, as if in respect for the quick visibility of invisibility, the sudden fact of a fall, the instant blast of devastation.

Then came the eye – like a hole in the real. The eye of a storm is a hollow, sunny place in the middle of devastation where a force that hit one way inverts itself and hits in reverse. Past and future at once, the eye is vacated of the present. A horrible stasis where an impulse that threw itself outward waits for ricochet, as a gaze, reflecting against glass, is thrown back upon itself in a moment of recognition. Or perhaps the uncanny calm in the eye of a storm resembles the force of a gaze which, meeting its object in a literal eye, stands for a moment uncertain of the force of the counter-gaze by which it may be expelled against itself, abjected.

In that unsettling space of silence when force circles back as its own counterforce, I began to rethink the notion of the object's eye and came, eventually, to reframe the question in terms of an uncanny counterpart, shrouded, or secreted, in the raging rush of invisibility. What is the danger in the uncanny calm? What is the danger in an unseen eye, or the eye of the unseen, suddenly seen? Perhaps attempts to rescue a female gaze or discover an object's eye – to bring, we might say, the seeming blinded to seeming sight – displaces or shrouds another, more complex issue. Can the drive to invest the objectified with a counter-gaze be considered relative to another notion: the unsettling eye of a secret? The eye of that which has been secreted? The eye, hidden and denied, which nevertheless sees and has seen? And what does the secreted see?

The storm passed.

I went back to thinking about Sprinkle, a make-up bedecked disaster in the natural.

In theory, "real" "live" prostitute Annie Sprinkle in her *Post Porn Modernism* lay at the threshold of the impasse between true and false, visible and invisible, nature and culture as if in the eye of a storm. As any "whore" is given to be in this culture, she is a mistake, an aberration, a criminal, and a hoax: a show and a sham made of lipstick, mascara, fake beauty marks, and black lace. But a "whore" is also somehow woman untamed, woman unsocialized, woman unclassed, woman uncultured – woman, that is, "natural." When Sprinkle lays literally at the edge of the stage and inserts a speculum into her vagina so that art-world spectators and porn fans alike can line up to catch a glimpse of her cervix, she one-ups holy precedence. If Duchamp presented the toilet seat as "art," Sprinkle presents the prostitute as artist. Indeed, a toilet stands at the left side of the stage throughout her performance, and she uses it at one point to demonstrate a "golden shower" as she douches and then pisses in a mock urination (Plate 2.3). Here we have Living Whore, icon of modernism, historic toilet seat of humanity, the oldest (illegal) profession, revealed in the frame of flesh and declaring herself, adamantly, with celebration and feeling, "Post."

But how "post" is "post"? While I am performing a reading of Sprinkle's performance that privileges critical analysis, albeit peppered with personal investment, Sprinkle herself most often articulates the hope that her performances would result in spiritual transcendence. Sprinkle's declaration of herself as "post" modern is fraught. At the same time that she presents her identity as masquerade, she looks to her profession as "holy." While this might lead to interesting thoughts on holiness as born of or linked to masquerade, or experience of masquerade as somehow "sacred," Sprinkle does not make such a leap apparent in her work. Rather, she reaches toward her "post" through a nostalgic search for a sacrality imagined as lost and finds it in the lore of "ancient sacred prostitutes." *Post Porn Modernist* ends with a ritual masturbation designed to transcend "sex-negativity" and offer a healing, spiritual union through mutual "sex-positivity" – a mutuality achieved, ironically, in a display of auto-eroticism. Indeed, Sprinkle has written that this "Masturbation Ritual" is her favorite part of the show:

> Everyone in the audience gets a rattle which they shake while I breathe, undulate and masturbate myself with a vibrator into an erotic trance, often to full-bodied and clitoral orgasms. It is a ritual originating from the ancient sacred prostitutes, which I re-create on stage. It is these moments in which I feel most powerful; a shaman/witch/ healer, capable of visions.
>
> (1991:112)

To the toilet and sex toys, Sprinkle adds healing, ritual, and a primitivism linked to shamanism. The speculum and the rattles became interchangeable and to the already competing frames of "porn" and "art" which collide at The Kitchen, Sprinkle adds spirituality.

Plate 2.3 Annie Sprinkle urinating on stage during a 1989 performance of *Post Porn Modernism*. Photo by Les Barany, courtesy of Annie Sprinkle.

But the tumult of competing frames Sprinkle brings to the stage is arguably part and parcel of her point. Her stage, her "post," is, after all, itself the question: porn or art? sacrilege or sacred? science or shamanism? In a tangle of class issues, The Kitchen as venue arguably retains its identity as a trendy "art" space versus an arty "porn" theater, but the challenge posed by porn at the post of art is redolent. The "post" in Sprinkle's declaration ricochets against the "modernism" like a question mark. It is the undecidability, the competition of frames, which allows us to read Sprinkle's work as a postmodern parody of a modernist aesthetic – a doubling back over modernist canonical obsession with the explicit female body, and explicitly the prostitute's body, as a primary foundation for the erection of high modern identity.

Perhaps Sprinkle's porn/art can be read as a "take" on precedent masterpieces such as *Origin of the World* (see Plates 2.4 and 2.5), Gustav Courbet's 1866 painting of a woman's belly, thighs, and genitals so "realist" that its one-time owner, Jacques Lacan, kept it veiled behind an abstract "hiding device" constructed by surrealist painter André Masson (Faunce and Nochlin 1988:178). Or perhaps Sprinkle's *Post Porn Modernism* can be read as a performative "take" on Manet's *Olympia*, taken a few steps further than *Site*, the 1964 remake of *Olympia* by Robert Morris with Carolee Schneemann discussed in Chapter 1. Sprinkle's version of *Site* might be dubbed *Sight*. Sprinkle spectators line up to get a peek at the scene of her cervix embedded in her exposed pussy, which is in turn embedded in her specific body, kinkily clothed in the raiment of a porn queen. The body, on a bed raked for visibility, is embedded on the stage of The Kitchen, which is an art space embedded in the tradition of the avant-garde, embedded in the larger frame of the art establishment, embedded in ideals of Western history, a history of a patriarchy which, broadly speaking, can be said to be embedded in the effort to manipulate and control . . . the scene of the cervix.

If we can dub Sprinkle's show *Sight* we can also see her piece as a performative riff on another modernist classic: Duchamp's final work, *Etant donnés* ("Given That . . . ") (Plate 2.6), in which a woman's naked torso lies in bracken on the other side of a hole in a door. The woman's head and one of her arms are not given to be seen. Her legs are parted to expose her genitals which lie at the center of the image. In this 1946 assemblage, Duchamp makes an overt depiction of Western habits of specularity: perspectival vision, with woman as vanishing point as well as origin – woman as infinite recession, infinite reproduction. Rosalind Krauss, after Jean-François Lyotard, suggests that Duchamp's piece is based on the system of classical perspective but is simultaneously "maliciously at work to lay bare that system's hidden assumptions" (Krauss 1993a:113).

What is perspective? What is perspectival vision? And what are its "hidden assumptions?" *Perspectiva* is a Latin word that means "seeing through." Signaling the science of sight, perspective is umbilically linked to Renaissance concepts of humanism. In early use, perspective was a term applied to various optical devices, but it also came to mean the art of delineating solid objects upon a plain surface so that a drawing produces the same impression of apparent relative

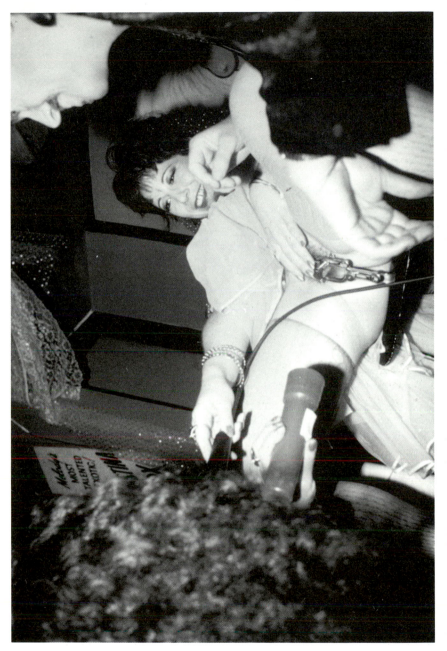

Plate 2.4 Annie Sprinkle with speculum inserted as spectators look at her cervix during a 1989 performance of *Post Porn Modernism*. Photo by Les Barany, courtesy of Annie Sprinkle.

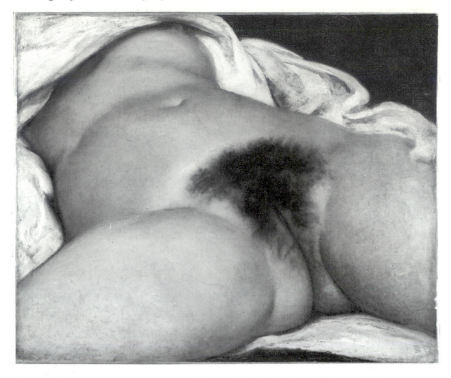

Plate 2.5 Gustav Courbet, *Origin of the World*, 1866. Musée d'Orsay; © photo
RMN–M. Bellot.

positions, magnitudes, and distance as do the "actual" objects when viewed from
a particular point. Perspective, then, is reproduction of the "actual," but it is also
construction of that real – a delineation, through representation, of the defining
characteristics of "actuality" as relative to and marked by *distance* – distance as
marked from an unremarked, unseen viewer. The use of perspective made use
of geometry (thus Lacan calls perspectival vision "geometral vision") by the
application of straight lines measured from the viewing eye to the
object in space as those lines cross a grid delineating the scopic field. Where the
receding parallel lines appear to meet is the vanishing point – and that point,
geometrically, is in exact proportion to the point of the viewing eye – an eye,
importantly, outside the field of its own vision.

   But here we must remark the hidden assumptions: within a patriarchal
economy of meaning, within, that is, the Symbolic Order of modernity,
perspective, like the worldview to which it gives symbolic form, is deeply
gendered. Within the terms of that order, the seeing eye is unseen. Its gaze penetrates a scopic field marked by distance. That gaze is rendered active, phallic, and
it is subject to and constituted by propriety of and anxiety about space. That
which is seen is, simultaneously, that which can never fully be seen. The scopic
field lays before the gaze but secret(e)s within it a point of vanishing, a mirror of

Plate 2.6 Etant donnés: la chute d'eau; le gaz d'eclairage, Marcel Duchamp, 1946–66. Philadelphia Museum of Art; gift of the Cassandra Foundation.

the viewer's own veil by which access of the field meets the black hole of infinite inaccessibility. The given to be seen, rendered passive, is feminized, made into an object of phallic (gaze) penetration, yet infinitely inaccessible even as "she" is infinitely accessed, surveyed, and purveyed.[11] This is the way we "know" how to "see." Perspectival viewing is a cultural practice at which we have been, to quote Erwin Panovsky, "habituated" (1991:34).

In Duchamp's *Etant donnés*, Krauss writes, "all the elements of perspective are in place, but in a strangely literal way."

> The role of the picture surface that slices through the visual pyramid of classical perspective is played, for example, by a brick wall, with the possibility of seeing-through that is normally a function of pictorial illusion now a matter of literally breaking down the barrier to produce a ragged opening. And the viewing and vanishing point, or goal of vision, is manifested by the dark interior of a bodily orifice, the optically impenetrable cavity of the spread-eagled "bride," a physical rather than a geometrical limit to the reach of vision. And the viewing point is likewise a hole: thick, inelegant, material.
>
> (Krauss 1993a:113)

Unpacking Duchamp's assemblage even further, Krauss, again through Lyotard, makes evident a veiled secret written into the geometrical underpinnings of perspectivalism. If perspective is orchestrated around the theoretical identity between viewing point and vanishing point, and if the vanishing point is inscribed as inscrutable lack, as always already vulvic, then "He who sees is a cunt." Here we glimpse an underpinning of patriarchal terror which the mechanism of perspective both institutes and secrets: when the peeping eyes "think they're seeing the vulva, they see themselves" (1993a:113).

In her "Public Cervix Announcement" section of *Post Porn Modernism*, Sprinkle takes Duchamp's literality, "maliciously at work," a step further. Sprinkle places her *particular* body, the artist's body, as terrain, as view. The "bride," in Sprinkle's piece, is not general woman (as in *Origin of the World* and *Etant donnés*), but particular woman with a particular life story – a story that ricochets out of the silence that surrounds the female body in modernist classics. Unlike *Origin* and *Etant donnés*, Sprinkle has eyes and a mouth, and they are often actively engaged in seeing and speaking, showing and telling. Sprinkle tells a life story in the course of her performance, showing slides of herself as a child when her name was Ellen Steinberg, and charting an abundance of identities from the porn queen Annie Sprinkle to the sex goddess "Anya." Her story underscores shifting subject positions, refusing primacy to any fixed identity as "artist," "woman," or "whore." Uniform self-hood is replaced by identity as a series of uniforms, are put on and taken off like lingerie or hospital whites, black leather or pinstripe suits. Even when she is naked on stage she plays with herself as if her body were a toy store or an amusement park, as if parts were as interchangeable as Lego pieces, as much fun as bumper cars. Some of the slides she shows of friends who have undergone sex changes or surgical alterations emphasize the element of choice and masquerade in Sprinkle's worldview. Even hardline feminist anger at the delimitation of women in patriarchy is questioned by Sprinkle's soft, cooing voice, emphasizing performativity and seeming to reassure her audience that there's nothing a knife, a needle, and thread can't take care of. After all, she says without bitterness or irony or political unrest, she made more money as a prostitute than she would have in other lines of "women's work." Anger, pain, disappointment – all can be dissolved with face paint, surgery, feather boas, or simply a radical sex-positive attitude shift and a dose of cross-gender, cross-class role play.

But the performative gender and class spoofing going on in *Post Porn Modernism* is far from simplistic. The performativity Sprinkle puts forward as "fun" has deep repercussions. The entire visual field is in revolt. Let us remember again Lyotard's formula concerning the vanishing point. Because of the geometrical identity between view point and vanishing point, when the viewing eyes "think they're seeing the vulva, they see themselves." But because Sprinkle is a particular woman and not "all women," because she insists on self as a set of unruly details, then when the peeping eyes think they're seeing the vulva — they *are* seeing the vulva: here, insistently, *Sprinkle's* vulva. And Sprinkle gets flagrantly to remark her pleasure: she is seeing the viewer seeing her vulva. Distance is remarked by a gaze emanating from *within* the scopic field, not penetrating into it from without, and, as such, distance twists against its framing, replayed across the traditional scopic field of the female body made explicit. Sprinkle's cervix is in fact made to be so blatant, so apparent, that it is clear she is taking voyeurism to a ludicrous extreme. The vanishing point becomes a spoof, the wink of complicity, a public secret turned into a public joke — a blind spot disavowed by the pink organicity of Sprinkle's show. And Sprinkle's body, unlike Duchamp's *Etant donnés* and Courbet's *Origin*, bears a head and a gaze which complicates the seeming identity between view point and vanishing point.

Might we consider Sprinkle's performativity as perspectivalism on the flip? A rupture provoked by the refusal of occlusion, the view *from* the blind spot — a chiasmatic twist by which a blind sight sited becomes a blind site sighted?

3 Permission to see

One face, one voice, one habit, and two persons,
A Perspective, that is, and is not.

William Shakespeare, *Twelfth Night*, v., i., 224

I watch a woman on a bed.

Scratch, glitch, break.

Like so many other women on so many other beds, this woman makes love. We watch, practiced in our cultural habits of viewing, reading the woman's body as the site of the sex that takes place. We have seen her so often presented in dominant culture as the prime terrain of visibility and we know how to view her as the passive, malleable emblem of desire. She is the landscape "seen through" the keyhole or the aperture or the eyeball, and according to the tenets of perspectival viewing, which is to say with Erwin Panovsky, the tenets of modernist humanism, all that we see, stretching from our eyeball to the vanishing point, is given to us to know – is, in other words, under the sway of our perspective (1991:27).

As we noted at the close of the last chapter, perspective is a deeply gendered way of seeing to which we are, after Panovsky, "habituated." The scopic field is riddled with desire, seeping into the infinite deferral of the vanishing point, and the gaze is disembodied at the same time that it is rendered phallic. To write the performance of Sprinkle on a bed in The Kitchen, or Schneemann on the bed in her own video, and to write my watching, is to summon the socio-cultural ghosts of perspective. Habituated, we are practiced at standing at the keyhole and, by the good graces of the painter or the photographer or the film-maker and his apparatus – apparatus historically modeled on the tenets of perspective[1] – we are practiced at viewing from a distance or a dislocation the properties of the seen. These properties – whether dictated by the verisimilitude of realism or abstracted into formal shapes to mirror what Clement Greenberg called the "conditions of vision" (1966:107) – are revealed and framed as secrets, exposed to an eye which is not seen seeing by that which is seen. Like a public secret, or the equally oxymoronic notion of a public private, the female body, or the body of the Other, becomes emblematic of the scopic field itself – as Duchamp illustrated in *Etant donnés*. This paradigm of perspective, as a historical habituation to any scene, haunts explicit feminist performance art. And performance art of the explicit body in turn interrogates the prerogatives of that ghosting.

GENDER IN PERSPECTIVE: HAVE WE REALLY GONE BEYOND?

In league with the humanist ideals of the Renaissance, perspective secularized the godhead into the eye of the beholder, and gendered that beholder after the gender of God. As John Berger remarks of this transformation, "The visible world is [in perspectivalism] arranged for the spectator as the universe was once thought to be arranged for God" (1972:16). Like God, the viewer is unseen. Conventions of perspective instituted and humanized the distantiation of omniscience, veiling and dislocating the viewer from the viewed by the secular science of mathematical proportion. As Martin Jay has noted, "The painter's own body . . . was effectively banished" (1993:56), even as the painter (and by extension the viewer) was presumed to be gendered, like God, male. The marker of the viewer/artist's godly gender was veiled, displaced onto his prerogatives of vision. In contrast, the given to be seen was rendered embodied object, reproducible by mathematical proportion and calculable distance: located, fixed, and blinded. The scopic field was feminized as passive – as accessible as it was, by virtue of the vanishing point, inaccessible. Men and women who appeared in the scopic field were fixed – sometimes in poses of pride and arrogance, as their portraits rooted their propriety into recessive eternity, beckoning an envy on the part of the viewer. Women were often undressed and spread across the terrain as emblems of the scopic field itself, beckoning the viewer to sense both the power of his gaze and the insatiability of his desire. She stretched across the field as an emblem of his desire to acquire that which, again by logic of the vanishing point, could never fully be acquired.

Classic perspective orients the field of vision to the viewer's veiled or vanished body, as if the scene itself emanates from the viewer's own gaze. The scene is subservient to that eye, at the same time that that eye is erased from implication in the visual field. Within the terms of perspective, there is no reciprocity – the seen does not see back. Classically, even if the seen is presented so as to be looking at the viewer (as in Titian's *The Venus of Urbino* or Manet's *Olympia*), what is acknowledged by the direction of her gaze (whether defiant or compliant) is the viewer's sight marking her as seen. She can only acknowledge that she is seen, but she cannot author vision, cannot see back. She does not render the viewer visible. Rather, she renders him sighted. Emblematic of the scopic field itself, she *is* the vision and he *has* the vision – she is the vision he has – just as Lacan would engender the logic of the fetish at the base of the Symbolic Order: she is the (fetishized) phallus, he has the phallus, she is the phallus he has.

Interestingly, the institution of perspective actually theatricalized the field of vision, creating "scenographic space" in which all that is given to be seen is, in a sense, staged for the viewer – laid out before him like his own future. In this sense, importantly, the seen became spectacle, an always already theatrical masquerade, a parade of desire, a dreamscape of wishes spread for potential consumption. This scenographic orientation in perspectivalism is, as Jay notes, "a notion of space congenial not only to modern science, but also, it has been widely argued, to the emerging economic system we call capitalism"(1993:57). The given to be seen grants an access to an "actual" marked by distance from the viewer. That distance beckons and simultaneously denies, invoking possession at the same time that it expands into an infinite, inaccessible dreamscape of masquerade hinged on the vanishing point. It is an inscription of distance and penetrability – a distance across which desire can be constructed as insatiable, and so constructed, can work its magic as the unending drive to accumulate, appropriate, possess, acquire.

Despite any number of attempts to find ourselves beyond the grip of perspectivalism or to locate nonperspectival roots in Western concepts of representation – such as Martin Jay's (1993) thesis that the denigration of vision in the twentieth century has led to the end of ocularcentrism, or Svetlana Alpers's attention to generally ignored nonperspectival traditions in painting – the historical primacy of perspectivalism, at the very least in our historicizing of art, is indisputable. Works which wrestle with the legacies of perspective reckon with the ghosts of those habituations. Sitting, watching, we conjure these ghosts, whenever we look for narrative line.[2] "Woman," wherever we recognize her signs, rebounds with the cultural construction of desire as insatiable, a narrative linked to the feminization of the scopic field as open for possession – a narrative replete with the heterosexual imperative[3] which renders the "phallic ghost" as modus operandi of seeing (Lacan 1981:88).

Critiques of perspective are arguably as old as modernity's signature for self-reflexivity – the modern's endless attempts to see himself seeing.[4] Indeed, modernist obsessions with vision as prime terrain of knowing are increasingly coupled, at the end of the nineteenth and into the twentieth century, with modernist suspicion and even fear of vision, provoking an increasing anti-ocularism. Modernist concern with ocularcentrism, however, may not have toppled the visual paradigm of perspective to the degree that some scholars contend, since the obsessional quality of modernist anxiety about vision exists in a tangled web of mutual dependency with modernist privileging of perspective's mastering subject. An anti-ocularism born of anxiety arguably serves to prop the perspectival paradigm more than erase its effects.[5]

But this question as to whether the late twentieth century has seen a shift in visual modality and has left perspectivalism behind is an important one. We can ask how radically habits of perspectivalism have been reorganized through the "relentless abstraction" of the visual field which has taken place in a long trajectory from Impressionist canvases to contemporary cybernetic and electromagnetic terrains, but we must be careful not to overlook the tracings or ghostings of perspectival habituation which remain. The mastering subject, figured so profoundly by perspectivalism, has been, Jay contends, undermined. Yet, contemporary pioneers of cyberspace can still proclaim that their medium will herald the death of the mastering subject, or at least the precariousness of his once omnipotent position, signifying that the ghost of that mastering subject continues to hold sway on our imagination, affecting our ways of seeing. Jonathan Crary, in *Techniques of the Observer*, puts the question this way:

> If there is in fact an ongoing mutation in the nature of visuality, what forms or modes are being left behind [and which are carried forward]? What kind of break is it? At the same time, what are the elements of continuity that link contemporary imagery with older organizations of the visual . . . ? The most urgent questions, though, are larger ones. How is the body, including the observing body, becoming a component of new machines, economies, apparatuses, whether social, libidinal, or technological? In what ways is subjectivity becoming a precarious condition of interface between rationalized systems of exchange and networks of information?
>
> (1991:2)

In asking these questions, Crary is advising caution in assuming that the herald of "new" is automatically a complete shift away from precedent models. Crary takes issue with what is so often historicized as a "new vision" brought about by modernist painters' late nineteenth-century seeming break with the long reign of perspectival realism.[6] Instead, Crary's analysis suggests a certain continuity of one of perspectivalism's fundamental tenets – the tenet of the detached observer.

Crary's analysis is worth examining closely. While looking to ways in which perspective has survived across the centuries, Crary simultaneously cautions against reading perspectivalism in a long and unbroken reign from Plato to the present (a continuity invested in by conservative and radical historians alike).[7] Instead of an unbroken line of perspective's primacy, Crary charts a "radical reconfiguration" of vision in modernity, one predating turn-of-the-century abstraction in painting – a reconfiguration that is importantly not an absolute rupture with perspectivalism but a reshaping in response to specific social, political, and economic pressures most concretely relative to the phantasmagoric role of the commodity and the "proliferation of circulating signs and objects whose effects coincide with their visuality"(1991:11). Crary sees the detachment, disembodiment, and objective (godlike) distance of the early modern observer transfigured into the subjectification and ultimate *dislocation* of the nineteenth-century observer when vision became not a privileged form of knowing but itself "an object of knowledge, of observation." Nineteenth-century science explored the biological properties of sight, reattaching the biological body to the viewer and reattaching the viewing eye to the field of vision. But such science simultaneously rendered that eye dislocated (if not detached) from that which it sees by virtue of the viewer's own mind, interpreting that which falls on his retina. The eye could no longer claim access to a "real world" through perception. Vision became a phantomic and phantasmic projection of the viewer's mind, dislocated from "reality," composed of mechanized formal elements subject to the terms of the viewer's always already subjective perspective.[8] Importantly, this shift from disembodied, transcendental and godlike detachment to embodied subjective dislocation maintains a partial contiguity with perspectivalism – a shift rather than an end. Though attached to the seeing body, vision remained separated, dislocated, from the scene before the gaze, isolated now in a kind of physiognomic, sensuous solipsism of "subjective vision."[9] Thus, in both early modern detached perspectivalism and later modern formalized, dislocated, and physiognomically sensual vision, the viewer is not in direct relation to something marked as a reciprocal "real," but is still detached in that the viewer remains unmarked, cut off, separated from the seen – either by extremes of transcendental objectivity or extremes of physiognomic and psychic subjectivity.

As perspective transmogrified across modernism, the fact of distance and dislocation between viewer and viewed has remained intact – a conceptual space for transactions of meaning determined always by the viewer's desire, like the conceptual space necessary for commodity exchange. If dislocation has remained intact, the viewer remains to some degree separate, un(re)marked by the scene before him. Perspectivalism had instituted a vanishing point within the field of vision, in direct mathematical correspondence to the seer, who was similarly vanished in that he was invisible to or dislocated from the seen which opened out before him. So, too, in nineteenth-century subjectivism and twentieth-century anti-ocular disillusionments with vision, the viewer remains dislocated (differently) from the scene in the anxious rendition Jay has noted as "visual indifference," by which "what you see" became "not what you get" (1994: 162–3). Either way, vision remains linked to "getting," acquiring – access or its denial. Either way, insatiability and lack, dislocation and distance, govern the interaction between viewer and viewed. Exchange across the visual field cannot admit mutuality, reciprocity, or even complicity. If anti-ocularists, as Jay charts them from Duchamp's "anti-retinal" to the hypervisuality of Baudrillard, could imagine vision as a two-way street, they nevertheless maintained a thoroughly untraversable median which rendered images as irrevocably severed from referents. In Jay's words, for perspectivalism's modernist discontents "what is perceived by the senses and what makes sense are split asunder" (1994:586). Still, however, in certain league with perspective, the viewer stands on the outside, unremarked by the viewed.

In late capitalist renditions of perspective, then, insatiability still reigns: the image/commodity does not "give" what it promises, the viewer does not "get" what he desires – he is destined to spend himself unseen, un(re)marked by the blinded object of his gaze, to try and try again, ritually stabbing at his own eyes like Oedipus. Ultimately he imagines he can give up on vision altogether in orgasmic thrall with his narrative of loss. The image, the object, is what must be "gotten" or abandoned. The given to be seen, like the commodity itself, is never considered to "get," but only to "give" or to deny.

To return to the roots of perspective, it is not inconsequential that the institution of the vanishing point and its logic of insatiability marked the institution, the "discovery," of a previously inconceivable notion of infinity (Koyre 1957). As Panovsky has explained, the vanishing point in perspective is relative to a shift in worldview from the concept of a closed universe to an infinite expanse, a never-ending recession and expansion of space, endlessly purveyable by an enterprising, colonizing and capitalizing subject/gaze.[10] The vanishing point, as mirror site of the viewer's dislocation, services enterprise and is elusively contained within the terrain of the envisioned, the commodified, as thus the feminine. The feminine, as emblematic of the given to be seen, became terrain, virgin territory made passive before a veiled masculine gaze. "She" is thus figured both as that which is traversable, the object possessable, and the inaccessible, the vanishing point of present knowledge – that which infinitely recesses, endlessly escaping the boundaries of phallocratic ordering. As that which is rendered visible as well as that which slips beyond vision, woman became emblematic of the modernist paradox of a possessable infinite – she is given to be origin as well as death in a universe which, paradoxically, contains no beginning and admits no end. Thus in the broad symbolic picture woman became, as Freud would acknowledge, a riddle – a riddle marked, above all, by sexuality.

As woman, like the horizon, contains the vanishing point of her difference – her sex marked as lack – then the aim to possess her could never be fully satiated, propelling infinite exchange, and the consumer's quest for the feminized object of masculinzed desire became, as Luce Irigaray put it, a "game of Chinese boxes. Infinitely receding" (1985b:134).[11] We read the female body as sex, but dominant tropes of heterosexuality play on both the overly visible terrain of bodily matter and on the slippery slope of language, "engenderment," the arena of language and its limits. Lacan placed language in symbolic league with the scopic field, catching language and vision in a thoroughly tangled embrace. To quote Jacqueline Rose, explicating Lacan, sexuality is conceived as "the vanishing point of meaning" (1982:47).[12] And thus, as feminist criticism has so often pointed out, "woman" – the traversable field, the site of sex – is constantly caught in a symbolic chase in which she is given to be uncatchable, caught as that which cannot be caught, known as that which cannot know or be known, meant as that which cannot mean. Emblem of consumptive desire and designated capitalist consumer, she sets out to consume *herself* in an anorectic frenzy of the logic of the vanishing point – attempting to consume her own inaccessible image, chasing after disappearance infinitely.

REFUSAL TO VANISH

Watching a woman (the sex that takes place), on a bed in a film is as familiar, today, as toothpaste. Though myriad sexual partnerings – men with men, women with women – exist in "alternative" venues, in general the "mainstream" admits a limited range of sexualities and even body-types to the big screen of Desire. Generally, exceptions in the mainstream tend to prove the rule. Inundated by dominant cultural habits of viewing, we are accustomed to tenets of naturalism, to watching as though we were not watching, or as though (a/the) woman, the spectacle, did not know we were watching. We watch, in other words, as though her role of being viewed and our act of viewing were some-how secret, not come to light, as if pleasure depended on the assumption that the seen cannot see back, or that she does not know she is seen. Even if the seen is presumed to know that she is being purveyed, we are practiced, as Lacan remarks in an aside, at assuming that pleasure is dependent on disavowal, dependent on our not letting her know that we know that she knows (1981:75). The viewer, in the long run, comes to know more.

Clearly, our habits of viewing are engaged in a number of secrets. Because we situate the viewed as not knowing, as blind to the seer and unable to see back, we are habituated to watching as a secret – a series of deceptions, or displacements.[13] This deception suggests a dominant voyeuristic paradigm in which, as in the TV show *Candid Camera*, a "real" person does not suspect that she is being implicated in a public scene, but rather assumes she is implicated in private, "real" life. As Baudrillard remarked about the documentary on the Louds in which a "real" family agreed to be video-taped going about their lives "as if TV weren't there," when the viewed know that they are being viewed, their mandate is nevertheless to behave as if they were not being viewed, secreting the contract of viewing.[14] The relationship between an assumed "real life," an assumed private sphere, and the public secret of representation impacts upon the situation of *woman* historically.

The feminine is emblematic of the private sphere – the home, the family, and consumption – while the sphere of production bears gender as a masculine domain.[15] Yet woman, emblematic of home, leisure, and the private property which that sphere implies, is simultaneously the prime terrain of the given to be seen, the obsessional hub of *public* display. She is the public private, as it were. Public production of the *signs* of privacy, like the "laboring" apparatus in representation, is secreted – "as if TV weren't there." Voracious popular consumption of "private" scenes suggests that the private is foremost a public concern. Public display marks and constructs the private, like the sign "Private Property." Is the displayed sign "Private Property" private, or public? Public display of the so-called private, of which woman is so often emblematic, services the gendering, the (masculinized) prerogatives, of "private" property, and secret(e)s the machinations of capital exchange. As the public sign or vessel of (his) privacy, her own privacy is complicated – a concept amply illustrated by the tenuousness of abortion rights. As Amy Robinson writes, "considered as a form of property, the problem of privacy is the problem of identity itself" (1996:261).

The explicit body performer wrestles with the secret service the "private" plays as public display by complicating the category of "private" at all. Many explicit body performance artists make the private so explicitly public (as underground porn is dragged into the frame of art, or as the "personal" is hailed as flagrantly "political") that a binary terror is evoked as the two terms, public and private, collide across her body. Such work also interrogates habits of deception and secrecy in viewing, the presumed passivity and ignorance of the given to be seen: She is "doing it to herself" – so she must "know."

I watch a woman on a bed in a film.

The film is Schneemann's 1964 *Fuses*, in which Schneemann makes love with James Tenney – again and again and again. As with *Vesper's Stampede*, here glitches and scratches, breaks and doubled images tell me "art film" or "avant-garde," locating me in the scene of viewing – a woman on a bed. I watch myself watching, wondering about an "approach." How should I wield her body in representation across my critical text? Like a good materialist, I want to de-familiarize the terrain of her body as given to signify masculinized desire. But defamiliarization is only part of the project. More complexly I want to show the impossible tangle of *heimlich* and *unheimlich*, familiar and strange, in which a seen woman is always already embedded – sited but blind, stretched between the canny and uncanny like a threshold, or a doormat. It is not enough to pick sides in the long-standing debate between art and anti-art that spans modernism. Dominant culture *and* counter-culture have often staged their positionings, their defenses and offenses, across the body of woman – making of that body a battlefield. For example, in 1963, the same year Schneemann mounted *Eye/Body* and one year before she filmed *Fuses*, the Metropolitan Museum of Art in New York exhibited the *Mona Lisa* to record crowds. Three Fluxists carried signs outside the exhibit bearing the Dadaesque slogans: "DESTROY ART! DEMOLISH ART MUSEUMS!" The next night, one of those Fluxists, Henry Flynt, gave a talk in a Manhattan loft. His audience entered the loft by first stepping on a print of the *Mona Lisa* that served as a doormat. The point here is that "she," in the body of Mona Lisa, signified the terrain across which both sides of the culture/counter-culture Oedipal battle was being waged. Thus the issue of an "angle" for feminists is more complicated than simply a taking of "sides" between dominant culture and counter-culture, as her body has often served as the symbolic foundation across which both art and anti-art have waged their proprietary battles.

I watch a woman on a bed, flickering across my screen from out of the mid-1960s. Looking for an angle, an "in," I pick about among the fray of debates on high modernism and its avant-garde relative to the postmodern, the post-modern in relation to feminism(s) and postcolonialism(s), and poststructural theory relative to all of the above.[16] But regardless of savvy in any positioning I can conjure, and regardless of a desire to explicate the mechanisms of narrative/ perspectival meaning ghosting and informing the significance of any woman writhing on any bed – regardless of any angle I can conjure, I am riveted by the medium: my eyes inhabit the familiar place of the lens, my mind infests the vacated space of the camera, doubling over the apparatus, standing in. Watching.

I watch her as I have watched other women on other beds – scratch, glitch – through the eyes of the camera, guided to the keyhole by the film-maker, with him in the dark, sharing, exchanging these "private" parts, watching.

Break.

Guided to the keyhole by the film-maker? Sharing with him in the dark? Here I meet the scratch and glitch, the cut and snip of the film in the realm of my own habituations – habituations denied. The film-maker, and by extension the seeing eye, is, in this case, precisely the woman I watch. Carolee Schneemann is the woman in front of the camera with Tenney *and* behind its lens, guid-ing me to the keyhole, with her in the dark. It is this doubling, intrinsic to the film, that complicates habituated reading. Writ(h)ing on this filmic bed is the film-maker herself.

Guided to the keyhole, standing in the shoes of the film-maker, sliding in behind her eyes, I slide simultaneously into her knowledge of her own pleasure. Female pleasure, *jouissance*, is given by the tenets of perspective and Symbolic Ordering to be unknowable. But Schneemann makes it explicit that she knows. She is showing me, "telling" me, disavowing the caveat of ignorance and insatiability with the wink and nod that are the textural glitches and scratches she brings to the film-making. Perhaps most unnerving to our cultural habituations to the ignorance of the viewed is that she not only shows me that she knows – being both subject and object at once – but that she takes pleasure – satisfaction, satiation – in being out about her knowledge. She is not horrified, or apologetic, or shamed. She sees, and admits that she sees.

Because Schneemann is artist and object she is on both sides of the keyhole. Thus she cannot be delimited to the scene. Nor can she be surprised by a third, paternal gaze, as in Sartre's model of "The Look" by which a viewer is caught at the keyhole of his perspective by an interrupting third party, turning the viewer into a viewed object and, thus, shaming or feminizing him (Sartre 1966). Schneemann cannot be caught at the keyhole and made into a shamed object because she is already that object – without shame – implicated in her own seen, even as she is situated as subject. As viewer, Schneemann exceeds the seen of her own body just as *jouissance* is said to exceed the organizing telos of the phallus/gaze, and yet, as seer *and* seen, she also plainly *knows* her *jouissance*, does not let it plummet into the Lacanian mysticism of the vanishing point by which woman is endlessly presumed not to know, to be blind to her own pleasure. Rather, Schneemann bald-facedly finds a very concrete and glaringly quotidian pleasure in her knowing, exhibited in an aesthetics of explicitude which, at the vanishing point, refuses to vanish, and at viewing point, refuses to be veiled. Here, ironically, Lyotard's explication of the anxiety at the heart of perspective is made literal. As Lyotard explicated that anxiety: when the viewing eyes "think they're seeing the vulva, they see themselves" (in Krauss 1993a:113). Here, the viewing eye is Schneemann's, but the vulva made public is also Schneemann's. The formula of co-identity between viewer and vanishing point is made literal, though in that literalization the distance between viewer and viewed is radically collapsed onto the person of the artist/object herself, and the anxiety of emasculation redolent in that equation is simply denied.

In making this film Schneemann was taking what she has called "permission to see."[17] Because she is seer and seen, Schneemann is (as seer) explicitly embodied, in distinction to the veiled, disembodied or dislocated viewer of classic perspectivalism. Of course, in *Fuses* we do not actually see her watching herself make love, but because Schneemann is both the film-maker and a primary object of the film, the double sense of seer and seen is pervasive, serving to embody the viewer by extension. Schneemann's camera, propped by Schneemann in her bedroom, silently surveyed Schneemann for Schneemann to survey later – making a seen of Schneemann, made for Schneemann to see. Since Schneemann refused to give up the object position while claiming the viewing subject position, she occupied both positions at once, making each precarious. In its chimerical flip between subject and object, "permission to see" ricochets vertiginously between the eyes of the spectator and Schneemann's eyes as the woman on the bed instantly re-doubles as the spectator again even as she climaxes repeatedly and impressively for her own pleasure and the pleasure of her partner.

Analysing scenes of voyeurism in early films, Judith Mayne makes the point that female voyeurism in and of itself is not transgressive. In fact, a woman at a keyhole displayed in classic film does not, unlike her male counterpart, require punishment. She is incidental and ineffectual. Mayne argues that this is precisely because of the female voyeur's implicit disempowerment and lack of active involvement. She is read as a woman over and above her status as voyeur, and thus she is like a blind voyeur. Her sex cancels her vision as she does not possess the penetrating gaze. A "female voyeur can peek, but does not possess the authority necessary to penetrate the room – a privilege reserved for the [male] detective" (1990:180). She can peek, but she cannot see. The threat of a female voyeur, it seems, is only the threat of empty vision – a vision without authority. What becomes interesting and disruptive to this paradigm is that in *Fuses* Schneemann boldly occupies all positions: she is at once voyeur, surveyed, and detective. As voyeur, she has penetrated the scene, being already in it as object seen, and thus her "permission to see" becomes a "permission to detect" and bears the authority of explication as she uncovers and accumulates details in her seen, details of her very explicit envisagement.

This envisagement – her explicit body – is immediately historical, though Schneemann's 1960s cultural feminism generally translated that history as auto-biography. Clearly, history accumulates around any woman on any bed, as a woman on a bed is always much more than "a woman" on "a bed." A woman on a bed cannot help but speak a history embedded in habits of representation: women embedded in a patriarchally marked and extra-visible sexuality that is given to signify a public private, fetishistically signifying the prerogatives of the phallus in a drive to mark the scopic field with desire and lack, fueling consumptive exchange. In any film or performance, a body marked female on a bed brings to that bed, either with consent or in resistance, an entire narrative backdrop of social Oedipalization, the history and habituation of reading "woman" as ignorant and blind (if she is not blinded by ignorance then she is blinded by pleasure or rage, and if she is not blind, is not ignorant, and is "beautiful," that beauty is blinding and she is a terrifying, castrating Medusa, and if she escapes the above then she bears a "stray masculine principle"). Over and above Schneemann's occupation of both the subject and object position (a position she sought for her male lover in the film as well by marking his body as the object of her active desire), Schneemann attempted, like other early cultural feminist artists, to cut Oedipal narrative ties, or to show them up against themselves by constant interruption – scratches, glitches, and breaks.

Within the field of vision, Schneemann sought to deny the organizing telos of male orgasm by beckoning the cultural feminist hope in a fluid and multivalent sensuality – almost a tactility. Thus *Fuses* is a conglomerate of visual bodily detail by which the lover's bodies, and other objects, are montaged. The seen is not organized around the operative imperative of the phallus – there is no singular logic of beginning, middle, and end. Instead the film is as a series of slippages: Tenney's body, Schneemann's body, their bodies together, the cat Kitch watching from the windowsill, the lover's bodies on the bed, intercourse by the window, joy across the face, her mouth on his engorged penis, his fingers at her labia, Schneemann running on the beach, Tenney driving in the car, his mouth on her on his, hers, theirs, the beach, the car, the cat, the bed, the window (Plate 3.1). At one point, in a flash, a close-up of Tenney's cock dissolves instantly into a close-up of Schneemann's vulva exacerbating, at the point of explicit detail, the labyrinthine flow of bodies in flux.[18] Schneemann's editing in *Fuses* is slippery and messy, as if the celluloid itself were wet. Her painterly texturing, scratching, and dyeing of the celluloid – "the touch of her hand on the film's flesh" (James 1989:320) – creates an insistent visual tactility and perceptual disorientation that mimics and reproduces the sensuous encounter which *Fuses* documents, allowing the medium to become both apparent (the film, scratched, becomes visible *as* film) and, even more strikingly, participant.

In line with Marilyn Frye's blunt contention, outlined above, that the "phallocratic scheme [can]not admit women as authors of perception, as seers," Schneemann's "taking" of the permission to see bore a flavor of criminality. It should not be surprising, then, that when the film was made in the mid-1960s it could, as historian David James put it, "hardly be seen" (1989:321). It was "too much," often even for avant-garde audiences.[19] The fluid interchange of imagery interrupts a conventionally narrativized climax, yes, but implicit in this fluidity is the taboo exposure of the penis to the scopic field as an everyday object of "equitable interchange."[20] That such exposure of the penis should occur through a woman's camera eye, cut and spliced by her hand, may be one factor which relegated the film to the near status of "unseeable." The film was too much for both the avant-garde establishment with its organizing telos of the male artist and for a fledgling women's movement which conjoined in the general labeling of Schneemann as narcissistic, fearful that her exaltation of her own bodily erotics too closely resembled the general heterosexist, fetishistic delimitation of woman to her genitalia. Ironically then, in direct relation to Schneemann taking permission to see, the picture was proclaimed hardly able to be seen. As unseeable, there would be nothing for Schneemann to declare she had seen.

Interestingly, this crisis of vision relative to the explicit feminist artist was still operative twenty-five years after *Fuses*. In 1989 C. Carr wrote of Annie Sprinkle's onstage display of her cervix on stage for the *Village Voice* claiming that "to look inside someone's body is to *see too much*." The dynamics of overexposure here reinscribe the blindspot as vision encountering a "too much" of itself. For Carr, Sprinkle's "too much," her overexposure, functioned to help the artist "transcend" sexuality. As Carr wrote: "All that remained were questions of vulnerability and power" (1993:176). But I would argue that sexuality is not at all transcended in Sprinkle's collapse of the binary distinction between public

Plate 3.1 Carolee Schneemann, James Tenney, and the cat Kitch in a still from Schneemann's film *Fuses*, 1964/65. Courtesy of Schneemann.

and private. Rather, Sprinkle's "too much" exposes sexuality as indivisible from social issues of vulnerability and power inscribed in ways of seeing. It is this provocation, not her actual cervix, that might be read as "too much." It is the politicized *link* she is making explicit between sexuality, vulnerability, and power that is "hardly able to be seen" – out of the bounds of vision for a society habituated to maintaining "perspective" by maintaining distinctions between sexuality and politics, nature and culture, or porn and art.

CASTRATION ANXIETY IN PERSPECTIVE

As Lacan and the feminists who have followed him have made abundantly clear, habits of perspectival vision are linked to habituations to the Symbolic Order of language. In Panovsky's wording, perspective gives form to the Symbolic – it is "symbolic form." Disrupting the form of perspectivalism unsettles the organizing telos of the Symbolic Order itself. To unsettle perspective by interrogating the logic of the vanishing point throws into question the operative thrall with insatiability and lack at the heart not only of perspectivalism, but of commodity capitalism. Instituting an object/subject which sees *and* is seen denies a foundational principle of perspective by which the viewer is dislocated from the scopic field and suggests that the one-way street of anxiety-ridden desire might become a two-way intersection allowing, heretically, mutual exchange, satiation, and reciprocity.

Lacan outlined geometral, or perspectival vision as constituted by castration anxiety (1981:93–4, 102). However, the anxiety inscribed within the Symbolic Order is arguably deeper than a fear of the loss of the penis. Rather, "castration" anxiety is a fear of the loss of the tenet of Loss itself. To deny the prerogatives of perspective is to deny lack and insatiability as the organizing telos of exchange. Thus castration anxiety can be reread as anxiety over the loss of anxiety about loss – anxiety propelling the infinite drive to accumulate on which the circulation of capital depends. In this sense, "castration" anxiety operates as a veil, secreting its own absurdity through the infinite dramatization of its paranoid tenets – a dramatization carried out in the form of perspective, a form *instituting* that very anxiety. Unpacking this distinction helps us to analyze the anxiety surrounding early (and later) feminist work of the explicit body, such as *Fuses*. Paradoxically, such works provoke anxiety *because they deny anxiety* – denying the organizing telos of castration anxiety. It is castration anxiety itself which is cut short. The fact that so much anxiety arose around *Fuses* suggests that castration anxiety itself is what must not be castrated – that castration anxiety is a fear of the loss of castration.

Because *Fuses* aimed to deny castration anxiety as the operative trope of its optic, it could "hardly be seen." The film was even "too much," in excess, of the genre of heterosexual pornography.[21] Schneemann's refusal to fetishize all details according to phallic agendas meant that, in David James's words, "contemporary pornography [was] shunned" (1989:320). Though extremely sexually explicit, *Fuses* did not fit the genre of pornography, was not recognized as pornographic, even as it was simultaneously too explicit for "art."

In porn, implicit socio-political anxieties about borders demarcating the appropriate and inappropriate *vis-à-vis* gendered, raced, classed, aged, and preference-marked bodies (as well as general anxieties about libidinal expenditure, leisure time, anti-productivity, excess, and waste) are translated across bodies in explicitly sexual terms, but those translations are recognized as "porn" only to the degree, ironically, that they align within the narrative, lexical, and grammatical confines of porn's "category of understanding." A vast underbelly to the socially appropriate arenas of art, commerce, and popular culture, pornography is more subterranean than marginal – a mainstream flowing underground. Socio-political anxieties above ground are played out underground in ritualized scenes of transgression. The invention of pornography as a regulative category was, according to Lynn Hunt, born of mid-nineteenth-century anxiety over the powerful democratization of culture made possible by mass reproduction and print media. Porn as a "category of understanding," to quote Hunt, arose out of fears about policing the boundaries of consumption – especially as consumption was a sphere increasingly associated with women (leisure, private, and domestic realms) versus men (work, public, and production realms) (Hunt 1993:10).[22]

As Jean Genet repeatedly illustrated, the illicit enactment of taboo is the ideological twin to licit or normative social orders of appropriate behavior – one buttresses the other, one mimics the other, one secret(e)s the other. In its blatant appeal to bodily function, porn plays underground upon normative habits of perspectivalism by transgressing one of its operative tenets. Porn aims overtly to involve a spectator libidinally, and thus it arguably invites a complicity that challenges the mythos of dislocation and disinterest on the part of the perspectival observer.[23] However, as porn transgresses one tenet of perspective it reinscribes another: the standard heterosexual pornographic scene replicates – in explicit terms – fundamental narratives of anxiety.

Gertrude Koch (1989) has written on the careful attention given to castration anxiety in the vast majority of heterosexual pornographic films in which the penis is again and again seen heroically to surmount the threat of death-by-drowning in the voracious black hole of female genitalia. Filming *Fuses*, Schneemann was not interested in heroism or survival. But she was similarly not interested in defeat, demise, or castration, as the penis appears, disappears, and reappears in her film as casually and without any more fanfare than the cat is seen to lick itself in the very same frame. Perhaps even more heretically, especially for 1964 and the category of "art" in which Schneemann framed her film, the penis became interchangeable with the vulva, the beach, the car, the face, the window, the breast. That is, the penis, too, was given as exchangeable signifier – not all signs read back to its primacy as phallus. The penis was presented in the scopic field as equally subject to exchange as any other feminized object – and yet *in literal terms* it remained an intact organ, hardly castrated. At the height of heresy, pleasure continued to occur though castration anxiety was apparently absent.

The standard pornographic scene resembles, Koch argues, Freud's inscription of a boy-child's castration anxiety. The standard heterosexual scenario depicts a frenzied search for that which is construed as woman's secret – the place where she must be "hiding her penis." The penis (or the eye) which hides behind the vanishing point is in direct geometral relation to the viewer's phallic gaze which is secreted behind the perspectival veil of dislocation.

> The castration complex gives rise to the persistent voyeuristic mania to look at the female organ, constantly and as closely as possible, in order to uncover the secret of the missing penis . . . Because this mania is the result of the castration complex, seeing lots of penises confirms their durability and intactness; castration anxiety is also reduced by inducing the feeling of phallic omnipotence. The restless search for something that can't be found – the woman's penis – is compensated by an appeasing display of erections and potency.
>
> (1989: 24)

Signs of female pleasure in standard pornographic films become fetishized displacements of the phallus itself (Ellis 1980:24). Yet a woman's orgasm – the moment when, by Lacanian paradigm, "woman is no longer the phallus, she *has* the phallus" – is the pornotopic moment to be surmounted, disavowed, overcome, repossessed, mastered by the ejaculating penis across the scopic field (see Linda Williams 1989).

As a result of pornographic narrative pandering to systemic "castration" anxiety, Koch notes that one hardly ever sees a coition in porn film that does not end with a penis ejaculating onto a woman. "The sight of an ejaculating penis seems to be pleasurable to the heterosexual male viewer, because to him it is a sign of intactness, an assurance that the vagina, imagined as insatiable and dangerous, has once again yielded its victim, unscathed, to see the light of day" (1989:26). If gender codings in the "underground" of porn can be read relative to the nervous networkings of the market economy "above ground," some provocative links can be uncovered. Remembering that the consumer is feminized and the producer masculinized, a certain "pornographic" rendering of the anxiety and lack that drives exchange between realms of production and consumption comes into relief. The penis is given to be productive, the vagina consumptive – but the producer must get the better of consumer, surplus value must be generated, and fulsome consumer satisfaction thwarted so that insatiability can be guaranteed.

And, just as commodity dreamscapes revolve around the "secret" of commodities, obsessively secreting the social relations of production, so the paradigmatic porn scene explicitly enacts a thrall to secrecy. Koch suggests that the abundance of sperm in standard porn films is an ecstatic sign of the inadequacy of representation to divulge the secret women are constructed to contain, to bring her supposedly hidden phallus to visibility. Thus porn endlessly reinscribes the very secret it sets out to expose. The "secret" of woman's hidden penis (eye) is substantiated through the ecstatic failure of the porn narrative to envision it, and castration anxiety is ritually reaffirmed even as it is momentarily appeased. Both woman *and* representation (woman *as* representation) become tangled in a mutual inadequacy – representation fails (this time) to represent woman's secret phallus and woman fails (this time) to castrate, though she continues to signify the threat of castration, just as she continues to be the terrain of representation. Constantly and ritually eclipsed by this ritual failure of representation, woman herself becomes the fetishized, orgasmic signature of that failure. In the paranoid and repetitive scenario of "castration" anxiety, woman does not *have* representation, is not represented, but becomes the sign and insignia of (inadequate) representation itself – she *is* representation. "Woman" becomes the simulacrum, a phenomenon underscored in pornotopia by the fact that, in Koch's words, women's pleasure is repeatedly "sacrificed" in the wake of coitus interruptus (1989:26). Operative here is the idea of female orgasm as given to exist in the majority of porn films "in the wake" of the penis, and thus precisely as after-image, mimetic copy, simulation. In representation, woman becomes a mirror, a double, of the ejaculating member. She is figured as mimesis itself.

Fuses could "hardly be seen" because, in large measure, it defied such categorical tenets of the scopic field. Even while its contents were blatantly sexual, it was not pornographic: castration anxiety found no organizing foothold or loophole in the flow of its object images. Schneemann was searching for something, certainly, but that something was decidedly *not* marked by anxiety. Her explicit sex denied any ecstatic reinstatement of her supposed secret, denied any mystery or danger threatening her lover's supposed anxious drive to mastery. Rather Schneemann's "search" adopted a cultural feminist counter-narrative form, and became more like a scan – there is no single element, no specific hidden penis obsessively sought in a search and surmount mission. Instead there is a scanning and interchanging of details, a concrescence and concupiscence of objects in relation, a multiplicity, an excrescence of signifiers in a kind of ecstatic accumulation in which the waves, the cat, the car, the window participate as much as and interchangeably with labia, breast, thigh, cock. Unlike standard pornographic fare, the concrete world of these objects is not funneled back into phallocentrist abstraction that organizes the perceptual field to fit a narrative of anxiety in which, citing Koch again, "all those visible, concrete penises and vulvas represent only a single symbolic phallus" (1989:28). Rather, the details themselves disorient any organizing telos, slipping again and again out from under habits of phallocratic organization.

Castration anxiety in the scopic field has to do with the fear of loss of the power of unitary, dislocated perspective even as it inscribes that perspective as powerful. Such fear of loss at the heart of perspective arguably drives its obsessive redramatization. If we are habituated to perspectivalism, then we are, it would follow, socio-culturally habituated to anxiety as well. Indeed, we can almost hear the anxiety in Lacan's phrasing, after Merleau Ponty, "I see only from one point, but in my existence I am looked at from all sides" (Lacan 1981:72). The seer bears the phallic authority of perspective, but is also blind-sided by that perspective. The degree to which the seer is invisible, shrouded in the detached authority of his dislocation, is the degree to which he bears authority within the terms of perspective, but it is also precisely the degree to which he is blind-sided – vulnerable to being caught seeing. To be caught seeing, to be rendered visible, is ironically to be blinded or, within the terms of the perspectivalism, to lose one's prerogatives as disinterested viewer. To be rendered visible is to be rendered blind, to be feminized, which is to say, castrated.

Within our socio-cultural habituations to perspective, the given to be seen – or woman as embodying "to-be-looked-at-ness" – bears the systemic burden of anxiety, the threat of castration, the "shadow of death" (Bryson 1988:92). But she embodies the threat of castration less by lacking a penis, than by lacking vision. She is stuck in the representational field as either blind (unable to look back) or castrating (blinding). Of course, to the degree that she is blinding, she cannot be seen – and so to the degree that she is visible, she must be marked as blind. Thus she symbolizes the threat of castration by bearing the symbolic effects of castration – by being structurally blinded, denied the authority of vision.

Freud linked castration anxiety to what he cited as horror at the sight of female genitals. Importantly, he saw such anxiety as linking fear of castration to an explicit fear of blindness. Reading closely in "The Uncanny," one finds that female genitals (offered as a "concluding" example) became intimately associated with a fear of blindness – they are, in fact, blinding. We can interpret Freud's link between the fear of the loss of one's penis and the fear of the loss of one's eyes as signifying a fear of the loss of the masculine-marked prerogatives of perspectival vision. For Freud, the fearful qualities of the female genitalia revolve around the trope of "home" – female genitals are, at base, "the entrance to the former *heim* of all human beings." Female genitals connote an inherent and unsettling ambivalence in that they signify not only what is known and familiar, like home, but what is strange, unknown, secret, hidden, or "former" – lost (1958:152–3). As such, his discussion exemplifies the social construction of the female gender as signifying home (domesticity and spheres of consumption), as well as bearing the terrifying potential of loss and the threatening potential to revolt – in both senses of the term.[24]

Freud's discussion of the uncanny articulates a systemic unrest at the base of the Symbolic Order, an instability at the base of binary distinctions where such distinctions threaten to implode as if sucked into the voracious black hole of the vanishing point. Elisabeth Bronfen has noted that Freud articulated the uncanny as the "effacement of the boundary between fantasy and reality [which] occurs when something is experienced as real which up to that point was conceived as imagined . . . when a symbol enacts a sublation of signifier into signified or an effacement of the distinction between literal and figural" (1992:113). If the threat of literality is relative to the fear of the uncanny, then for the patriarchal imagination there is nothing more literal and threatening to the prerogatives of the Symbolic Order than the sight (seeing back) of the female genitalia. The vanishing point as a seeing eye.

Though inherently threatening to the prerogatives of vision, the uncanny vanishing point is nevertheless coded into the nervous networkings of perspective at all times.[25] The explicit mark of the female body threatens the ability to see at the same time that that body, as representative of desire in the scopic field, reminds the viewer that he wields the prerogatives to master, to acquire, to possess – the prerogatives of uniocular, one-way vision. Perspective depends on its blind spot – but more specifically, on its blind spot remaining blind.

But let us return for a moment to Lyotard's equation that, following the logic of perspective, "He who sees is a cunt." Perspective is organized around the theoretical identity between viewing point and vanishing point, so it would follow that if the vanishing point is inscribed as lack, as always already vulvic, then "He who sees is a cunt." But while Lyotard's equation is geometrically correct and while this equation makes explicit the narrative of anxiety that is endlessly redramatized across the scopic field, nevertheless, everything in perspective is organized around the concomitant disavowal of this equation – the effort to make sure, to reassert, that he who sees *has* a phallus. By geometric alignment he who sees is a cunt, *but as long as the cunt is continually reinscribed as blind, then as long as he sees he cannot be a cunt.* The viewer's detachment from the scene saves him: as long as he is dislocated, she cannot locate him, she cannot see him. He is saved from "castration," or symbolic equivalence with the feminized, only as long as the object seen is obsessively located and continually reinscribed as blind.

Of course, the disconcerting suggestion in *Fuses* is that the cunt does, in fact, see, but does not castrate. The apparent lack of concern with castration anxiety, however, may suggest that what is castrated is anxiety itself – and that *that* dismemberment, that disregard, is the most unnerving to habits of knowing. What Schneemann exposes is not a heretofore "hidden penis," but an eye that is not a mimetic displacement of the phallus in that it does not reflect back the scripted terrain of concerns. There is no phallus to hide, and no sense of shame.

If one could see while being at the same time positioned as seen, there would be no fear of being blinded when seen, no fear of losing authority in locating oneself. If the feminine could wield prerogatives of vision there would be no threat in feminization. Put another way, there would be no reason to fear "castration." If women can see as well as be seen, then castration anxiety – fear of loss of the prerogatives of vision as linked to *gender-marked* prerogatives – becomes patently absurd.

The operative, driving fear inscribed within the patriarchal Symbolic Order is misplaced. It is not a fear of castration, but a fear of the loss of anxiety about castration, a fear of its discovery as absurd. A fear of the loss of the penis is a masquerade of symbolics, veiling a deeper, market-linked sacrality: the sacrality of anxiety, unrest, and lack which pitches an economy dependent on insatiability into a fever of accumulation. More systemically fearful than any castration is the fear of the loss of Loss as modus operandi.[26] Without the fear of lack as the operative organizing telos of the scopic field what would happen to the desire for accumulation? It is interesting to conjecture: If anxiety were to cease to masquerade, and to pass, as desire, perhaps we could acknowledge, practice, and circulate a desire based on something other than the thrall to loss, deferral, displacement, misrecognition and insatiability – a satiable desire, built on present satisfaction, reciprocity, and mutual exchange.

GHOSTLY HORRORS: LOOKING AT THE PAST, SEEING THROUGH THE BODY

> Now I stood up and, with Simone on her side, I drew her thighs apart, and found myself facing something I imagine I had been waiting for in the same way that a guillotine waits for a neck to slice. I even felt as if my eyes were bulging from my head, erectile with horror; in *Simone's* hairy vagina, I saw the wan blue eye of *Marcelle*, gazing at me through tears of urine. Streaks of come in the steaming hair helped give that dreamy vision a disastrous sadness. I held the thighs open while Simone was convulsed by the urinary spasm, and the burning urine streamed out from under the eye down to the thighs below . . .
>
> Georges Bataille (1967:84)

> To ask a woman to read [or see] as a woman is in fact a double or divided
> request. It appeals to the condition of being a woman as if it were a given
> and simultaneously urges that this condition be created or achieved.
>
> Jonathan Culler (1982:49)

Bataille was a modernist writer extraordinarily attentive to the paradoxical
condition of detached vision and enthralled with the experience, often the
horror, of its demise. His inverted anthropologies repeatedly returned to a
thinking through the body and its organs. If distanced, flaneur-like vision was
the primary modern sense for knowing, then the eye as a visceral and material
organ, the literal mechanism of sight, became particularly provocative for
"anti-ocularists" thinking through the body. In its materiality as a literal thing,
an enucleated eyeball garnered a special kind of horror in that it could collapse
the split, implicating both body and mind at once. This is also a horror at the
base of Hoffman's "The Sandman" which Freud adopted when attempting to
explicate the "uncanny." Bataille provides, in a sense, a careful and provocative
biopsy of the modernist obsession with perspectival (which he calls "horizontal")
vision and the separation of the visual from the visceral which ensues – an
obsession, however, which he simultaneously exemplifies through his endlessly
self-reconstituting horror at the very blindspot he attempts to make literal.
That the separation of the visual from the visceral is enacted across the blindspot made literal on the site/sight of the explicit female body (or elsewhere
for Bataille on the site/sight of the explicitly castrated penis) is far from
insignificant.[27]

   In a close reading of the quintessential scene from Bataille's notorious *Story of
the Eye*, we find an enucleated eyeball of one woman (Marcelle) peering out
of the vagina of another woman (Simone). We also find the narrator transfixed
by horror before the scene he envisions. We can remark how the narrator's
horror depends upon a literalization of the blindspot sighted, but also note that
Simone's own eyes, the ones in her head, are not admitted to the scene, as her
body is on its side and her gaze is simply unacknowledged. A reader is given to
identify with, or certainly to see through, the "erectile" eyes of the male narrator
as he "draws" apart Simone's thighs and sees the eyeball of Marcelle peering
out of her vagina. He suggests that this vision will result in his own beheading,
or castration, as he likens his experience to the guillotine.

   Reading this scene I find myself associated with a male narrator, spectating a
classic female split: the acephalous body of one woman (the sexually liberated
Simone) and the envaginated eye of another woman (the sexually repressed and
victimized Marcelle). If I imagine the vaginal eye looking back at me, as the eye
peers at the narrator with whom I am identified, then I, as reader, find myself
misrecognized through the vaginal eye as male. On the other hand, if I shift
my reading to identify *as* a woman *with* the woman given to see in the text, if,
that is, I choose to identify with Marcelle rather than the narrator, I choose
to see through the envaginated eyeball. Standing outside the narrator's identity
and seeing through Marcelle's envaginated eye, I witness the narrator's face.

From this position I witness the gaze of the modernist author at the critical scene of his own authority in revolt as he peers at Simone's vagina, his own eyes bulging from his sockets, "erectile with horror."

It is significant here that the envaginated eye and the narrator's gaze are the only eyes admitted to the scopic field of erectile vision. There are the eyes in the head of the sexually active woman, Simone herself, but they are not admitted, remaining unseen in the scene. When a reader shifts to see through Simone's unacknowledged eyes, she finds herself beyond modernist peripheries, authoring an unwritten perspective. Though lying "on her side," Simone's eyes might not be averted. Unwritten, they might nevertheless look across her shoulder, witnessing the frenzied author in his culminating scene. From this "space off,"[28] the reader would watch the author's predictable shock as he sees, or thinks he sees, the eye of another woman between her legs. In this reading, Simone witnesses the narrator's authorial horror at encountering what he has conceived – his terror at what he has written as an explicitly female (envaginated) gaze.

As Bataille's horror illustrates, the institution of a "female" gaze necessitates, within modern imagination, the re-embodiment of detached or disinterested vision. If detached vision is disturbing, the notion of re-embodiment is even more horrifying, as re-embodiment is necessarily figured by the particularity, the literality of the marked body. Re-embodied vision bears the horror of the marked body, a horror linked inexorably to woman. Re-embodied vision bears the savagery of feminization, here literally framed by the female genitalia. Thus re-embodiment of the detached gaze is rife with the horror of feminization, destroying the veil of disinterestedness shrouding supposedly "distanced" vision. A re-embodied gaze threatens the prerogatives of disembodied perspectivalism, the prerogatives of the veil, and doubles as a terror of female sexuality. This re-embodied female gaze is authored by and relative to patriarchal horror, or anxiety in the explicit extreme. Again, it is important to remember that the female gaze given to see from Simone's vagina is not Simone's own but the victimized and virginal Marcelle, herself radically disembodied – the female gaze as the gaze of the disembodied re-embodied, always relative to a female body she herself does not possess. The *eyes* of the woman with sexual agency (after all, she put the eyeball there herself) are relegated to the space-off. Simone is not *admitted to witness* how an explicitly female gaze is sited as horrific, authored as always already dissimulating, or duplicitous, as never of *a* woman, but always already that of an *other* woman, infinitely recessing, split off from her own agency.

The project of looking back at the modernist in thrall, amid the admittedly self-splintering notion of reading "as a woman," here exemplified in a reading back through Bataille, becomes not only a looking back in time, but even more provocatively a looking back *in space*, which is to say, across the "savaged" bodies which demarcated modernist perspective. The contemporary feminist project to turn the eye of the visceralized, marked object back on to the detached eye of the modern attempts not simply to re-enunciate modernist horror, but to examine the terms of that horror, to survey the *entire* field of her visceralization from the (space-off) perspective of the visceralized. What is uncovered rather than reconstituted in this project is a plethora of patriarchal fears.

At the close of the last chapter, I posed the question of whether we might imagine feminist works such as Schneemann's *Eye/Body* and Sprinkle's explicit performativity as perspectivalism turned upon itself, a view from the vanishing point of the terms of that vanishing. Linked to Bataillean fascination with the literal body and the envisaged blindspot as sites of subversive potential within Western symbolic systems, how might such a performativity nevertheless avoid the endless self-reconstitution of horror and "castration" anxiety Bataille's literalization exemplified? In her "Public Cervix Announcement" in *Post Porn Modernism*, porn queen Sprinkle smiles, chuckles, and exchanges quips with her peeping spectators, watching the scene unfold across her own body in the frame of "art." The display of the cervix becomes a kind of ludicrous moment in which voyeurism is taken to a certain extreme where the viewer encounters not an infinitely recessing negative space, a vanishing point of "Origin," but explicitly, and somewhat clinically, a cervix. If the cervix can be imagined as an eye, catching the viewer at the keyhole as it were, any horror that scene might occasion would be noted by the author, Annie Sprinkle, and remarked. "Oh look," she might exclaim, letting her audience in on the scene, "Your eyes are erectile with horror! Take a picture, quick so I can use this image in my next 'Show and Tell.'"

Schneemann's eyes as film-maker in *Fuses* or artist in *Eye/Body* similarly rebound across her scene. Unlike Simone's, Schneemann's and Sprinkle's eyes are not secreted. Rather, the artists provoke an interruption in the thrall to horror and anxiety and invite a critical (and/or humorous) analysis of the terms of obsessive horror. Here, the interrupting third eye – the eye that catches the peeper at the keyhole, as in Sartre's imagination – are "object's" own eyes upon the scene of her body. The interrupting eye is acknowledged *within* the scene, implicated upon the body of the seen itself rather than in an intrusive third, implicitly paternal party.[29] The "seen" takes on an agency of her own and wields the unnerving potential of a subversive reciprocity of vision, an explicit complicity, or mutual recognition between seer and seen, who become seer and seer, subject and subject, object and object in the scene of viewing. Such reciprocity threatens in that it suggests a disavowal of the terror and anxiety that demarcates subject from object in Western cultural habits of knowing. In the wake of such reciprocity, in the explicit avowal of Simone's eyes, horror at re-embodiment has the potential to be replaced by acknowledgment – acknowledgment of the historical terms of anxiety as those terms are re-enacted and made explicit across the stage of marked body.

The feminist project to open an eye of the visceralized (blinded) object, to *see and remark* her own delimitation is to open Pandora's eye/box and discover there not Pandora as "newly born woman" but to dis-cover a plethora of the patriarchal terrors and desires propping woman as symbolic of the terror of blindness/castration. In the Pandora story, as Ludmilla Jordanova points out, "secrecy is

reified as a box" (1989:93).[30] Both looking into and looking out from her box –
from the delimitation of her own patriarchally over-determined, over-exposed
body – what would Pandora see? The terror of the patriarch at his own scene –
gazing at her, to borrow Bataille's again, "erectile with horror." Pandora opened
her box because she couldn't resist the desire to "see" and thus know what it was
she was constructed to hide. However, the box she opened – called Pandora's box
and often theorized as female sexuality – was really Zeus' box in that it was given
to her by Zeus together with the order not to open (see) its contents which held
"all the evils of the world." In effect Pandora's great transgression was her desire
to see/know the patriarch's own box, or with the Freudian equivalence between
the box and the female genitals, to see/know the father's femininity, marked by
him as consummate terror.

4 The secret's eye

Veiling implies secrecy. Women's bodies, and, by extension, female attributes, cannot be treated as fully public, something dangerous might happen, secrets be let out, if they were open to view. Yet in presenting something as inaccessible and dangerous, an invitation to know and to possess is extended. The secrecy associated with female bodies is sexual and linked to the multiple associations between women and privacy.

Ludmilla Jordanova (1989:17)

To keep the secret is evidently to tell it as a nonsecret . . . To keep a secret – to refrain from saying some particular thing – presupposes that one could say it . . . The stratagem of the secret is either to show itself, to make itself so visible that it isn't seen (to disappear, that is, as a secret), or to hint that the secret is only secret where there is no secret, or no appearance of any secret.

Maurice Blanchot (1986: 133, 137)

Secrecy is wrapped up in the cultural construction of femininity. Femininity is wrapped up in socio-political manipulations of secrecy. Dynamics of hiddenness and mystery are scripted into the drama of "woman" as she has been set to dance on the stage of modernity. That stage, as this chapter sets out to explore, is the theater of "private property," the theater of capital.

The theatricalisms by which commodities are displayed and circulated put on a good show, and historically that "show" has scripted the female body as emblem of desire and property in general. Consumers are meant to recognize their own wishes, their own dreams, the network of their desires in the drama of display. Commodities become fetishes, displaced insignias of consumers' private dreamscape wishes – "private," that is, as ruse, in a completely public terrain of a social and collective "optical unconscious."

Walter Benjamin first used the term "optical unconscious" in 1931 in his essay "A Small History of Photography" (1979) in which he sought to explore the sensuousness of photographic display, a sensuousness he saw as potentially disruptive to Cartesian distinctions between mind and body, viewer and viewed. As Michael Taussig has written, the "capacity of mimetic machines [cameras] to pump out contact-sensuosity encased within the spectrality of a commoditized world is nothing less than the discovery of an optical unconscious, opening up new possibilities for exploring reality" (1993:23). Key to Benjamin's and Taussig's use of "optical unconscious" is the way in which the reproduction of an object, an image, deploys a sensuality of mimesis, implicating the body of the viewer at the same time that that viewer is, by tenets of perspectivalism, seemingly dissociated from that which is seen. The object in display plays on the sensuousness of the (dislocated) viewer, beckoning the viewer to enter (purchase) the object presented.

Benjamin's optical unconscious can be "opened up," as Taussig writes (1993: 24), to explore ways in which the cultural, perspectival separation of viewer and viewed is undermined by its own secrets – the "secret" of physiognomic tactility as always already inherent in mimetic display. The secret is that the viewer and viewed are entangled in sensuous contact, sensuously complicit in the scene – bodies *are* engaged. Thus, even as we are "habituated" to tents of dislocation in perspectivalism (Panovsky 1991:34), the sensuousness inherent in copying, in mimesis, as well as the way in which the eye is always already an organ of tactility, resists the very separation to which the perspectival viewer habitually subscribes.

Sensuous contact, explicit and ready tactility between viewer and viewed, exists as an optical unconscious, as a secret of perspectivalism exploited to the hilt by commodities in advertisements which rub up against the supposedly dislocated viewer every chance they get. Why must sensuous contact between viewer and viewed be disavowed? Why a "secret" of perspective? Why the realm of a collective optical *unconscious*? The separation of viewer and viewed is fundamental to capitalism. Like the historically gendered distinction between producer and consumer (by which men get to produce and women get to consume), the (gendered) separation between viewer and viewed functions as a conceptual space for commodity exchange in which the viewer (male) is marked as separate, possessing desire for the sensuous (residing in the commodity, female).[1] The separation between viewer and viewed institutes an insatiable desire across the divide by which the viewer has the desire, the product is the desired. Sensuous complicity, literal and immediate contact between seer and seen as always already operative must be disavowed to service the status of "desire *for* contact" which keeps commodities circulating. Tactility is deployed and simultaneously secret(e)d, becoming an optical "unconscious" as we are consciously habituated to a seemingly a-sensuous dislocation between viewer and viewed. As explored in Chapter 3, the viewed does not (must not) engage actively, does not see back, but rather vanishes, just beyond grasp.

The sensuous properties of mimesis are both exploited and secret(e)d by commodity capitalism. The theater of commodities hopes that consumers respond to the mimetic representation of desire by another mimesis: a miming of the promoted desire on the part of the consumer, a dreaming the dream suggested, a trying it on for size – a "mimesis of mimesis" (Taussig 1993:63). But sensuous contact while employed is disavowed. If a commodity object is acquired – say, a pair of Reebok sneakers or a BMW or a cordless phone – it is as if after the fact, as an insignia of desire itself. Owning the commodity becomes, in a sense, a display of the ownership of insatiable desire, a member-ship in the landscape of collective social desire. What is enacted in engaging the scene of the commodity is, beyond the acquisition of a product, the engagement of a cultural scene, perhaps even a ritual scene, of the continuous circulation of desire as modus operandi of humanist individualism (see Kojève 1969). It is desire itself, rather than any sensuous, satiate object, that circulates in a system of infinite deferral replicating the vanishing point of perspective.

The sensuousness of objects acquired is secondary to the insignia of infinite desire those objects have signified in the scopic field of the dreamscape. Rather than (or beside) any concrete thing, what is often acquired in a commodity is the social accouterment of desire, not its satiation. Acquisitions augment rather than satisfy desire, insuring that the consumer will not achieve a state of completed/depleted desire, but will participate in a perpetuation, a heightening of desire, as ritual perpetuates its own terms and solidifies its membership. Like the complex infinity of an afternoon soap opera, the social dynamics which engender commodities and shroud them in networks of social fantasy set an effective stage for the continual circulation of a particular socio-cultural notion of desire – a desire marked by habituations to perspective which disavow the sensuousness of contact in favor of the infinite of the vanishing point, a desire which only allows that it will never be fully satisfied, never depleted, never fully met.

Feminist artists of the explicit body explore capitalist mimetics across their bodies in their "art," looking to open up the optical unconscious and disallow the disavowal of sensuous contact between viewer and viewed – making sensuous contact literal and explicit. Barbara Kruger's billboard art *Your Gaze Hits the Side of My Face* (Plate 4.1) is a case in point. In 1981 Kruger collaged the slogan across the face of a woman in profile taken from a '50s photo-annual of a female bust. Kruger's work mimics and talks back to ad-scapes across which women have so opulently been objectified. The "hit" of the gaze against the object(ified) and the hit of the object against the gaze is at issue in a radical reassessment of the tactile effects of visual dynamics upon bodies in relation.

Writing on advertisements, Benjamin found the optical unconscious in full, tactile swing: an advertisement "all but hits us between the eyes with things as a car, growing to gigantic proportions, careens at us out of a film screen" (1986:85; see also Taussig 1993:29–31). In its mimesis of ad-scapes, Kruger's slogan "Your Gaze Hits the Side of My Face" takes on multiple meanings. As Hal Foster has written, Kruger makes "an equation . . . between aesthetic reflection and the alienation of the gaze: both reify" (1982:88). But, as Craig Owens points out, Kruger is simultaneously addressing "the masculinity of the look, the way in which it objectifies and masters" (1983:77). On the one hand, the gaze of the viewer hits the side of the face of the woman in the "ad," projecting the habitual inscription of desire across her body (as we habitually read her according to tenets of desirability). On the other hand, with Benjamin, the "ad" itself hits the face of the viewer, in the way that commodities, such as cars or women's bodies, careen across ads repeatedly to grab us, catch us, implicate us in the lure of their

Plate 4.1 Barbara Kruger, *Untitled (Your gaze hits the side of my face)*. Photograph, 55" by 41", 1981. Courtesy of Mary Boone Gallery, New York.

constructed vanishing points, even as they loom in the enormity of reproduction. Kruger's art seems to suggest a ricochet. A woman viewing the woman's face hit by the gaze is hit in return by the manifestation of her own mimetic representation as given to service the "hit" of the commodity.

Feminist address – and especially address relative to the explicit body, the object, the historical "vessel" of her sex – is deeply riddled with the complexities of commodity distress. This should come as no surprise given, as explored in the last chapter, the feminization of the object in perspectival vision. After all, the structure of desire in commodity capitalism is intimately linked to perspectivalism which determines that a viewer is fundamentally dislocated from the scene of the object, set to striving after an object, even as, as Benjamin has noted, sensuous contact is everywhere manifested by commodities on display. Examining the dynamics of commodity distress relative to the female body in the field of vision can begin to expose some of the deeper nervous networkings of social engenderment situating the particular provocations of feminist performance art of the explicit body.

NO ACCIDENT: COMMODITY BODIES

I owe my first actual contact with the notion of infinity to a tin of Dutch cocoa, the raw material of my breakfasts. One side of the tin was decorated with an image of a farm girl in a lace cap, holding in her left hand, an identical tin, decorated with the same image of the smiling, pink girl. I still get dizzy imagining this infinite series of an identical image endlessly reproducing the same Dutch girl who, theoretically shrinking without ever disappearing, mockingly stared at me, brandishing her own effigy painted on a cocoa tin identical to the one on which she herself was painted. I suspect that mingled with this first notion of infinity . . . was a somewhat sinister element: the hallucinatory and actually ineffable character of the Dutch girl, infinitely repeated the way licentious poses can be indefinitely multiplied by means of the reflections in a cleverly manipulated boudoir mirror.

Michel Leiris (1984:11)

The determination of the magnitude of value by labour-time is therefore a secret, hidden under the apparent fluctuations in the relative values of commodities. Its discovery, while removing all appearance of mere accidentality from the determination of the magnitude of the values of products, yet in no way alters the mode in which that determination takes place.

Karl Marx (1977:168; translation as found in Zizek 1989:15)

Commodity dreamgirls recess forever. Within the pages of Michel Leiris's *Manhood* quoted above, a "confessional" autobiography written by the surrealist in 1939, dreamgirls fall into the infinities of their own blind gazes, their own "mocking stares," forever receding into themselves "without ever disappearing." Dreamgirls possess recessive vision, "staring" at the viewer but empty – full only of their own infinite vanishing. The recessive gaze is the opposite, after all, of the penetrating gaze – such a gaze cannot see, with any authority, into the scene of the viewer, but only into an infinite of deferral (see Mayne 1990:180). Recessing into themselves, forever at hand but always out of reach, commodity dreamgirls sing a paradox – they cannot be that which they are given to be. They slip out from under themselves in parades of anorectic desire. Though always out of reach, dreamgirls can be acquired through exchange, but when they are bought and possessed, what is discovered? The predictable deception – this time in the form of powdered chocolate ready to mix and serve.

Such deceptive relations between commodity dreamworlds, such as cocoa-can dreamgirls, and everyday "realities," such as breakfast, are not accidental. Such relations belie the intricate armature of the secret of "accidentality," as Marx put it, secreting the value of the commodity itself. I am reminded of the girl-child on the Coppertone ads that graced US highways in the 1960s – as an eager pup pulls down the girl's bikini bottoms to expose her bum, she looks out at passing motorists with a coquettish smile of surprise as if to say "Oops! An accident!" Right. An accident – orchestrated across billboard after billboard to steal the glance of the driver away from the race of the road. But an accident orchestrated is no accident at all, rather an accident like Oedipus's own, re-enacted as the drama of human nature, crystallized across the stage of Western understanding. An "accident" predetermined, pre-formed, and performed.

Commodity-land dreamgirls,[2] angels of billboards and emblems of desire, recess into the mockery of their own empty stares and whisper of inaccessibility. This recessive inaccessibility simply argues for the desire for access, propelling the purchase of the commodity pitched. Acquiring the object – say, a can of Dutch Cocoa – one is blessed in the bargain with the assurance that one can never fully possess that which one has acquired. Though the chocolate is infinitely acquirable, one can never deplete the chocolate's elusive double, the dreamgirl. Thus one's desire is never entirely exhausted – there is always more, just out of reach, for tomorrow. The value of such a bottomless cup is the immeasurable value of infinity, the imperial value of landscapes forever open for conquest. Dreamgirls have been the insignia. Recessing into the glint of the imagination, they are marked with a teasing sexuality of "cleverly manipulated boudoir mirrors" as they sing the inexhaustible value of what you can't possess though it's in your own hands, propping up the nonaccidental "appearance of mere accidentality," the rush of misrecognition. Yet Marx's reminder is important here, if paradoxical. The recognition of misrecognition – the "discovery" of the ruse, the explicating, or demystification of the myth of accidentality – in no way alters the stream of desire ignited by the myth, much less the social mechanisms responsible for the erection and manipulation of the so-called "accidents." This is the conundrum of the public secret. The secret that everyone knows is still prized, paradoxically, as secret. The pleasure, in part, is the seeming infinite of the paradox itself.

As with commodities, so too with the social dynamics of sexual politics. Much has been written on the performative ruses of gendered identities – identities routinely enforced, blindly accepted, valiantly rejected, or deftly masqueraded in a tangle of phallocratic and counter-phallocratic means and ends. Much textual effort has been spent analysing and debunking the myth of "nature" regarding gender, exposing engenderment as relative to the product and habit of social and cultural power brokering. Following Foucault, not only the overlay of gender but the supposedly deeper grain of sexuality itself can be wrested free from the sense of accidents of nature and read as bred within socio-political discourse, instigated, corralled, and maintained by an ideological network of orchestrated repressions for patriarchally determined desires (Foucault 1980a). Marx's analysis of the secret of commodities can be transposed onto an analysis of the ruses of gender to caution that though gender can be "found out," and the myth that it springs "out of the blue" as an accident of birth can be unsprung, such a debunking does not automatically collapse the cacophonies of desires and counter-desires set in place by the circulation of that secret nor "alter the mode in which [gender] determination takes place."

It may seem paradoxical that the secret discovered, the accident exposed, does not alter the effects of secrecy – but simply consider that patrons of funhouses experience "fun," all the while knowing full well that someone veiled behind a curtain operates the show, pushing buttons to make floors seem to tilt on their own, mirrors ripple, clowns burst out in canned spurts of Bataillean laughter. Similarly, film-goers suspend their disbelief, willingly forgetting that the woman they weep for, the "accident" they hold their breath about, is a staged display of colored light. So too the chimerical embodiment of the commodity dreamgirl only thinly veils the secret that she is *disembodied*, is never what she appears to be – in Leiris's case, she whispers of infinity as she slips through his hands into a breakfast drink, a fast car, a stiff umbrella, the suds of soap. Ironically, her impossibility, her overly visible recessive invisibility is, like the absurdity of a public secret, the sum total of her alarming charm.

All of this is reminiscent of Simone de Beauvoir's explication of the secret that the female body *in representation* is not what it appears to be, and sets the stage for the particular manipulations of the female body that have become prevalent in much feminist performance art. By de Beauvoir's and later Irigaray's explication, the overwhelming habit of Western representation of the female body has not signified "woman" at all, but has simply been the effective insignia of so-called masculine desire. Yet just as "feminine" form has been propped throughout the modern period as a scrim for the machinations of masculine desire, so too "masculine" desire can be read as guise, its mythic stature erected in representation. Like feminine form, masculine or phallic desire becomes a ruse, its mythic stature, its ordinances and anxieties manipulated and maintained through habitual ways of seeing. Such "decided" orchestrations of and perspectives on form and desire propagate the accident and the mythos of "basic human desire," the network of social factories where "nature" and its "accidents" are rigged and oiled to make the machinery of society and capital run smooth. Here, the construction and dissemination of desire promoted as primally phallic secret(e)s the machinations of a more organless social body by which only a few reap the big benefits of monetary privilege (Irigaray 1985a).

To sustain an everflowing spring of desire, the socio-cultural pact concerning the relation between the representational and the real becomes highly significant. It is important to a culture propped by the economics of commodity exchange that fantasy and reality remain distinct categories of understanding, set apart from each other in dialectical tension. Fantasy may affect everyday actions designated "real" – my fantasies of owning a product may propel my buying that product and making it "real," which is to say making it private property – but my fantasies are not, in our Western cultural way of knowing, themselves already real. Indeed, fantasy gestures toward reality, tells us something *about* reality, even constructs the dream of achieving the "reality" fantasized, but fantasy is never fully coextensive with the "real" which it intimates through desire and representation.

Indeed, Lacanian psychoanalysis buttresses this scenario by suggesting that any true "real" is essentially impossible, always mediated by desire which gestures toward but never fully accesses the real it constructs through fantasy. This model of "human nature" suits commodity capitalism, suiting and sustaining the perspectival gaze as well. The desire for the real is impossible to realize, Lacan believed, but, as Peggy Phelan notes, "that impossibility maintains rather than cancels the desire for it." The desire for the real is marked, continually, by loss, but that loss is what fuels the desire. Phelan goes on to note that "the physiological understanding of vision, like both the psychoanalytic conception of the gaze and the technologies of aesthetics, is also a theory of loss and distortion" (1993:14).

The real as marked by dislocation and loss is necessary to the continual circulation of desire in commodity exchange. Fantasy or desire must suggest a direct enough link with some notion of actual satisfaction to propel exchange, but it also must never fully usher in that which it intimates – must never fully achieve the "real" toward which it reaches – so that the frenzy of accumulation will not be assuaged. The "real" which desire desires must fail to be fully realizable. In this sense, and with all the force of modernist paradox, insatiable desire becomes the only dependable reality. Everyday exigencies of material objects, as well as "actual" persons in social relation, become only the signatories of that desire.[3]

The phantasmagoria of commodities on display must, to propel exchange, be both separate from reality and suggestive of a reality, indeed productive of the real toward which it infinitely propels itself. The phantasmagoria of the market constructs a real that cannot *yet* be, or a nostalgic real that once was and might be again (if a product is purchased). That is, it constructs a real that is impossible, that needs always to be brought (bought) into existence by consumers in a scenario of desire *which can never be fully satisfied*, even as the "hit" of the commodity promise smacks with sensuosity, squarely between the eyes. The real, in this scenario, is always nostalgically or futuristically outside over there, on the other side of fantasy, recessing away from the viewer like the vanishing point of perspective.[4]

The circulation of insatiable, dislocated desire as an accidental "fact" of nature secrets the ways such desire is scripted across bodies. Through a network of socio-cultural taboos regarding the appropriate and inappropriate body in display, bodies fall into the service of signifying the systemic insatiability of desire. In particular, bodies marked (young, thin, white, female) have come to serve as insignia of insatiability.[5] These bodies in display dance a phantomics of impossibility – what can never be acquired though it is in your hands. "The phallogocentric mode of signifying the female sex," as Judith Butler put it after Irigaray, "perpetually reproduces phantasms of its own self-amplifying desire" (1990b:12–13). The habitual scene of the female body is thus a locus of culturally inscribed misrecognition – an image of such a body, say, draped on a car, is agreed to be misrecognized as "woman." While the imaged "she" is read to mean "desirable" and is read to mean "I am what you lack and what you want," she is simultaneously displaying "I am what you already are" insofar as she implies "I reflect you back to yourself as your own (culturally prescribed) desire." Here, "she" reflects the status quo of the prescribed desire of the veiled viewing self, "he" – or whomever stands in for "he," of whatever gender, as potential consumer.

Ironically, the primary consumer in modern capitalism was given to be female. Indeed a strict gender division between production and consumption augmented a conceptual space for commodity exchange. Production, figured as active and generative, necessitated a consumption driven by lack. Women, whose "work" was rendered invisible and often unremunerated, were the perfect vehicles for a consumption driven by lack.[6] As cornerstone of the bourgeois home she was given to spend "his" money to fill up "his" home with products of "his" labor and thus, as consumer, she was given to look through "his" eyes. She was, herself, a very double to the commodities she acquired, as one of her main tasks was to appear as "his" prized possession. Thus it was in her best interest to buy the best, and buy the best again and again. Updating her commodities was updating her very self, which is to say updating her man. In this sense, and according to an infinite whirlpool of displacement, the body signifying desire (historically the white female body[7]) becomes the automatic emblem of misrecognition by which someone or something is taken for "other," when in effect that "other" is the infinite amplifying mechanism of self.

Historically, the body marked female is not alone, but stands in league with myriad other feminized displacements. For instance, this dynamic of self-displacement is exemplified in the myriad ways the modern West imaged its own identity, its civilization and modernity, through displaying the spoils of colonialism. Modernity became recognizable in and through the trappings of the primitive, very often conjoined with the female body, on display or in representation. The "primitiveness" of the artifacts and images of other cultures produced an "other" in and through which the modern self could distinguish and recognize its own identity. The dynamics of self-image deflected onto the other as dangerous or exotic or wild object is a dynamic intricately twisted into the self-perpetuating crisis of capital, in the "hysteria" of the market, and the histrionics of the commodity whose promises must always exceed their ultimate ability to deliver the self they purport to reflect.[8] It is amid these phantasms of self-displacement that we struggle to define ourselves, a little absurdly after all, as "men" and "women," or, conversely, wake to find ourselves wondering if the categories themselves are not phantasmic, obscuring or secret-ing or displacing a more complex understanding of our own social and cultural nervous system which generates the natures we find ourselves striving to emulate.

Contemporary performers of the explicit body bank on the possibility that though, as Marx reminds us, the mode in which identity determining takes place may not change, and though secret-making and the mechanisms perpetuating the social underpinnings of the construct "nature" are not altered by exposure, nevertheless, that which is secret-ed by such mechanisms may be malleable, playable, *performative*. In other words, the terms of the secret, if not the thrall to secrecy itself, may shift. In such an effort, performers confront the dominant habit of accidentality with accidents of their own, or counter-accidents. Lynda Hart makes note of this dynamic relative to misrecognition. Misrecognition as mode of knowing may not disappear, but the terms of mis-recognition – its habitual, obsessional terrains – may be altered. As Hart writes: "The trick is to premeditate the misrecognitions, to interpret before, not after, the event" (1993a:10). The trick is to acknowledge and manipulate the dynamics of misrecognition, making explicit the historic locus of the body in service of that dynamic. Like the child's game of telephone, the *meaning* of the secret message, if not the mechanisms of secrecy, comes out the other end radically changed. In the telling and retelling, showing and reshowing, copying and recopying, we manipulate our own misrecognitions, our own slippages.

> Bandage any part of your body.
> If people ask about it, make a story
> and tell.
> If people do not ask about it, draw
> their attention to it and tell.
> If people forget about it, remind
> them of it and keep telling.
> Do not talk about anything else.
>   Yoko Ono[9]

EMBODYING DISEMBODIMENT

Benjamin flipped on its head the easy habit of bemoaning the so-called alienating or damaging effects of advertising's phantoms and capitalist mimetics by suggesting that we look instead at their draw – the potential in these phantasms and dreamscapes (as in the shadows of film or the power of mannequins) to show us to ourselves in our own symptomatic displacements (1969:217–52; 1979). In this effort to decipher dreamscape displacements, historical materialism and the critical theory it has spawned can be linked to psychoanalytic theory. However, Lacan's concern, after Freud, was with the subject and his desire, rather than with collective social dreamscapes informing and instituting subjects and desires. In the psychoanalytic paradigm, the "Real" is lost, relative always to an individual subject's desire, and can only be apprehended as missing, as lack – it falls by the wayside as impossible. For Benjamin, the real also falls by the wayside, but it does not disappear, is not impossible, but rather accumulates as wreckage. In his runic "Theses on the Philosophy of History," a montage of philo-fragments, Benjamin wrote of storms and angels and Paul Klee's painting *Angelus Novelus*:

This is how one pictures the angel of history. His face is turned toward the past. Where we perceive a chain of events, he sees one single catastrophe which keeps piling wreckage upon wreckage and hurls it in front of his feet. The angel would like to stay, awaken the dead, and make whole what has been smashed. But a storm is blowing from Paradise; it has caught in his wings with such violence that the angel can no longer close them. This storm irresistibly propels him into the future to which his back is turned, while the pile of debris before him grows skyward. This storm is what we call progress.

(1969:257)

This often cited fragment is like a hieroglyphic hurricane, twisting on itself in an effort to mark out the insight found in debris. In it, we can catch flying shards of meaning. Because the dreamscape is privileged in the compelling "storm" of capitalism's "progress," subjects are rendered ineffectual relative to the real. But rather than impossible, rather than lost, the real actually accumulates, like dust or outmoded commodities, as only too possible. The real, discarded, actually dirties up and interrupts the dreamscape, cluttering a culture which, systemically bent on privileging the dream of progress, institutes a certain blindness toward the "wreckage upon wreckage" produced by the storm.

The real as overly possible, the clutter of debris the dreamscape attempts to render invisible, prompts us to reread the thrall to loss and the psychoanalytic impossible real. Psychic loss and social loss, or "wreckage," intersect. "The social actually gets into the flesh," writes Teresa Brennan, on the need to examine even more closely the spaces between social (materialist) and psychic (psychoanalytic) critical analyses:

The commodity is a point at which the social and psychical converge . . . The relation between psychical and social determination has been conceived as a one-way street, when it should allow for a two-way traffic. The social actually gets into the flesh, and unless we take account of this, we cannot account for the extent to which socio-historical realities affect us psychically, and how we in turn act in ways that produce and reinforce them.

(1993:10)

Anne McClintock finds predilections of the social to "get into the flesh" productively explored in examining the social contract on relationships between commodities and women. Again, the space between the "prostitute" and the "normal" woman flashes into critical relief around the scene of the commodity:

What is it about the act of shopping that turns a prostitute into a "normal" woman? The female shopper, trawling the grocery aisles for bargains, shows her proper place in the market. Bending to commodities that flash at her – to borrow Marx – "their flirtatious gaze," the shopper genuflects to the family, to domestic order, and respect for consumption. Getting and spending, she lays waste her powers. Shopping for others is work a woman generally does for free, and constitutes, as such, the hallmark of gender normality. Trawling for men, by contrast, the female prostitute puts a price on her labors. The sex worker cocks a snook at Johnson's famous edict that "on the chastity of women all property in the world depends" . . . Where they are not tightly fettered by men, prostitutes interfere with the male control of cash and commodities . . . Small wonder that the Parisian public official, A.J.B. Parent-DuChatelet, called them "the most dangerous people in society."

(1993:1)

Rather than the simple solution that capital and its theatricalisms are "bad," "evil," "destructive," the challenge becomes one of learning *through* capitalist mimetics.[10] Feminist performance artists can be said to mime, or twistedly counter-mime, capitalist mimetics in a concatenation of mimicry designed to explicate the machinations of our social habituations to a desire marked as insatiable. In the service of this effort, contemporary theorists study the ruses of "performance" – the ways bodies play their parts in the dramas determining social "reality." Such contemporary performers mimic the history of the way women have been mimicked, tapping out a counter-mimicry on their physical exigencies in a strangely frenzied ghost dance of the living body (see Kilkelly 1994; Diamond 1989 and 1990/91).

Material Girls dancing with Ideal Girls. Counter-mimicry. Madonna "does" Marilyn Monroe but refuses to vanish, insisting on her status as "material" girl. Schneemann "takes" Olympia. Sprinkle "takes" the Holy Whore. Bernhard does the Bunny. And as we will see, Ann Magnuson dons the House Wife. Modernity's dreamgirls thus ghost-dance in the arms of performance artists – but are these performance artists putting themselves forward as "real" women in opposition to the representations they wield?

To present themselves as "real" would be to recapitulate the very naturalized separation between dream and reality, phantom and true, that these artists are interrogating. Rather, these performance artists embrace their ghosts with irony.[11] Instead of denying dreamgirls validity, these artists provoke a binary terror: their embrace suggests a collapse of the space between phantomic appearance and literal reality, interrogating the habitual ease of our cultural distinctions.

By now it is a well-known conundrum in the wranglings of feminist theory: the "appropriate" female body signifies masculinity (as in masculine desire), while the male form has signified masculinity as well. Thus, what we want to call "real" woman falls apart as her body (that which marks her "woman") is read as always already relative to the phallic signifier which marks her as his insatiable desire, the terrain of his obsessions.[12] Women both signify masculinity (they are the mark of "appropriate" male desire) and are simultaneously excluded from the privileges afforded that term (they are not "real" men). This double bind can be seen to place "real" women in a paradoxical situation regarding their own bodies. Women are invisible to the degree that they are visible – that is, as visible, woman will be read relative to man, while man is also read relative to man. This being rendered invisible by her visible markings creates a cultural scenario in which a "woman" striving to be other than representative of the phallic order can find herself striving to appear as invisible, to *appear as disembodied* – a paradoxical drive which resonates with the recessive logic of the vanishing point and the infinite deferral of desire in commodity capitalism.

The effort to emulate disembodiment can be seen across the board in women's reactions to phallogocentrism: both in the literal self-starvation of teenage girls leading to anorexia and bulimia (see Bordo 1993) and in contemporary feminist theories exploring invisibility as political practice (Phelan 1993). In feminist performance art, however, disembodiment is explicated rather than emulated. The paradox of disembodiment is played out, made explicit, across the literal bodies of performers on stage who "take" the bodies of modernist dreamgirls onto themselves *as if* they themselves were disembodied, only to wield those dreamscapes with a voluble, "in your face," embodied vengeance.

Here, the notion of the secret's eye begins to gain resonance. To attempt to grant vision to the blinded object of the patriarchal gaze results in the disquieting sense of a doubled gaze – of spirits and shadows and ghosts. The gaze returned from the position of an "object" must be a gaze not simply from the object fetishized but from that secret-ed by the object – the gaze of the object's secret that that object is not what it has been given to appear to be. The eye of the object's secret bears the twist of a gaze recognizing misrecognition. To face the secret's eye, rather than simply objects' so-called "flirtatious gazes" as posited by Marx, is to face the challenge of recognizing misrecognition, like seeing blindness, or blind sight. This conundrum of the secret's eye must be taken into account when considering the dynamics of the gaze of the objectified, the feminized, the colonized *vis-à-vis* the cultural master narrative she has been given to serve. The very idea that the unseen might suddenly be seen to see, or that an eye in a socket of a body might belong to a disembodied being as much as to the socially marked body it inhabits smacks of horror, of the uncanny, of body-snatching, of voodoo, of possession. In short, the secret's eye suggests basic modernist obsessions and colonialist terrors, obsessions expressed in explicit terms of gender and race in so much modernist art through the female form and the primitive fetish which science sought, through heightened "objective" prurience, to know, understand, and master.

In feminist performance art of the explicit body, the cultural ruses of dis-embodiment are made apparent by foregrounding the literal embodiment of the tactile body. White performance artist Karen Finley makes her body explicit as a stage across which she enacts and critiques the cultural dramas of disembodied bodies. Finley resolutely resists the dynamics of the vanishing point. She is hardly coy or recessive in the standard "dreamgirl" genre, but relentlessly present and somehow solidly visceral. She stands before her audience and ushers forth an onslaught of identities like some virus run rampant – a virus she insists her spectators take seriously. Though the personas that pass across her may be mangled, multiple, and even manic, the rush of identities across Finley's bodily stage is never apologetic. More like testimony or religious/political witnessing than aesthetic performance, Finley's monologues, both by the ribald content and her testimonial style, disallow conventional distance by which a spectator sits back and suspends disbelief or "appreciates" art. Rather, disbelief is the constant question that bangs at the door of the viewer – I dare you to disbelieve, Finley seems to say, when I'm shoving this material squarely in your face. In an almost complete inversion of naturalism, disbelief rather than belief is put forward like a dare: viewers have to suspend their belief in order to look at some of the nasty underpinnings propping those belief systems. Go ahead: try to *disbelieve* that I am "real," that I feel these things, that I am angry, that I am fed up with a culture that ignores AIDS, that promotes poverty, that condones domestic violence while purporting to be righteous, free, and brave.

In *The Constant State of Desire* (1987), Finley chanted a series of monologues with a fevered ferocity, her rhythmic wail rising and falling with unremitting passion. She has said that she performs her monologues in a "trance state" as opposed to realist narrative delivery because when she performs she "wants it to be different from acting." She wants her audience to be aware that she is "really feeling" as opposed to a dislocated re-enacting (Finley in Schechner 1988:154). In her opening monolog in *Constant State*, Finley tells of a woman who dreams of strangling baby birds. The woman's dream and her doctor's reactions are punctuated by shards of stories of incest, rape, suicide – the status of which, dream or recall, is never clear. But nor is that status ultimately important. The problem, Finley chants, is not in the distinction between reality and dream, but in this woman's performativity relative to that distinction: "The problem really was in the way she projected her femininity. And if she wasn't passive, well she just didn't feel desirable. And if she wasn't desirable, she didn't feel female. And if she wasn't female, well, the whole world would cave in" (1988:140).

Finley stands beside a table and takes off her clothes. She has just finished one of her trance monologues, dropping it as she now drops her dress. In distinction to the monolog she begins to speak nonchalantly and extemporaneously, addressing her audience with casual jokes and asides. On the table beside which she undresses are Easter baskets, Easter paraphernalia, and pastel-colored stuffed animals. After she strips down to a pair of distinctly unremarkable high-waist white underpants, Finley turns her concentration to the jumble of stuff on the table. She puts the colored eggs from the baskets together with the animals into a large, clear plastic bag. She explains as she goes, joking with her audience in an everyday, "I'm on stage but it's no big deal" kind of voice. Indeed, Finley's punctuation of her trance chants with these unrehearsed asides function as Brechtian interruptions: as she told C. Carr for the *Village Voice*, "I want the audience to see what I'm going through. I want to demystify this process you go through when you're trying to expose yourself. Also, these issues can't be packaged and polished" (Carr 1993:127).

Finley explains casually that she will smash everything together – which she does – smashing the bag and checking it to be sure the unboiled eggs inside have smeared all over the fake animal fur. When she's sure that the mixture is good and ready, like some kind of nightmare Betty Crocker she takes out the dripping animals and uses them as applicators to paint her naked body with colored egg muck. She then sprinkles glitter and confetti on her body and wraps herself in paper garlands (Plate 4.2). She looks like a birthday present, or a boa-ed starlet gone amuck. A dreamgirl in a nightmare. In a flash she is fevered again:

> So I took too many sleeping pills and nothing happened.
> So I put a gun to my head and nothing happened.
> So I put my head in the oven and nothing happened. So I fucked you all
>   night long and nothing happened.
> So I went on a diet and nothing happened.
> So I became macrobiotic and nothing happened.
> So I went to the Palladium, the Tunnel, and nothing happened.
> So I went down to Soho and checked out the art scene and nothing
>   happened.
> So I quit drugs and nothing happened.
> So I worked for ERA, voted for Jesse Jackson and nothing happened.
> So I put out roach motels and nothing happened.
>
> (Finley 1988:140–1)

In *Constant State of Desire* Finley has said that she "wanted to show vignettes of capitalist, consumer society where people go far out, stretch the boundaries – but still can never be satisfied. So they take things into themselves, and this is what incest or abuse is all about" (in Schechner 1988:154). Her monolog continues with tales of sticking Cuisinarts and racquetballs and cordless phones up the asses of entrepreneurs who are looking for graffiti art, entrepreneurs who then "lick the piss and shit off me on Avenue B" – 'cause they like it:

> So I take you Mr. Entrepreneur, Mr. Yuppie, Mr. Yesman and tie you up in all of your Adidas, your Calvin Klein, your Ralph Lauren, your Anne Klein, your Macy's, your Bloomingdales. I tie you up in all your fashion, your pastel cotton shirts of mint green and lilac and you know what? You like it. You like it.
>
> So I open up those designer jeans of yours. Open up your ass and stick up there sushi, nouvelle cuisine. I stick up your ass Cuisinarts, white wine, and racquetball, your cordless phone and Walkman up your ass. And you look at me worried and ask "but where's the graffiti art/" and I say "up your ass." And you smile 'cause you work all day and you want some of the artistic experience, the artistic lifestyle for yourself after work and on weekends.
>
> (Finley 1988:142)

The graphic quality of Finley's monologues combined with the explicit use of her body as a stage serve to suggest the impact of social symbolics, social hieroglyphics on literal bodies (see Pramaggiore 1992). The consumption of commodities as stand-ins for identity, the notion that purchased objects are purchased self-hood, indeed the Marxist notion that commodity capitalism makes social relations appear "as relations between material objects" is translated, in Finley's work, literally – with all the threat to symbolism that literality entails.

Plate 4.2 Karen Finley during a performance of *The Constant State of Desire* in New York. Photo by Dona Ann McAdams. © Dona Ann McAdams.

Racquetballs, Cuisinarts, cordless phones, and graffiti art are literally driven into the body, get stuck "up your ass." The space collapsed in commodity capitalism between material objects and social relations (by which material objects *symbolize* social relations) is here collapsed in a *literal* sense – objects as insignias of enviability do not float in a dreamscape of insatiable desire but are dragged screaming into visceral and finite social bodies. Objects inhabit the place of bodies by a contract Finley makes violently explicit – they are driven into the *satiate* body as she says "I'll show you the burden of private property . . . " The symbolic, here, is translated with a ferocious and unsettling literality of over-satiation.

Jill Dolan has written that "rather than offering her body as a sadistically inaccessible commodity, an idea for . . . spectators to consume in a masochistic exchange, Finley offers herself as already consumed" (1988:65–6). Finley disallows the dreamscape of insatiability by showing the show of that dreamscape – exposing the stage across which the dream of infinite consumption is erected as being her own consumptive and finite visceral body, viscous, present, and resistant. She is the very opposite of a recessive dreamgirl. Finley's vanishing point refuses to recess but rather regurgitates the terms of vanishment across her literal body. Insisting on her literal body as the exigent stage across which the codes of insatiability have been manipulated, she relentlessly drives home the abusive impact of that staging.

RADICAL SEX ACTIVISM, SATIABILITY, AND THE COMMODITY

Current feminist performance terrorizes the careful socio-cultural binary distinguishing fantasy and reality that props phallogocentric desire and fuels the continual crisis of commodities in late capitalism. Postmodern criticism has strengthened the foundations, laid by psychoanalysis and materialism, for interrogating cultural distinctions between fantasy and objective reality, buttressing assertions that fantasy is the vehicle for our construction of the real. But much current feminism insists on remembering the flipside of this equation: that the impact of those social fantasies is, nevertheless, inexorably real. Feminists have an obvious stake in focusing not only on the fantastical production of reality but the simultaneous sensuous reality effects of those socio-cultural fantasies.[13]

Looking at the relations between reality and fantasy, we have noted above that commodity culture has a stake in their precise distinction. It is in contradistinction to this socially constructed insatiability of desire and the impossibility of the "real" explicated above that we return to Annie Sprinkle and the dialectical image of the living commodity – the whore – to consider the trend in recent feminist activism toward a "radical sex politics" which champions a loud, insistent, and deliberately troubled notion of explicit *satiability*.

The term "radical sex activism" is writer Susie Bright's term, but Annie Sprinkle falls under this rubric as do myriad and diverse other artists and performers. As if jumping directly into the social divide which pits reality in a binary distinction to fantasy, Bright offers a ribald *reality of fantasy*.[14] For Bright, as for Sprinkle and Finley, the reality of socio-cultural fantasy impacts the body directly, again bringing to mind Kruger's: "Your Gaze Hits the Side of My Face." Unlike Kruger or Finley, however, Bright puts an overtly "sex-positive" twist on the binary terrorism implicit in the declaration "everything we make up is REAL."

You don't have to wait for any equipment to have a virtual experience. You've already had it. Every time you close your eyes and touch yourself, the mind pirouettes, and every sort of feeling floods your body . . . Fantasy is the

ultimate virtual experience because it feels so real and requires no accessories
. . . I have been captivated by the idea of "virtual reality," by the recognition
that our fantasies and fears – especially the sexual ones – are more real
than the "real" forces we have reckoned with historically. I figure the virtual
revolution is just a breath away from smashing our institutional state of
mind.

(1992: 10)

In interesting ways, this politic is the trouble-making twin of the postmodern
dictum that reality is a fantasy of representation in that it proclaims inversely
(though not in opposition) that fantasy is always already real – and not simply
in and through its effects.[15] Here, the "real" rebounds out of the realm of the
impossible, abdicates its status as secondary to or produced by fantasy, to find
itself in an arena of excessive satiation – of the overly possible.

Satiability as exigent, as *not* always just out of grasp, is a notion against
the grain of the circulation of commodities, and especially antithetical to the
female body as emblem of desire, emblem of circulation. As the "appropriate"
female body has been positioned to signify insatiable desire itself – posited as
mysterious, self-recessive, and dangerous – her satisfaction, but most especially
her self-satisfaction, challenges the distinction between fantasy and realization.
After all, how can desire itself satisfy desire? (see Doane 1987). Interestingly,
autoeroticism and explicit masturbation appear liberally in performance art
of the explicit body. Women have been given in representation to masturbate
or to exhibit pleasure for the stimulation of desire in others. But contemporary
performers from Madonna to Susie Bright advocate a masturbation explicitly
touted as geared to satisfy the desire of the self-proclaimed exhibitionist as if to
say: watch if you want to, get off if you want to, but I'm doing this for my own
pleasure.

The question of whether such work simply recapitulates the delimitation
of the body marked female to the realm of sexuality is an important one. It is
possible to argue that work which employs overt sexuality buttresses rather than
shatters the patriarchal delimitation of women to the realm of sex. It is also
possible to argue, however, that this work, rather than positioning itself against
the sexualization of the female body, attempts to wield the master's tools
against the master's house, to force a *second look* at the terms and terrain of that
sexualization. Sprinkle's masturbation at the close of *Post Porn Modernism*, for
instance, while performed for her own pleasure repeatedly marks the spectator for
complicity, and, in the frame of "art," as suggested in Chapter 1, the prostitute
poses questions of authorship and agency relative to the canon of sexualized female
bodies that ghost the work. Often, the explicit use of sexuality in works authored
by women employs appropriation across gender lines. For example, Madonna's
explicit grabbing of her crotch in the late 1980s and early 1990s smacked of the
pop star's well-known ribald autoeroticism, but it was also an obvious appropriation of the mark of male rock-star virility – appropriating the masculine-marked
gesture of phallic virility and applying it to female genitalia (see Madonna 1993,

cover of *Interview*).[16] In the midst of the popular culture wars over the significance of women's pleasure (and for whom that pleasure exists), Madonna was awarded a mock trophy at the 1992 Oscars. Designed as a sexy undergarment with a jock cup attached, the trophy, awarded by Billy Crystal, disavowed Madonna's auto-eroticism: If she gives herself pleasure, she must really be male, hiding a phallus. If she grabs her crotch for pleasure, she must be grabbing the only acknowledged instrument of pleasure: the phallus. Everyone got the joke because the correlation of *active* female desire with gender confusion – or with the notion of a hidden phallus (see Chapter 3) – is a socio-cultural given. The trophy and its jock cup reinscribed the phallus as modus operandi of pleasure strapped onto the female body as modus operandi of desire.

The politic of autoeroticism and explicit self-satiation are not simply an inevitable product of the post-1960s "me generation," but can be read against the grain as a politic poised against the thrall of infinite capital-driven deferral. As phrased succinctly in the *San Francisco Weekly*: "If Bright's agenda works out, we might all be so busy sighing with satisfaction that we'll forget about capitalism's consumption treadmill."[17] The implication here, which smacks of heretical power by dint of its simplicity, is that if fantasy is fully experienced as always already real then, in a world that might present a somewhat silly face, perpetual satisfaction would rule the day rather than perpetual accumulation fed on insatiable desire. In an almost Foucauldian paradigm, history would have to acknowledge the force of social fantasy alongside the normative history of, as Bright puts it, "real forces."

Interestingly, pleasure-oriented sex activism doubles with the radical gender activism propounded by queer theory feminists such as Judith Butler. Though Butler can be critiqued (erroneously) for her potentially too-easy privileging of gender's performativity and resultant dismissal of the historical reality effects of gender,[18] nevertheless her theories employ an important notion of agency: that thinking a world makes a world. Following from the notion that continuing to think in phallocratic categories of gender sustains a phallocratic world, Butler writes "We need to think a world in which acts, gestures, the visible body, the clothed body, the various physical attributes usually associated with gender, *express nothing*" (1990b:281). Here she is advocating the force of thought/desire/fantasy as immanent, as a concrete means of countering the persistent reality effects of dominant phallogocentric fantasies of engenderment. Butler's elegant explication, following the general postmodern complication of the real as social fantasy is, again, the flipside of Susie Bright's insistence that fantasy is reality. From both directions, the terms fantasy and reality collapse into each other in a tangle of complicity. From either direction, efforts to interrogate the given socio-political divide between fantasy and reality allow us the important space to ask: What (whom) has that divide protected? And what (whom) does it secret(e)?

TWO-WAY STREETWALKERS

> A dialectical image . . . is provided by the whore, who is seller and commodity in one.
>
> Walter Benjamin (1973:171)

> We're all prostitutes, in our own way.
>
> Madonna (1993:102)

The argument that provocations such as Susie Bright's aim, at least in part, at the solidly social and political space erected between fantasy and reality seems more secure with some artists' work than with others. When speaking about this topic on various college campuses, several people immediately objected to my inclusion of Madonna because she "cashes in" so enormously on her provocation, a fact which, along with popularity, seems automatically to cancel anything vaguely associable with "feminism" or with "politics." The same issue is raised with Annie Sprinkle relative to her being a prostitute. Monetarily "cashing in" seems to be the same, for many, as "selling out." Prostitutes have sold out and cashed in (criminally) on the general objectification and commodification of women since "time immemorial" (the infinite recession of the "oldest profession"). But Benjamin was fascinated with prostitutes precisely because they straddle a treacherous conceptual line, illegally walking the street between subject and object, being both "salesgirl and commodity in one." Prostitutes – and especially aging whores Benjamin cited as hanging out in shopping malls among heaping sales bins of outmoded commodities (Buck-Morss 1989:101) – are exemplary dialectical images. By showing the show of their commodification, by not completely passing as that which they purport to be, dialectical images can talk or gesture back to the entire social enterprise which secret(e)s them, providing a kind of history of objects accumulating in the cracks of capitalism's "progress" which can be read back against the pervasive myths of nature, value, and accidentality.

Writing on the socio-cultural dynamics of mimicry, Taussig sees in Benjamin's notion of the dialectical image the dynamics of a "two-way street" – a street which runs both one way (fantasy) and another (reality) *at once* – like a public secret which is both secret and known by everyone (1993:251). The trick in engaging dialectical images is to explicate not only the phantasmagoria of, say, makeup, or not only the seeming authenticity or "truth" of the skin that lies beneath face paint, but to read the history and present moment of their *interrelationship* as constructive of the real – to see the interdependency, the complicity, the reciprocity – the flow of both directions simultaneously. For Taussig, dialectical images "satisfy the demands of the two-way street," giving us a glimpse at the ways history is naturalized at the same time that we struggle to historicize nature. Most often dolled in the accoutrements of femininity, prostitutes (of whatever biological sex), it is true, insistently, and in this socio-historical moment illegally, stand in the median crack of traffic, interrupting the flow, selling social fantasies inscribed across literal bodies and concretizing the complicity between fantasized realities and realized fantasies. But they also make evident, as dialectical materialists such as Benjamin completely ignore, the gender dynamics at the structural base of the signifying system propping the circulation of commodities.[19]

One way the gendered dynamics of dialectical images is overlooked is in the implicit gender coding inscribed in reading such images. Benjamin's dialectical images seem to wait *passively* for the intervention of a historical materialist who, discovering them, is viscerally struck by a flash of insight and proceeds to interpret the images as mysterious runes, translating their leaking secrets for the purposes of his materialist history. Benjamin's object awaits the capacities of a gifted materialist observer who, like some Great White Emancipator, can "invest it with the ability to look at us in return" (Benjamin 1973:148) – as if that object did not possess a "look" of its own, whether we are habituated to recognize it or not. But if the "prostitutes" in this study – feminist performers one and all – can function as dialectical images, it is important to note that they resist any appellation as passive runes. These performing "women" function as dialectical images but they are also the image interpreters, loudly voicing their own interpretations – sex commodities and materialist philosophers in one! Put another way, these dialectical images bear dialects of their own, coming out with their secret(ion)s and making a mess across a number of high holy divides – not only the divide between art and porn, reality and fantasy, desiring and desired, but perhaps even more compellingly the divide between theorized and practiced, historian and historicized, materialist and materialized.

Making no secret of her relation to the exchange of capital, the "out" prostitute makes a scene (and possibly lands in jail). The political whore, the object who doesn't wait to be "invested" in order to look back, is a trouble-making whore. The whore who does not sit silently in the sales bin but, in a flash of insight of her own, talks back to her positioning is an unruly commodity. So is the prostitute who, perhaps like Madonna or Sprinkle, publicly "gets off" on herself, becoming commodity, salesgirl, *and buyer* in one – something Benjamin certainly did not imagine even if Luce Irigaray did. Irigaray read the cultural taboo on lesbianism as intimately related to the link between women and commodities, positing lesbians as commodities refusing to circulate, except among themselves.

> It is out of the question for [women] to go to "market" on their own, enjoy their own worth among themselves, speak to each other, desire each other, free from the control of seller-buyer-consumer subjects. And the interests of businessmen require that commodities relate to each other as rivals. But what if these "commodities" refused to go to "market"? What if they maintained "another" kind of commerce, among themselves?
>
> (1985a:196)

In October 1992, while appearing at The Public in her one-woman play *You Could be Home Now*, white performance artist Ann Magnuson published a parodic spread in *Paper Magazine* of explicit pictures of herself having sex with an enormous teddy bear, among other images intended as her own sarcastic version of Madonna's *Sex* book (see Plate 4.3). Using her own body as dialectical image, Magnuson can be read as playing out Irigaray's idea of "commodities among themselves" with a *literal* vengeance. With a politic of ribald satiation, Magnuson says about the teddy bear: "Forget the Vault [a hip downtown sex club], there's a lot more fun to be had at FAO Schwarz. The fur may be fake, but the orgasms are real."

In a printed monolog titled "Free-Range Chicken Pussy," Magnuson describes having sex in a heterosexual foursome in which the only other women is, literally, a chicken, suggesting a bestiality in league with Schneemann's *Vesper's Stampede to My Holy Mouth*, but also suggesting that to be a "woman," or to remain a woman, is to be a chicken – too chicken to challenge the codings marking "woman" in the heterosexual paradigm of patriarchal culture. With classic avant-garde irreverence and sarcasm, Magnuson quips that the chicken is as much a "woman" as she is, implying that she is as much a "woman" as she is a "chicken": "Since I'm the only woman there with hands I soon find myself fully occupied." The monolog is followed by a picture of Magnuson as a classic 1950s housewife – naked except for an apron and a hair-do, holding a glass of milk and a plate of white bread under the boldfaced heading: "Honey I Ate the Kids" (1992; Plate 4.4).

At the end of the vignette Magnuson is driving around a "sleepy suburban neighborhood":

> I can't help noticing all the beautiful pine trees that are around here. I see all those housewives through their kitchen windows making dinner for their husbands who should be returning from work around this time. I start to feel cheap. *Is this the fulfillment of a fantasy hoped for?*
>
> (1992:22)

In Magnuson's terms the image of the suburban ideal is a fantasy hoped for, rather than the fulfillment of a naturalized fantasy. In this sense, fantasies become possessions themselves, hoped for – rather than simply fantasies of hoped for possessions. Magnuson's character speaks of a "fantasy hoped for," a fantasy, marked as "natural," which nevertheless she does not automatically possess – the desire for mainstream desire: husband, house, kids, suburbs. Thus Magnuson presents fantasy itself as a possession. The dream itself – here in 1950s family values guise – becomes a commodity one buys into. This adds a twist to Bright's dictum that fantasy is real – like a "real" object, fantasy itself is acquired, taken on, even bought – if one can afford the cost.

With a related if somewhat different twist, in their performance piece *Anniversary Waltz* lesbian performers Peggy Shaw and Lois Weaver wrestle with the effects of social fantasies which relegate the "norm" as markedly heterosexual. Writing on Shaw and Weaver's *Anniversary Waltz*, Lynda Hart notes that because the Symbolic Order is "the social order of a masculine imaginary," then within its terms "lesbian identities are hallucinations." When lesbian identities refuse to vanish like daydreams but resolutely appear as literal and embodied, "they indicate that the symbolic order is itself a fantasy construction" (1993b:135). In

Plate 4.3 Ann Magnuson with teddy bear. Photos by Len Prince.

Plate 4.4 Ann Magnuson as housewife, from *Paper Magazine*, 1992. Photos by Len Prince.

Shaw and Weaver's work it is precisely the *real* – here the real of lesbian desire marked as impossible – that throws the fantasy construction of the Symbolic Order into relief. Shaw and Weaver make sure that their lesbian identities appear in explicit terms, often mapping their desire for each other explicitly across their bodies (see Hughes, Shaw and Weaver 1989; Schneider 1989a; Patraka 1992). As Hart explicates, "When Shaw says in *Anniversary Waltz*, 'All my fantasies were becoming realities, so I went to see a shrink,' she indicates that 'awakening' to the reality of the Symbolic would be entering into a fantasy where the real of her lesbian desire could not take place" (1993b:135). Shaw and Weaver prefer instead to awaken to the fantasy of the Symbolic Order – to expose the phantasmagoria of its dreamscape, making explicit the ways in which that dreamscape inscribes their reality as impossible, as hallucinogenic.

In her Off-Off Broadway one-woman show *Without You I'm Nothing*, Sandra Bernhard asks her audience to "Pretend it's 1978 and you're straight." She then belts out a popular song about what it feels like to be made love to by a man: "I feel real . . . I feel so real." She is mocking, of course, but her mockery is intended to hit hard at the social symbolics constructing a "real" as a fantasy dictation of the Symbolic Order. "Remember," she tell her audience once her song has wound down, "it's 1989 and you can pretend that you're straight."

Sandra Bernhard is a white performance artist who has labored, in the name of spoof, to make desire explicit as appropriation. In *Without You I'm Nothing*, which she made into a film in 1990, Bernhard "appropriates" with a vengeance. She makes a show of the attempt to *be* appropriate, desirable, and in so doing she becomes the queen of the inappropriate, a Hollywood bad girl extraordinaire. In the process, she outs the minefields of fear and envy by which desire is bought and sold. *Without You* is set in Los Angeles, in an anonymous club where her audience is entirely black. Bernhard presents a flagrantly failed act, attempting to pull off a series of songs and personas appropriating everything from black jazz to country and western to Israeli folk tunes (ostensibly, as Bernhard is Jewish, this would be her "appropriate" terrain, but she is clearly mocking that notion as well). Significantly, Bernhard's black audience is clearly unimpressed, and now and then disgusted. "The audience [doesn't] respond to me at all. They're just staring at me like 'Who is this white bitch?'" (Bernhard in Chua 1990:38). In a seeming last ditch effort to move her audience, Bernhard eventually does an abysmal striptease, winding up in a G-string and pasties in sequins of red, white, and blue.

When she first appears on stage at the club, Bernhard is wearing a pseudo-African headdress and a bulging dress of African print. She sings a sultry song, accompanied by an all-black jazz ensemble:

My skin is black.
My arms are long.
My hair is woolly.
My back is strong.
Strong enough to take the pain

afflicted again, and again, and again.
What do they call me?
They call me: Aunt Sarah.

She finishes with an emotional finale and waits for applause. There is none. Her act is followed by a blonde Madonna look-alike, presented by the black emcee as the "act you've all been waiting for . . . the one, the original, Shoshana." Bernhard's appropriation of Madonna, herself a queen of appropriation who has repeatedly spoken of her desire to be black (to the consternation of African American critics like bell hooks (1992:157–64)), is one of the signature spoofs of her show. Sham Madonna, presented as original, gyrates to a drumbeat, stripping down to next to nothing.

When Bernhard comes back on stage, she attempts to rouse her audience with a round of Israeli folk tunes, and then tells stories of growing up Jewish in America. She elaborates a detailed fantasy about being named Buffy and sitting around a Christmas tree with her oh-so-nice Gentile family. She sings a Christmas carol, accompanied by a group of black carolers in winter hats, scarves, and mittens. Fake snow begins to fall as they sing. At first the snow falls gently and romantically, but it increases in intensity until it's almost a blizzard when Bernhard calls out wistfully: "May all your Christmases be white."

Bernhard has called her show a "mockumentary," but her successfully failed appropriations both show up the tangle of racial envy in popular representation and land her in an ironically powerful position. The fashion market scrambled, as the 1980s turned to the 1990s, to re-appropriate the lure of Bernhard's counter-appropriations. Revlon enlisted Bernhard for their "Most Unforgettable Women" ad campaign and Barneys New York dolled her up in Armani drag as a promotion for their men's store. Bernhard herself plays designers off her own body like a spoof – wearing Romeo Gigli, Isaac Mizrahi, Michael Schmidt, and LA couture while spitting and sneering and mocking her way into sham stardom – or a stardom made explicit as sham.

As for being the "most unforgettable woman," Bernhard gets to the heart of that institution in *Without You I'm Nothing* when remembering a woman she can't forget. Talking about her desire to be a *real* woman, she reminiscences about what she grew up thinking such a woman should be like:

> I remove my boots giving my lower back a full range of motion, as recommended by *Cosmopolitan* magazine. I feel confident stepping into my bath remembering that I've already applied my Rubbermaid daisies. I soak for hours in Calgon Bouquet with cool cucumber slices on my eyes. I shampoo my hair with Herbal Essence shampoo. I smell like a garden of earthly delights. I step out carefully, grabbing my Fieldcrest 100 per cent cotton oversized towel and rub vigorously, bringing much needed blood to the surface of the skin. I glow as I splash on Loves Fresh Lemon. I choose to put my hair up and put in some babies breath. I look real pretty.

Later in the show, Bernhard falls into melancholy remembering Andy Warhol. All the women Andy had immortalized from Candy Darling to Marilyn have gone. She feels left behind. But then she realizes, in a flash of insight, there is one woman who remains: her lunch – a steaming bowl of Campbell's Soup. She doesn't feel so alone anymore.

EXPLOSIVE LITERALITY

> A literal rendering of . . . syntax completely demolishes the theory of repro-
> duction of meaning and is a direct threat to comprehensibility.
>
> Walter Benjamin (1969:78)

Radical sex activists such as Bright and Sprinkle have been criticized for looking only at the pleasuring side of fantasy and ignoring more disturbing, damaging effects. As Modleski writes, such activists can be accused of "minimizing the issues of power and violence" and thus failing to explicate the ways that dominant patriarchal fantasies and the control of the apparatus of representation have wielded reality effects which have been far from pleasurable for women (1991:152). But a pleasure-oriented radical sex activism is not the only orien-tation possible when exploring the reality of fantasy. Recent explorations of sadomasochistic role playing across bodies attempt to focus not only on effects of pleasure, but on social commentary potentially affected by the mimetic manipulation of the cultural dynamics of domination. Because the division of public and private sphere is the primary social sphere for gender domination, Jessica Benjamin has suggested that sadomasochism gives this division *literal* or "objective" form – a concrete arena for making explicit and manipulating the implicit bodily terrain of that division (1988:79; see also Ben-Levi *et al.* 1992/93; Adams 1989; McClintock 1995:155–60).

Karen Finley's use of her literal body as a stage resists a reading of fantasy as the hand-maiden purely of pleasure. Instead, Finley provokes the violence inherent in "Your Gaze Hits the Side of My Face." Finley's work may not be pleasure-oriented, but her use of the literal and often blatantly sexual body shares common ground with radical sex activists. Both make the body evident as affected by a network of socio-cultural fantasies. Radical sex activists such as Bright are intent on reclaiming the control mechanisms for those fantasies, carving out an active arena for female desire historically marked as passive and phallocentric, liberating the body marked female from the confines of infinite deferral. Finley also makes the body evident as impacted by the reality effects of socio-cultural fantasies, though her work does not "reclaim" any pleasure, or reclaim any pure bodily site. Finley's body – as terrain, landscape, stage across which patriarchal fantasies of domination are carried out – serves to make evident the artist's rage, a rage which, through her politic of literality, "talks back" to the social dreamscapes which rack her frame.

Karen Finley presents a veritable theater of Zeus' box misrecognized as Pandora's, in that Finley re-performs, across her body, the myriad patriarchal terrors and desires woman has been inscribed to contain. She opens "her" box to find, instead of some true body or some pure self, a cacophony of socio-cultural disturbances – "all the evils of the world." Her "vision" is, then, a replay in excess of the way she has been envisaged to contain and symbolize patriarchal anxiety. It is a vision looking out from inside envisagement.

Finley's performance practice can be read as a politic of literality as she relentlessly reads social symbolic codes for their literal exigencies. Consider the following two quotes:

> The feminine situation is only established, however, if the wish for a penis is replaced by one for a baby, if that is, a baby takes the place of a penis in accordance with an *ancient symbolic equivalence.*
>
> (Freud 1965:113, my emphasis)

> I take that mama and I push her against that washer. And I take her baby, a bald-headed baby, and put Downy fabric softener on baby's head. Then I strap that baby around my waist till it's a baby dildo. Then I take that baby, that dildo, and fuck its own mama . . . AND THEN I BLACK OUT/AND IT'S TWENTY YEARS LATER/AND I'm in my mama's house.
>
> (Finley 1988: 147)

Though the first quote, taken from Freud's "Femininity," does not appear in Finley's script for *Constant State* and is not mentioned directly in her performance, it is translated with all the force of obviousness in her graphic monolog on the baby as dildo. In literalizing the details of such "symbolic equivalences" upon her own body in performance, Finley unleashes a counter-mimesis that steps outside the bounds of the appropriate (and thus loses her her funding and, in the late 1980s and early 1990s, her acceptance by feminists).[20] Finley's is not a literality opposed to interpretation, as fundamentalist Christians might insist on a literal reading of the Bible, but a plea for an *interpretation of the literal implications* of any symbology which orchestrates the "hit" of its "equivalences" across socially marked bodies. The force of the latent made suddenly blatant impels interpretation of the literal reality effects of Symbolic Orders. As Maria Pramaggiore has written in conceptual league with Julia Kristeva, Finley "undermines one of the basic tenets of Freudian psychoanalysis – the positing of the unconscious as a realm cordoned off from the material and intersubjective world of patriarchal power relations" (1992:274).

In *A Certain Level of Denial* Finley chants, "You want hysteria? I'll give you hysteria."[21] Nineteenth-century hysterics have today become well known for their performative re-enactments of the repressions of the Symbolic Order upon their physical bodies in a display of tics and twitches, scratches, glitches, breaks. Depending on how one reads back over the nineteenth century, hysteria was either a pathology or a political statement of the unruly detail – or both, in the more complex terms of the "two-way street." Though the condition of hysteria is no longer recognized by the medical profession as viable, contemporary performers and theorists continue to wrestle with the conditions which gave rise to hysterical effects – conditions which have not necessarily disappeared.[22] Indeed, hysteria is often played back with a vengeance in arenas of feminist performance – or at least in critical analysis. Joy Press and Simon Reynolds argue in *The Sex Revolts* that Lydia Lunch performs as if "one of Charcot's female patients had taken charge of her own theater of hysteria and transformed the humiliation of being an exhibit into an empowering exhibitionism" (1995:262).

Feeling the intangible slap of the gaze as it "hits the side of the face," and the intangible slap of the commodity image as it "hits us squarely between the eyes," the hysteric's head jerks in response. A hysterical woman is a woman who has lost a sense of the boundaries between sign and signified – the supposedly arbitrary signifier and the supposedly distanced signified[23] lose both their mark of randomness and their distance as they are collapsed onto the space of her body. Under the unruly sway of symptomatology, the return of the repressed, symbolic signifiers bear weight, correspond, inscribe, impact upon her body. In the logic of hysteria, all things mark. The relation between signifier and signified is not arbitrary, not purely "accidental," but deeply imbricated in patriarchal prerogatives and therefore cannot be shrugged off as "oops, oh well, another day, another arbitrary sign of my inscription as woman, as negative term, another 'accidental' exclusion from and repression by the Symbolic Order." Unable to shrug it off (and thus compulsively shrugging), hysterical women seemed to say, in their counter-language of ticks and gasps: "Wake up! – relations between sign and signified are *orchestrated* accidents which secret(e) and disavow their literal impact. The correspondence is sensuous, like the side of my (scratch, glitch, break) face."

Writing toward a "feminist mimesis," Elin Diamond has examined the complicity between realism and hysteria, suggesting that the real is always hysterical in that it is always symptomatic of its construction (1990/91:59–92). To bring hysteria in realism into focus for purposes of feminist explication, Diamond advocates an *explicitly* hysterical realism – a performance practice which shows the show of realism, unveiling its basis in hysteria. With an emphasis on an explicitly hysterical realism, versus an implicitly realistic hysteria, a performer's body would, like a hysteric's, speak its historical signification and *reflexively* or ironically re-perform its symptomatology.[24] The trick is that in so speaking her symptomatology within the explicit frame of performance (that is, explicitly showing the show), the performer would simultaneously have to escape the very signification her body speaks – the performer would have to comment on that hysteria at the same time that she exhibits it. This is the trick of the dialectical image at the median of the two-way street, speaking her own interpretation. In speaking/showing her symptomatology – standing beside her own hysteria as Doctor Charcot once stood beside his hysterics on display – she could not, following Brechtian logic of the "not/but," be solely the symptom, not *only* the symptom, as she would also have to be her own vehicle for transference (see Diamond 1988).

Imbricating Irigaray's notion of hysterical mimicry[25] with a historical-materialist perspective, Diamond articulates the need for a feminist mimesis that functions as an alienation effect, framing the way systems of meaning are marked upon literal bodies and exposing the reality effects of those engenderments upon those who live in and wield patriarchally marked, engendered bodies (1989:66). Reminding her readers that feminism "has a stake in truth," like a stake in "reality," and determined to articulate a mimesis with an access to that stake, Diamond explores linking Julia Kristeva's notion of the "true-real" with Irigaray's irreverent mimicry (1989:59). A politic of the literal that side-steps signification, the true-real (the literal concretization of the signifier) could be said to reverberate in syncopated time with the Symbolic Order and to be imbricated in bodily detail. Thus it is *stable* referentiality which is potentially troubled by any irruption of the true-real – the troublesome sensuousness of the concrete particular (1989:69). In the language of hysterics, details are not displacements or sublimations of a generality, but the signified *is precisely taken for* the real, "side-stepping the sign-referent model" (1989:68). The symbol *is taken as* literal, just as the literal female body has so volubly been taken for the fetishizing purposes of patriarchal symbolics. In this flip-flop counter-mimesis there is a collapse of the bridge erected to maintain the separation between sign and referent. Diamond implies that side-stepping this bridge, jumping into the gap as it were, holds a potential for performative resistance which is productively "parasitic" on patriarchal mimesis – problematizing Truth (capital T) by showing up the show of its cultural erection. Such a performance is resistant, Diamond implies, precisely because in collapsing (hysterically) the space of distinction between the figurative and the literal, the symbolic and the real, the theatrical properties of that space are revealed.[26]

Finley's literalization of symbolic equivalences is also a spatialization. That is, Finley *maps* the "hit" of engenderment, the violence of patriarchal gender symbolics, upon her bodily parts. When Finley renders Freud's "ancient symbolic equivalence" literal, that equivalence becomes wholly unpalatable. When Finley collapses the aesthetic distance propped between a symbol and the signified, she threatens comprehensibility. Freud's symbolic equivalence between a baby and a penis is made safe by distance. But Finley's literal translation makes explicit the embodied foundations on which Freud's symbolism is propped. Made explicit, it is unbearable.

LITERAL SHROUDS AND DREAMSCAPE RE-INTERMENTS

As explicated above, women are invisible to the degree that they are visible – that is, as visible, woman will be read relative to man, while man is also read relative to man. Thus "woman," striving to be other than representative of the phallic order, can paradoxically find herself striving to *appear as invisible* – to make her disembodiment apparent. We have discussed the explicit body technique of denying disembodiment by replaying its tenets across the overtly embodied presence of the performer, as in Finley's, Schneemann's and Sprinkle's work. But other artists manipulate this paradigm by making the body explicit as vanished.

Ana Mendieta made performance pieces in the 1970s which documented erasure – bringing the dynamics of disembodiment explicitly into relief (Plate 4.5). Mendieta talked back to the issue of the female body as secreted or

Plate 4.5 Ana Mendieta, *Untitled* (from the *Siloueta* series), 1977. Carved earth silueta in swamp area, Iowa. Photo courtesy of the Estate of Ana Mendieta and Galerie Lelong, New York.

shrouded by representation through creating, literally, shrouds. Her *Siloueta* series and her "fetish series" from the mid-1970s consisted of effigies traced from her own body and carved in limestone, sand, wood, or mud, chiseled into cave walls, or set to burn in flames (see Barreras del Rio and Perreault 1987).

Like Schneemann's *Eye/Body*, Mendieta's earth/body works invoke the cultural feminist Mother Goddess, but, also like Schneemann, these Goddess invocations are simultaneously linked to her own physical body. But here, the body is traced in effigy – its literal erasure, rather than its voluble presence, is underscored. Mendieta's pieces both illustrate and disallow the service of her body to the infinite recession of the vanishing point, or the insatiability of desire, because they are so insistently *finite* – shrouds of sand, mud, stone, tree, or the fertile grave-bed stuff of dirt. Here is no infinite recession: vanishing has already occured. Here is only the blindspot, rendered literal as absence, left to stand and stare back at the viewer. Loss is not an anxious flirtation, not riddled with desire, displacement, or dislocation. Loss is present – literal, exigent, palpable. Tragic and beautiful at once, the pieces are haunting, umbilically tied as well to Mendieta's experience as a Cuban exile and redolent with her aim that her work help to "end colonialism, racism, and exploitation" (Mendieta in Barreras del Rio 1987:33).

Mendieta made explicit the vanishing of her body, at the same time – the 1970s – that the young white female body was the over-abundant site of representation in the West. The pressure she was under to conform, to Americanize, was a pressure to disappear, to erase and forget her cultural heritage, or to commodify it. In a real sense, the pressure was to disappear into disappearance, since the American woman she was given to emulate was a personification of the commodity logic of disembodiment itself (the object, fetishized, is not that which it is given to symbolize). Mendieta's vanishings still resonate in the 1990s as popular representation increasingly presents a standardized body of desire in a panoply of "multicultural" colors, genders, and ages. Difference is increasingly commodified as simply mix'n'match style, an anything-goes palette of variety. Difference, like makeup, is something not to be "taken too seriously," as if histories of oppression and experiences of exile or exploitation were simply nasty particulars, easily ignored by applying a "fun" face to a history of colonial appropriation.

Like Mendieta's, much of Cindy Sherman's work aims at making the dynamics of disembodiment *vis-à-vis* the female body in representation apparent for critique. Sherman, like Finley, uses her own body as the stage across which she mimics cultural habits of marking the female body for the services of dreamscape representation. When one looks at Sherman's photograph *Untitled #153* (1985; Plate 4.6) alongside any number of popular advertisements which figure the female body as infinitely inhabitable vessel for desire, the force of Sherman's "second look" at these images becomes obvious. An ad for Ferre Boutiques from *Vogue* shows a model (as models signify general "woman") draped upside-down over a couch, looking as though she has just been murdered (Plate 4.7). The ad, like all ads, is intended to ignite desire for purchase. Manipulating the "hit"

Plate 4.6 Cindy Sherman, *Untitled #153*, 1985. Color photo, 67.25 × 49.50". Photo courtesy of the artist and Metro Pictures.

Plate 4.7 Advertisement, Gianfranco Ferre, as it appeared in *Vogue*, 1993. Gianfranco Ferre, Autumn/Winter 1993/94 Women's campaign. Photographer: Steven Meisel; model: Linda Evangelista.

of the commodity, Ferre intends to capture the female consumer in her effort to emulate the drive toward disembodiment her culture offers as "femininity." But a strikingly similar image, cast across the particular body of the artist Sherman in mimesis, is obviously confrontative. The disembodiment re-performed in *Untitled #153* "looks back" through the eyes of a particular woman-as-artist, seeing herself in the appropriate(d) scene of general "woman" – woman as disembodied desire. The violence in this contract rages into relief.

But if making erasure and dismbodiment explicit has been a strategy of politicized aesthetics here explored in feminist performance art, the explicit body, the dreamscape of capitalism, has recently been mining erasure and disembodiment and even impoverishment for the "hit" of the commodity, as if to aestheticize the political unrest such issues invite. Though it is possible to argue that erasure and impoverishment are standard fare in commodity dreamscapes, the images employed have become increasingly "explicit." An ad selling expensive clothing in *Vogue* (April 1992) can stand as exemplary: the ad features a double-page spread of a dilapidated city street with a burning carcass of a car at a sidewalk and only the words: "United Colors of Benetton." No clothing, no dreamgirls, no "dreamscape," but an image of the "wreckage" of the real itself. Indeed the absence of dreamscape bodies is staged here to catch the viewer's attention with the question: What is this ad about? Is it simply an image of impoverishment, violence, and explicit loss to provoke accumulation, all in the name of fashion? Is it a re-appropriation of threatening sites of disappearance and unrest into the reassuring dreamscape of commodities?

Of course, concave dreamgirls such as Kate Moss often smack of impoverishment as much as any burned-out car. The drawn, emaciated, and unhappy faces of so much contemporary high fashion raises fascinating questions about why late capitalist desire appears so often libinally invested in the opposite of prosperity: unrest, poverty, and lack. A recent Guess Jeans ad in *Elle* dressed blonde leggy models in bust-revealing clothing and set them to work in rice paddies. Their backs are bent. One model wipes her brow as if overcome by her workload. Is this ad saying: Buy Guess clothing and you too can work for long hours for very little wages in horrific conditions? Is this the Third World as First World fashion theme park? Is this envy across privilege, fear across privilege, in the guise of desire? Is this appropriation of disenfranchisement: the attempt to "pass" as oppressed? Another image in *Elle* featured absolutely bone-thin models with concentration-camp haircuts exhaustedly trying to climb chain link fences. The text reads: "Upwardly Mobile and Very Versace . . . green viscose suit, $2,500."

The rampant mimesis of disprivilege across emaciated bodies dressed in extremely expensive clothing compels questions about the envy of disprivilege in a culture of insatiable accumulation. Perhaps the imaging of despair, violence, and loss attempt to appease anxiety about reality effects – claiming ownership or control over the signs of the wreckage in the wake of capitalism's "progress" – turning them into artifacts of privilege. Appropriating such images to the dreamscape may reassure the consumer with one of postmodernism's dictates:

that even the most troubling "reality" can be considered masquerade, hype, sham. Such tragedy is not "really real." Impoverishment becomes a choice one can buy into, wearing its signs like blackened eye-shadow, re-appropriating fear of the disenfranchised "other" into the belly of high-cost consumptive desire. If one were to encounter a bombed-out car on a city street (as opposed to one in an ad), one could now safely consider it a fashion statement. Women in sweat shops or rice paddies or homeless shelters must have bought into their "look," freely. If Mendieta and Sherman make erasure and disappearance explicit in their artworks, flipping through contemporary glossy magazines it becomes immediately apparent: such efforts in the name of subversive political awareness can be re-appropriated, consumed, re-interred by capitalist mimetics.

Capitalist mimetics have also recently been employing in the "hit" of gender subversion and femininity as masquerade as transvestites increasingly grace the pages of print media and TV ads. Of course, femininity as masquerade is nothing new to the aims of capital, but recently advertisers have been willing to trade more openly in the depths of artifice at the heart of gender distinctions. In 1995, for example, the successful young MAC Cosmetics Company announced that its spokesmodel would be RuPaul, a seven-foot, leggy blond, African-American transvestite who had appeared in myriad ads selling not only makeup but Baileys Irish Cream. Judith Butler has written that transvestites "can do more than simply express the distinction between sex and gender, [they can] challenge, at least implicitly, the distinction between appearance and reality that structures a good deal of popular thinking about gender identity" (1990a:278). The distinction between appearance and reality is, as discussed above, a distinction upon which commodity dreamscapes depend: reality must always be deferred in favor of the lure of appearance. In this sense, femininity as masquerade has been a quintessential signature of the dreamscape; a signature which the transvestite can sign with some precision.

Frank Toskan, the creative director of MAC, told the *New York Times Magazine* that RuPaul was chosen as spokesmodel because "the company's makeup is for everyone – all races and sexes, not just a 25-year-old model with pale white skin." More interestingly, and in a move that may seem ironic, RuPaul was adopted in an aim to sell "reality" rather than "appearances": "They are not selling dreams. They are selling the right shade of eye shadow and the proper applicator brush. They assume that if a customer has sought them out, she [sic] must be sophisticated and clued in to fashion" (Mary Tannen 1996:58). But the fact that the *Times* did not print "he or she" to mark their potential consumer is hardly a slight slip. The dreamscape of capital has a long-standing practice of relegating men to the status of producer, women to the status of consumer. Women, in fact, are represented (or have value on the market) as, in Irigaray's words, "the product of man's labor" (1985a:175). Thus women have long been accustomed to the task of buying themselves back, wearing themselves, painting themselves across their own faces as if, without the mask, they could not be recognized but would float in some netherspace as an unspeakable (public) secret. They would be disembodied.

RuPaul may "out" the secret of masquerade – or make it more explicit. But the degree to which she disrupts the impact for those bearing bodies marked "woman" is open to question. RuPaul has considerable social effect in part because of the play with disembodiment (and dismemberment) that she suggests as she manipulates a show of woman across a body constructed by "man." Her glitzy feminine wiles get to be lots of "fun." Fun or play becomes the selling point, obscuring the more poignant and incendiary political significances behind much drag performance (Butler 1993:121–42; Phelan 1993:93–111; hooks 1992:145–56). Indeed, Toskan has declared that his company has "never taken makeup [and by extension their spokesmodel] too seriously. It's something to have fun with" (in Tannen 1996:58).[27] This "not taken seriously" sadly echoes the condition of women historically, and such ad-scape utilizations of trans-vestitism seem to bank on the continual force of this condition, not on its demise, even as they mime and mine, as Mary Tannen put it for the *Times*, drag's "subversive messages."

In the same way that high fashion has adopted the transvestite, designers have begun to pose male models to appear "as if" gay. Writing on Jenny Livingston's Harlem drag ball documentary *Paris is Burning*, Peggy Phelan notes the contem-porary phenomenon of the mainstream attempt to re-appropriate "passing" – an appropriation, ironically, of an appropriation in an ever-reflective Baudrillardian hall of mirrors. Phelan cites Matthew Barney's fall 1991 show in New York as a fashion appropriation of the tropes of "(white) gay contemporary art" (1993:96). So, too, John Bartlett's 1996 line liberally "quotes" gay male aesthetics, posing men in femme makeup and hair-dos demurely touching urinals in *Detour* (March 1996). Designers like Versace drape dour-faced teenage female waifs in the arms of bored-looking men and boys wearing (appropriating?) gay identity-markers across glossy backdrops signifying everywhere: from scruffy subway stations to palatial estates.

But so what?

If commodity capitalism re-appropriates subversive practices brought to visibility in contemporary art, performance, and street life, should we bemoan such rampant re-appropriation? The effort of confrontative art and performance to bring oppressive structures to visibility – to *take them seriously* by making them explicit – runs the risk, always, of a re-appropriation of the counter-appropriate under the ad-scape rubric: "not to be taken too seriously." However this risk, as Phelan has noted, bears a positive political pay-off:

> The risk of visibility is the risk of any translation – a weaker version of the original script, the appropriation by (economically and artistically) powerful "others." The payoff of translation (and visibility) is more people will begin to speak in your tongue.
>
> (1993:97)

But do such ads as Benetton's burned-out car, which bank on erasure, impover-ishment, and violence, really speak in the same tongue as, say, Mendieta's literal shrouds? Benetton's ad is not a "weaker version of the original script," as Phelan suggests – in counter-appropriation there is no "original" but a concatenation of mimicry, an appropriation of precedent appropriations. Still, such ads do appear to talk back to subversive practices which have talked back to, or made explicit, oppressive structures of the Symbolic Order. If this is true, then the "pay-off" of such re-appropriation does appear, at the very least, to be dialog.

But, having said this, I was struck dumb by a series of ads in the March 1996 edition of the fashion magazine *Detour*. A series of glossy Gucci spreads presented female models in pink boxes as "blow-up sex dolls." The boxes were presented as commodity packages with phrases like "Flesh Like Skin" and "4 Different Positions" and "My Arms and Legs Move" printed across one side. A sultry vacant-looking model appears to be stepping out of each box. Four white models stand upright in four boxes. An Asian model, her arms and lower legs apparently amputated, sits spread eagled in another. An African-American model in zebra-striped lingerie crawls out of a sixth box on all fours.

This is an ad quoting the sex industry in the name, or in the frame, of *haut monde*. If these porn-quoting sex-doll images had been authored by an explicit body performance artist, would I have included them here as "resistant," "subversive," "talking back," or "counter-mimetic"? Would the frame of "art" authored by a "feminist" have altered the significance of these same images for me? With the re-appropriative drive of capital, these sex-doll ads appear to have ingested the "sex-positive," counter-mimetic art of Annie Sprinkle, Susie Bright, Veronica Vera, or Sandra Bernhard . . .

Almost, but not quite.

The Gucci models are once again mute. Like Manet's *Olympia* or Courbet's *Origin of the World* they symbolize "general woman." The images partake of the symbolic and secret, again, the literal, the particular woman, the artist/model standing beside herself, taking a second look at the way she is ghosted by the history of her conscription to the service of the dreamscape. The satiate and particular championed by feminist performance artists who make their bodies explicit as stage is re-interred into the symbolics of insatiability once again, deferred into some future exchange. The force of these images deliberately hits the side of my face with all the tactility of sensuous contact as the optical unconscious, opened up by feminist artists, closes down once again, slinking back, with increased vengeance, into the netherworld of dreams.

5 After us the savage goddess

After Stephane Mallarmé, Chavannes, after my own verse, after all our subtle colour and nervous rhythm, after the faint mixed tints of Conder, what more is possible? After us [symbolists] the Savage God.

W. B. Yeats (1958 [1896]:233–4)

The particular conjuncture of the dream of femininity with the dream of primitivity in modernism is the subject of this chapter. Like the feminine, the primitive stands as emblematic of the vanishing point of knowledge and provokes a related terror and fascination that tangle race and gender in significant ways. "Primitivity" is an attribute historically ascribed to "lower" races just as "femininity" is ascribed to the "second" sex. Unpacking this confluence, the strategic confrontations of contemporary feminist performance of the explicit body provoke us to take a second look at the shock of the savage body in historical avant-garde performance.

SEEING BACK THROUGH

If "seeing through" is the etymological root of perspective then seeing *back* through implies a postmodern turn on that perspectivalism, a doubling back over uniocular vision, to see, paradoxically, the uniocular a second time. Looking back in time at the legacies of perspectivalism becomes a looking back through perspectival space – redressing a space structured to render being seen and being blind identical, to render bearing vision and being dislocated (invisible to the seen) synonymous. The feminist postmodernist "take" on modernist tenets of visibility becomes tangled in the inherent paradoxes of that space, as structural "riddles" surround her project like the proverbial thorny bracken spatially guarding Sleeping Beauty from the ravages of time. Articulating the tongue-twisting speech of subject and object at once, the feminist artist after modernism, hacking her own way through the bracken from the inside out, finds herself ghosted by the modern inscription of "woman" as always already double, split, always already riddled by the inscribed pathologies of her sex.[1]

In making her split explicit for purposes of explication, the explicit body performer invokes her historic delimitation at the same time that she attempts to redress it as "seer," showing the show. That the historically feminized "dark continent" of insatiable recession – vanishing point *and* scopic field – should expose her secreting to "look back" out of her own vanishing, like a blindspot sighted, exists as one of the closely inscribed terrors of the modernist subject. She invokes that terror at the same time that she attempts to expose it as seeded in patriarchal aims.

Split subjectivity is infinite and insatiate and tangled in its own thorny paradoxes. Endlessly proliferating like Leiris's Dutch cocoa girl who splits into her own representation (Leiris 1984:11), the dream girl spanning the modern era is never only one – never "one," as in speaking subject, at all – but comes to signify the splitting off (like a rib) of sign from signified in a fetishistic frenzy of displacement.[2] To signify the splitting of sign from signified is a paradoxical project par excellence. "Hallucinatory and actually ineffable," as Leiris wrote of the Dutch cocoa girl, the image of "woman" has signaled the mysterious glory of negative space, approached with fear and envy but desired above all (1984:11). Defined *as* split (she is not man but not not man) and then defined *by* that split, "woman" in/as representation appears to invite one in and in and in as infinitely recessive, never quite attainable – the essence of commodity in display, ultimately silenced into a glass castle of her own rebounding echoes – as Leiris says, "theoretically shrinking without ever disappearing."

Though the influence of more women reading, more women voicing, more women publishing their "takes" (like the influence of previously inscribed "primitives" publishing today as postcolonials) has been undeniable on the general rethinking of the Western canon taking place in academia under the embattled banner of (multi)cultural studies, it is still the case that rereading the various legacies of modernism "as a woman" and publishing or performing those retakes cannot pretend to be a redemptive project or bear any one revolutionary reading, erect any singular new world order. The project itself is splintered. On the one hand, "woman" is exposed as constructed, shown to be the dream of patriarchy and ultimately a ruse servicing the mold of a desire determined by capital. On the other hand, there is the resiliently physical fact of bearing a body marked female and experiencing the resultant social reality effects of bearing those markings. On a third hand, even as "outing" the masquerade appears to promise an end to the naturalization of femininity, the issue of the inhabitability, the performativity, the "masquerade" of femininity rings of the historical habit of imagining woman as an endlessly inhabitable, impregnable, male-identified space.[3] And on yet another hand, the instant "real women" are held up to counter the historical construction of woman as infinitely inhabitable, those very physical exigencies marking woman as somehow real quickly re-splinter into women's myriad differences, such as class, sexual preference, race, age, experience. That is, just as we begin to posit "woman" as an active subject, she explodes again into women – brilliantly, importantly, she bursts into her million-handed variations as if disappearing, again, into the infinite of her own multiplicities.

Like "woman," modernism itself becomes a thorny bed of mirror shards when looked at across a historical plane. The notion of "post" can quickly lose temporal currency as the continual modernist splitting off of disciplinary "ologies" and aesthetic "isms" can be seen as leading inexorably to the combustive hetero-geneity we celebrate as beyond (post)modernity (Raymond Williams 1989:53). For Rosalind Krauss, the terms of modernism are only revealed, made apparent, in postmodernism. Postmodernism is not beyond the modern but rather "openly" modern, like a secret explicated.

> It is, in fact, from within the perspective of postmodernist production that issues of copy and repetition, the reproducibility of the sign (most obviously in its photographic form), the textual production of the subject, are newly brought to light within modernism itself – revealed as the matter that a euphoric modernism sought both to signal and to repress. Postmodernist art enters this terrain (the theoretical terrain of structuralist and poststructuralist analysis) *openly*.
>
> (1988:6)

In the spirit of secrets told, modernism's internal fragmentation and thrall to splintering "isms" can be seen as directly related to the general obsession with an infinitely fragmented female body. This relation is not incidental, is no accident (see Buci-Glucksmann 1987). Rather than positing a postmodernist and a feminist reading as beyond modernism, it is imperative to see the feminist postmodern as relative to modernity – an "open" or "out" modernity – making explicit the myriad secrets modernism sought, as Krauss has written, both to "signal and to repress." In this vein, we see the feminist postmodern as openly wrestling *within* the conundrum of reading the infinitely recessive dreamscapes of capitalist culture as they coagulate across the infinitely resplendent and splintering body of the feminized other. As Schneemann says in her 1989 performance piece *Fresh Blood: A Dream Morphology*, "His dream of us [women] is so culturally pervasive that we *still* ask: Are we dreaming ourselves or dreaming the dreams of the men dreaming us."

Though it may be reductive to say with Carol Duncan that modernist dreams covered a "remarkably limited set of fantasies" (1988:59), it is nonetheless true that certain motifs predominated – especially whores, primitives, crowds, and thieves (or criminals who "take" property, breaking boundaries between public and private without being seen). As explored in the preceding chapters, these modern phantoms were set to dance around a burning obsession with the vulnerable authority of vision and visibility – a vision distinct from a visceral, dangerous tactility, a vision dislocated from the visualized. The solitary, dissoci-ated observer, alienated flaneur, came to symbolize the condition of the modern subject who found himself separated from yet obsessed with those marked for a criminal or primitive or sexual or uncontrolled viscerality – a viscerality standing in for, fetishized as, his own anxiety, his fear of and insistence on "lost" connection. Enucleated or dissociated vision became a powerful trope of modern experience just as disinterested, objective vision had been its science-driven promise.[4] And dislocated vision is umbilically linked to the structure of desire fueling the modern machinery of consumer capitalism.

The modern arts responded to the condition of dislocated vision in a number of ways. Primitivism – the twin nostalgia for and confrontation of the insignia of the "primitive" in the space of the "civilized"[5] – was often employed in the strenuous effort to redress distance, to jettison beyond alienation, and catapult a spectator/art viewer into the "danger" of primal, "uncivilized," visceral experience.[6] "Primitive" practices and artifacts of "other" cultures, most notably African and Oceanic cultures,[7] were considered less evolutionarily developed and thus, rife with racisms of the day, were associated with a temporal remove (to the point of a prehistoric "vanishing") as well as a spatial remove from modernity, signaling a prelapsarian connectedness to all that modernity had "lost" (Fabian 1983). The nostalgic drive backward of modernist primitivism (which was sometimes confrontative and not nostalgic, as this chapter will explore) had a concomitant if ironic counterpart in the avant-garde romance of a break into the future – the ribald machine-loving ideology most crystallized in Futurism.[8] This twinned impulse, backward and forward, frames the structural institution of modernist detachment and alienation from the present "reality" of experience. Dictated by the desire machines of late capitalism and the legacies of perspectival ways of seeing/knowing, the impossible modern "real" relegated an impossible "present," tangling the flaneur in infinite deferral and endless displacement of identity. Efforts to understand and even heal the effects of dislocation and displacement spawned myriad philosophies, such as phenomenology, historical materialism, and psychoanalysis – philosophies which focused on "experience," material objects and relations, and slippages of the unconscious in the aim to interpret that which was considered hidden by modern dreamscapes and redress, by means of "suspicious" investigation, modernist incapacity to accessing that hidden meaning.[9] Arguably, if reductively, the foundational premises of such philosophies were, at their origin, tangled in the operative trope of perspectival viewing, faithfully following the modernist dictate that meaning, like the viewer, is essentially dislocated, thus reconstituting the dictates of mystification even in the aim of demystification.

Formalist abstraction, too, serviced the drive against alienation, the anxious search for an inscribed "lost" visceral connection, even while founded on its operative premise. Formalist artists sought to emulate the physiognomic mechanics of "purely" visual states and effects – to mimic the visceral mechanics of the eye itself. Oddly, the drive to reignite a viscerality, or at least to create a truly modern connection (versus detachment) to the modern world, was often orchestrated as a drive to take detachment to its extreme. Clement Greenberg described the attempt to inhabit the "*condition* of vision" in the creation of abstract paintings into which "one can look, can travel through, only with the eye" (1966:107). The modern arts would take perspectivalism to a certain extreme, absenting the image from the scene of perspective. The abnegation of the "realistic" scene which the perspectival grid had been developed to enhance was replaced by the romance of the grid itself. In place of the real-ized scopic field would come a mimicry of optics without the visualized (Krauss 1988:10, 15). The formalist version of the concern to mend the apparent breach between visuality and viscerality carried the hope that following disinterested and detached vision to its own extremes would facilitate a re-entry through our own detached eyes – to see ourselves seeing (versus seeing ourselves as seen) and thus know ourselves as the detached beings we had become. In knowing ourselves as detached, in the "condition" of "pure" perception, we would somehow no longer be detached.[10]

This modern impulse to master the "condition of vision itself" relates in important ways to the modernist thrall with the colonial subject, the "primitive." Using *Heart of Darkness* as an example, Marianna Torgovnick cites Joseph Conrad's thirst for the immediacy of perception as relative to his character's (and the modern West's) disillusionment with language: "a belief in *perceptual* versus conceptual experience [was] an attempt to recoup for the West the direct, unmediated experience associated with primitive societies" (1990:151). Certainly André Breton's invocation of "savagery" in the opening to his tome *Surrealism and Painting* carries weight in this regard: "The eye exists in its savage state . . . I feel that I have the right to demand a great deal from a faculty which, more than almost all others, allows me to exercise control over the real" (1972:1). The thrall of vision in modernism was thus complex. On the one hand, the separation of viewer and viewed as manifested in modern life was alienating from a notion of "the real." On the other hand, if vision could be captured in some kind of *primal* essence, that "real," it was believed, could be gloriously (re)accessed in a perceptual and primitive immediacy. Woman, Primitive, and Primal bodily function were linked and their images were employed in aesthetic representation in the effort to bust out of the dislocation of alienation to retrieve primal, visceral connection. But at the same time that they were employed to redress dislocation, their representation symbolized the "loss," the vanished connection modernists both desired and feared, and so they reconstituted the very alienation they were employed to redress.

PRIMITIVE TECHNIQUES

> There is no document of civilization which is not at one and the same time a document of barbarism.
>
> Walter Benjamin (1969:256)

Before looking more closely at primitivism in the historical avant-garde, it is important to set the stage of contemporary "savage" confrontation in the arts. In 1990, a conservative thrust to "clean up" art was in full swing. It seemed that "family values" were deeply threatened by such artists as Andres Serrano, David Woynarowicz, Holly Hughes, Tim Miller, John Fleck, Robert Mapplethorpe, Dred Scott, Karen Finley, and Annie Sprinkle – artists who were generally either homosexual, women, people of color, or a combination of the above. "Barbarians," wrote Hilton Kramer in a 1990 letter to prospective subscribers to *The New Criterion*, were taking over the museums, "putting on shows that are trivial, vulgar, and politically repulsive" (in Ben-Levi *et al.*

1992/93:8). The primitivism inherent in Kramer's accusation of "barbarism" has particular resonance that links contemporary anxiety about the explicit body in art to modernist fascination and fear of the feminized other.

Historically, women have been closely aligned with concepts of primitivity, and primitivity has been closely aligned with racial difference. Early cultural feminist performance art practice saw the opportunity to embrace primitivity as a strategy for reclaiming "woman" while simultaneously challenging the terms of a "civilization" which marked her as primitive. It is no coincidence that the explicitly marked body was a tool wielded in the service of this strategic primitivity, as the primitive, in distinction to the civilized, has been aligned with the infinitely splintering, visceral and tactile "body" side of the Cartesian mind/body split. In their utopian aim to free woman from patriarchal delimitation, cultural feminists found themselves necessarily wrestling to free the "primitive" as well, and though they rarely explicated inherent racial implications, the conjuncture points to some of the deep anxiety-ridden imbrications of race and gender.

In an essay on the rise of "obscene" body performance in the 1980s, Elinor Fuchs (1989) distinguished '60s and '70s feminist body art and body ritual work from later, seemingly angrier, raunchier, and anti-essentialist works of the '80s. To mark this distinction, Fuchs employed the categories "sacred" and "sacrilegious." Cultural feminist performance art in the '60s and '70s carried a reverence for the female body and often a nostalgia for a lost matriarchal heritage. This reverence and nostalgia sometimes took the form of ritual invocations of Gaia, the Goddess, aligned with Earth, Nature, and the Maternal body denigrated by a history and force of language marked as Patriarchal. Fuchs cites Carolee Schneemann's 1963 *Eye/Body* as exemplary of the sacred, celebratory female body in early cultural feminist performance, juxtaposing such work to the later "aggressive, scatological and sometimes pornographic" body in performance she terms "the obscene" (1989:33). The primitivist nostalgia of cultural feminist works was invested in a search for sacrality, for lost connection, while their more materialist progeny, suspicious of any essentialism or nostalgia, became more invested in problematizing or blaspheming the body than redeeming or celebrating it. Riddled and wrapped in a history of patriarchal inscription and haunted by habitual ways of reading gender, the "body" became Benjaminian wreckage of the real (see Dolan 1988:83–97).

Yet such distinctions between the cultural feminist "sacred" and later materialist feminist "sacrilege" are by no means neat. It is certainly true that the '60s and '70s female sacred also employed aggressive confrontations and "obscene" confrontations. Consider Suzanne Lacy's 1978 piece *There Are Voices in the Desert* in which three skinned lambs, adorned with pink feather plumage of Las Vegas showgirls, were propped as if dancing against a backdrop of women's testaments about rape (see Roth 1988:50–1). Or Lacy's 1977 *She Who Would Fly* in which naked women, painted in blood, crouched on a ledge beside a skinned lamb cadaver which, adorned with wings, dangled from the ceiling (see Roth 1983:114–15). Though body painting in viscous substances such as blood or egg or clay often invoked a sense of (primitive) ritual "ablutions,"[11] the cultural feminist "sacred" body did not always present itself as transcendent of patriarchal inscription as some materialist historians would have it. For instance in her *Interior Scroll* (Plate 5.1) performances in 1975 and 1977, Schneemann stood naked before her audience and outlined her body parts in paint in an invocation of "ritual" before pulling a thin cord of text from her vagina. The text, which had been literally interiorized by her body, was not a nostalgic celebration despite the invocation of the Goddess that Schneemann intended in the snake-like uncoiling of the envaginated "scroll." Rather, the text she read as it emerged quoted a "happy structural film-maker" on men's unwillingness to respect work made by women and included her critical commentary on his attitude:

we cannot look at
the personal clutter
the persistence of feelings
the hand-touch sensibility
the diaristic indulgence
the painterly mess
the dense gestalt
the primitive techniques

(I don't take the advice
of men who only talk to
themselves)
PAY ATTENTION TO CRITICAL
AND PRACTICAL FILM LANGUAGE
IT EXISTS FOR AND IN ONLY
ONE GENDER[12]

What literally comes out of Schneemann's incontinent body is, as in Finley's later exorcistic trance monologues, deeply conflicted, split between an invocation of sacrality and a recitation of the history of her delimitation within patriarchy – not, as some cultural feminists might have hoped, a transcendent "newly born woman."[13]

In the above excerpt from *Interior Scroll* I added emphasis to the words "primitive techniques." The confrontation of the explicit female body in performance relates in important ways to the thrall and threat of the "primitive" so intrinsic to modernism. The properties of this thrall and threat ghost contemporary feminist work with the explicit body, linking that work umbilically to the roots of the performative avant-garde dating to the turn of the last century in Europe.[14] In the following sections of this chapter, I will explore the uses of primitivism in the modernist avant-garde in order better to situate contemporary feminist manifestations. It is important to note from the outset that in distinction to modernist primitivism, contemporary feminist explicit body performance art works less to invoke or mimic the primitive other, as women are already, by virtue of the historical inscription of their sex, the primitivized other themselves. If

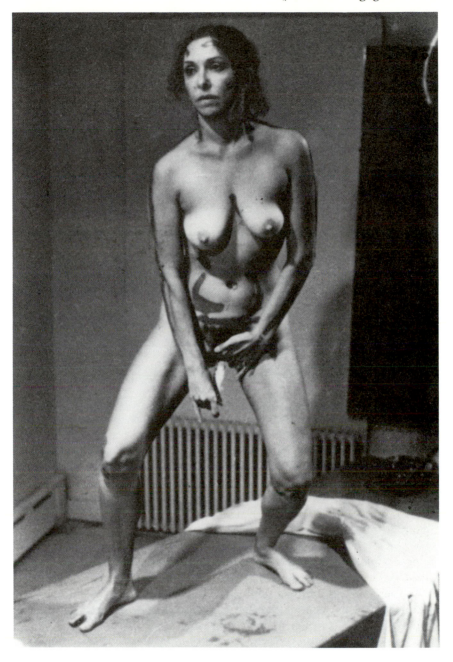

Plate 5.1 Carolee Schneemann during a performance of *Interior Scroll*, 1975. Photo by Peter Grass.

anything, these performers mimic their mimesis, mimic the ways they have been mimed by patriarchal representation – doubling back over the historical mimesis of their sex in a kind of counter-mimicry. Unlike the primitivism of their modernist predecessors, in contemporary work it is the primitives themselves, or the primitivized, who (re)perform their own primitivization, an exercise indelibly linked to the feminized who (re)perform feminization. Indeed, one of the criticisms of early cultural feminist performance art is that it did not explicate the problematic foundations of reading the primitive, did not reperform primitivization with critical distance (thus Fuchs's use of the appellation "sacred"). Nevertheless, it is useful to read both nostalgic explicit body feminist performance and more current "sacrilegious" material feminist performance of the explicit body as "looking back through" modernist primitivism as well as through the thrall to perspectivalism and commodity fetishism outlined in the preceding chapters.

DARK CONTINENCE: READING THE THRALL AND THE THREAT

> Thus I learned to battle the canvas, to come to know it as a being resisting my wish (dream), and to bend it forcibly to this wish. At first it stands there like a pure chaste virgin . . . and then comes the willful brush which first here, then there, gradually conquers it with all the energy peculiar to it, like a European colonist.
>
> Wassily Kandinsky (in Duncan 1988:63)

High modernism made use of the nostalgic "return to man's roots" implied by mimesis of primitive form,[15] but nostalgia for the noble savage had a confrontative, barbarous twin in the savage savage. Allusions to the savage primitive were employed by modernist avant-garde "anti-artists" as a confrontation to the tenets of high modernism.[16] Though sometimes laced with nostalgia, art-critical movements such as Dada made use of the perceived threat to civil values inherent in primitivism by mimicking the masks and drum rhythms of the uncivil "savage" African. Later, Surrealists, though less art-critical than Dadaists, embraced the "savagery" of the unconscious, celebrating a "degeneracy" associated with the primitive. Though founded in racist notions, Surrealist primitivism, by virtue of being celebratory, directly confronted contemporary denigratory racist tenets of fascism (see Foster 1993:12–13).

Though Kandinsky was not an anti-artist in the rebellious Dadaist sense – his above-cited battle was with the canvas and not with the social and political institutions buttressing high art[17] – the characters in his battle were iconic players in both the high modernist avant-garde and its more belligerent discontents. Women and colonial subjects raised, after all, key questions about the perimeters of modern humanist identity, and their near obsessive representation in modern art iconically marks concerns about the perimeters of art's changing relation to a changing modern society. Primitivism was, to quote Daniel Miller, "essential" to modern art's self-definition because of the "paradoxical foundations" of modern art practice. Modern art was saddled with the attempt to, on the one hand, characterize the "new" times, the splintering or fragmented nature of modernity itself, while at the same time representing other worlds as models for totality against which to distinguish that fragmentation. The racism inherent in primitivism both provided reference to the fragmentation of identity (into selves and others) so endemic to the imperialist history of the West *and* provided the nostalgic terrain of a vanished "whole," the "image of a world lost" (1991:55).

Avant-garde movements inclined toward politics, or toward a politic of anti-aesthetics, from Jarry's *Ubu* to Dada to Brecht's *Baal*, exploited the "primitive" for its racism: its link to all things base, especially bodily function. As such, the primitive in anti-art was evoked more for purposes of critical shock than aesthetic nostalgia. The body which repeatedly surfaced to confront the social tenets of high art was, then as now, a body made explicit – a body, like Jarry's Pere Ubu's or Brecht's Baal's, of physical functions, obscene specifics, and details of differences – sex, race, and class. Looking even cursorily at instances of primitivist shock as well as primitivist nostalgia in the modernist avant-garde(s) one discovers collusions of contemporary narratives of sexology and ethnography, illustrating the deep imbrications of issues of sex and race (the Woman Question and the Question of Colonials) in the development of modern Western identity.

Mimetic incorporation of the spoils of colonialism out of exhibitions and museums of ethnography and into the halls of Western art simply extended the general appropriation and incorporation into the body of European culture of "the diverse cultures of the whole world and of all history" (Coutts-Smith 1991:24). A massive consumption of others into the bellies of Western "masters" was underway. Mimesis through art – or reproduction with aesthetic distance – could help assure that the assimilation of the colonial other took place on Western terms. Picasso's 1907 painting *Les Demoiselles d'Avignon* (Plate 5.2) is most often cited as the influential origin of modernist primitivist art. Though primitivism in art predated Picasso, historians refer to Picasso's initiative in form which mimicked and incorporated formal properties of primitive style versus presenting "realistic" depictions of primitive scenes in European form (see Leiris and Delange 1968:8). Significantly, Picasso's *Les Demoiselles* depicts naked women in African masks, bringing "Woman" and "Primitive" into clear iconic conjuncture at the very inception of high modernist formal primitivism.

The interrelation of primitivity and femininity is key and deserves close scrutiny. The "dark continent" of female sexuality, as Freud put it in an unmistakable allusion to Africa (1953–74:212), was indelibly linked to the inferiority, indeed the feminization, of colonial subjects in relation to their civilized "superiors." The scientific foundation for Freud's linkage can be found in Darwinian evolutionism. When science moved with Darwin away from teleological theories of nature's grand design toward a concept of evolution based on random adaptability, this concept articulated in a new way the old hierarchy of black as lower than white, and woman as lower than man – it did not dismantle that hierarchy. Random adaptability pivoted on the notion of

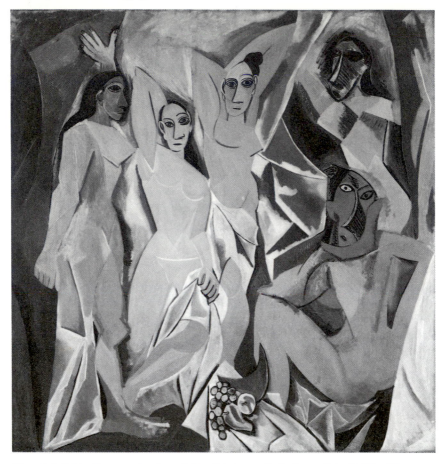

Plate 5.2 Pablo Picasso, *Les Demoiselles d'Avignon*. Paris (June–July 1907). Oil on canvas, 8' by 7'8" (243.9 × 233.7 cm). The Museum of Modern Art, New York. Acquired through the Lille B. Bliss Bequest.

differentiation. Differentiation, or specialized adaptation to the environment, equaled superiority in that successful specialization in the course of evolution increased fitness for survival. Though Darwin's theory of random adaptability carried a critical impulse that countered theological myth and dogma ascribing a God-given basis for superiority, "natural selection" nevertheless allowed those who interpret difference to confer "scientifically" a "natural" hierarchy that matched precedent teleological configurations. Phylogeny was interpreted to recapitulate ontogeny, and thus the male (differentiated and specialized by his penis and, for Darwin, his beard, from a primordial, fetal and female sameness) could be considered mentally and physically more advanced than the female[18] (whose clitoris, an atrophied remnant of her failure to differentiate herself, is veiled or invisible and marked by shame).[19] To underscore her inferiority, the female was written into scientific understanding in the canon of sexology as closer than the male to the primitive, just as, to underscore their inferiority, "savage" races were feminized as less specialized, less advanced, less differentiated than the civilized.[20]

Thus, the imperial white male became culturally and biologically superior to those from whom he *differentiated* himself – the "colored," the colonized, the female. In both sexology and ethnography, the act of writing or documenting the "other" was primarily an act of differentiating – an act of "civilizing" and ultimately creating the modern "self" – a self that bore the insignia of that self-hood on the white male body. Setting this scientific stage is by way of remarking what so many postcolonial theorists have made clear: the signatures of primitivity and civilization have been *inscribed upon the markings of the body*. What was civilized became the self speaking/viewing differentiation, while the primitive was the body (and body of culture) as spoken and re-viewed by that civilized, differentiating self.

Thus the sexologist and ethnographer marked differentiation by articulating the other, bringing her/him to the terms of his vision, onto the field of his perspectival gaze. And yet those very terms of vision necessarily set the wheels of inherent paradox to spinning. According to the habits of civilized perspective, the primitive was paradoxically *seen* as the terrain of the "dark," unknown, even *unseeable* non-self from which the self differentiates, even as details of that other were laid out for observation and analysis. Another important irony here is that though the civilized self differentiated himself from the dark continent of primal, irrational primitivity, that civilized self became invisible, unseen by the other, unmarked, in direct proportion to his mapping or marking the feminized other. As the one who saw, and in perfect keeping with tenets of perspectivalism, he who differentiated through observation observed and wrote as if he were unseen and un(re)marked by his object. The observer, the civilized, was there-fore cloaked or veiled by his own practice of differentiation – a situation amply addressed if not solved by postcolonial theory, poststructural narratology, and various strains of contemporary ethnography from "interpretive" to "dialogic" to "cultural critical" and even to "fictional."[21]

In keeping with the paradoxical foundations of modernity (the contradictory logic of late capitalism), one thing the differentiated claimed to see was that the differences of the less differentiated woman and primitive were mysterious, unknowable, dark, and unseeable (even as "seen" in his text), ultimately "secretive and insincere" (Freud 1962:17).[22] On the surface of the body the woman and the primitive became infinitely observable but (and here's the twist) that visibility (the markings female, black) became the visible insignia of their un-seeable dark mysteries. The advantage of the civilized self was, then, the privilege to disappear as a marked body, to veil the sign of one's initial specialization/differentiation and hide the markings of one's "random" privilege while citing the differences of others as "undifferentiated," less evolved. Thus, historically, the anthropologist and the sexologist disappeared in the text that exposed an other, though that text was precisely what the anthropologist, the sexologist, spoke to create his own, and his culture's, civilized distinction.

What is important here is that in this twisted dance of visibility and invisibility, signs of the dark, mysterious, unseeable primitive were inscribed *on the body* in a social vocabulary of seeable differences. Disembodiment was signified bodily. That which was primitive/feminine became understood as uncanny, possessed of a threatening duplicity (insincerity, secretiveness) in the ability to be both seeable and unseeable, visible and invisible, at once – an ability wholly imagined by the absented speaking self through the magic of civilizing narrative and scientific authority.

DARK INCONTINENCE: *UBU ROI* AND SAVAGE PRIMITIVISM

The avant-garde exploited the terms of this uncanny inscription. The body of physical function and explicit markings, in all its tactility and base assignation, was coupled with notions of primitivity, and as the body was associated with the primitive, the primitive was associated with "life" versus "art." In the opening decades of the twentieth century, as Picasso and others began mimetically incorporating primitive form in their painting, tribal masks and sculpture were displayed in ethnological exhibits as "artifacts" and barbarian "fetishes." Such objects were first displayed to the European public in exotic *cabinets de curiosities* in the late nineteenth century, then in traveling ethnological exhibitions, and eventually in museums of ethnology such as the Trocadero where, until after World War I, artifacts were mixed "helter skelter" with everyday objects such as "harpoons, arrows, oars, and axes" (Goldwater 1938:7). Tribal artifacts were thus linked to the everyday ritual-rich expression of primitive life and not to Western habits of distanced aestheticism. In 1915 ethnographer Carl Einstein (who was also a Dadaist poet and later a member of the Collège de Sociologie around Bataille, Caillois, and Leiris) energetically declared that European contempt for tribal expression was only a "reflection of our ignorance," a proclamation Robert Goldwater cites as instrumental in the reassignation of tribal expression as aesthetic (1938:35). Though the aestheticism of artifact could arguably be read as a colonialist assimilation and commodification – even, ironically, a fetishization – Einstein was concerned to afford African artifact what he saw as due respect. And respect meant, in Western terms, the authorizing signature of "art."

Until the first decades of the twentieth century, however, primitive art was not "art" at all but "ornament," and of magical, ritual, or quotidian rather than aesthetic importance. The nonaestheticism of such artifact, its connection to life versus art, underscored its early application as a means of confrontation to the tenets of high art. Before Picasso's initiative in style incited the long migration of African fetish objects out of museums of ethnography and into art museums, "savage" primitivism was practically synonymous with physical affront – the punch of the base necessities of everyday life in the face of higher transcendent ideals – the punch of the artifact in the face of art – the punch of the lowly literal or real in the face of the lofty symbol or dream. But in the marketplaces of colonialist exhibitions, primitive artifacts had already become exotic insignias of colonialist dreamscapes and "art" was following behind, granting the aesthetic distance to the fetish which the market had already effected through commodified "display." When artists such as Picasso incorporated tribal artifact through mimesis, the punch, or Benjaminian "hit,"[23] had already been appropriated, captured as display in the realm of exotica, suiting the aims of capital.

Before the migration from the Trocadero to the Louvre, in art primitivity signified scandal. In the history of performance, Alfred Jarry's 1896 staging of his play *Ubu Roi* at Théâtre de l'Oeuvre is a famous case in point. For many theater historians, Jarry's theatrical primitivism marks the birth of the performative avant-garde.[24] An affront to Symbolism (one of the prevailing theatrical styles of the day), *Ubu Roi* employed primitivism and the explicit body to spoof Symbolist attempts to transcend corporeal detail and invoke a psychic ideal. Symbolist theater drew heavily upon images of the archaic and classical. Avoiding allusion to everyday corporeal experience, Symbolist staging searched for dream-like expressions of an inner life, preferring scrimmed shadow figures of eternal nature and monotone incantation rather than "the active presence of man."[25] Though Symbolists did envision the ideal theater as a "ritual function," it was a ritual in celebration of an ideal "harmony" of aesthetic form, not a primitive ritual perceived as connected to the cacophonous expression of everyday life (Henderson 1971:32).

In some basic respects Jarry was a Symbolist. He promoted the use of masks because they could convey "a character's eternal quality" and he sought universal gesture and the delivery of lines in a conventionalized manner (Jarry 1965:72). But the symbolic invoked in *Ubu Roi* was antithetical in almost all respects to high Symbolism in that it was indelibly linked to the physical and quotidian – "physick," "phynance," and "pschitt" as Jarry punned in the program notes to the play (1965:80) – as if the symbol ultimately collapsed into the very literal thing it attempted to transcend. In *Ubu*, Jarry presented as his ultimate symbol something so profane and corporeal that it could not offer transcendence, could not invoke for his audience any higher ideal. That symbol was excrement. Jarry chose to have his character Pere Ubu exclaim, as the very first line in his play, "shitr" (*merdre*). The addition of the "r" to the expletive was not meant to disguise it, but rather, as Roger Shattuck has argued, was Jarry's way of "appropriating [the expletive] to himself" (1955:207). That obscenity, resounding in the hallowed halls of the theater, sparked pandemonium among the fashionable art-appreciating audience in attendance. As fist fights broke out in the orchestra section, it took a full fifteen minutes for the house to regain enough equilibrium to allow the show to continue.

But even before the curtain had gone up on his play – before, that is, the famous opening line – Jarry himself had come on stage to deliver preliminary remarks. He was, not insignificantly, made up to look like a streetwalker and his introduction and eccentric self-presentation set the stage for audience uproar. He declared that the play "takes place in Poland, that is to say Nowhere," but the program notes made clear that "Nowhere is everywhere, but most of all it is the country we happen to be in at the moment" which was why "Ubu speaks

French." Ubu, a name employing an obvious Africanism, was presented first and foremost as *both* an upstanding French citizen *and* all that is "ignoble . . . which is why he is so like us all (seen from below)."[26] As Roger Shattuck put it, Jarry's preliminary remarks "did not exactly insure a sympathetic response" from his audience (1955:206).

The curtain opened on scenery painted "by a child's conventions," representing indoors and out of doors and all kinds of climate at once, without distinction.[27] That is, a window and fireplace were painted against a blue sky, apple trees in bloom and snow falling in a bedroom – sense all akimbo, which Jarry hoped would symbolize eternity. Fermin Gremier, an established and well-known actor with the Comedie-Française, stepped forward as Ubu to deliver the infamous first line. The explicit excremental affront was coupled by the parallel confrontation of the character and body of the fat and whiney Pere Ubu – Gremier's already large body exaggerated in a pear-shaped costume. Not only did Gremier deliver the infamous line, but he simultaneously mimicked Jarry's own everyday voice and gestures – well known for their eccentricities – confusing, as Jarry often did, the distinction between art and life and making symbolist transcendence of the corporeal and the everyday that much more difficult. Indeed the riots themselves contributed to the confused space between art and life as the actors standing on stage waited and watched, wondering if they had become spectators of a performance in the house. When the initial pandemonium in the house died down – only after Gremier improvised a jig on stage – the play carried on, with repeated audience outbursts. Ubu murdered and pillaged his way to the throne of Poland, was unseated by the czar's army, and fled to France where he pledged to begin his riotous escapades anew, all the while obsessing on his digestion and peppering his speeches with scatological references.

The force of Ubu's excremental symbolism confronted tenets of aesthetic distance arguably because of Jarry's collapse of the space differentiating noble and ignoble, civilized and primitive, as well as his collapse of the space differentiating symbol and literal, art and life. Jarry presented "Ubu" as a white male Frenchman, indeed an upstanding French citizen,[28] at the same time that his name alluded to primitivity and his body was repeatedly made explicit, presented as in every way out of control. The King Primitive, obsessed with details of his bodily functions, threatened distanced aestheticization or any dreamlike transcendence of the corporeal, causing symbolist playwright W. B. Yeats to write sadly after the first riotous performance: "After us the Savage God."

Ubu Roi caused riots in the house on the three nights of its performance in 1896 in part because the play sparked a binary terrorism in the collapse of distinctions between civilized/primitive, art/life. But even as the riots were occurring, the "primitive" was being ingested into foundational understandings of the modern in society. By 1897 the "father of sociology," Emile Durkheim, had published *Suicide*, attentive to the secular alienation in modern society which he saw in relation to the sacred integration of primitive or "lower societies." Durkheim turned to primitive societies not to catalog exotic practices but to look for origins of the human sacred – to find the modern in the primitive.[29] In 1896, the very year *Ubu* caused its famous riots, Freud, confrontational in his own right, read his "Aetiology of Hysteria" before the Society for Psychiatry and Neurology in Vienna. From this work on hysteria Freud would eventually postulate the existence of a dynamic unconscious and eventually interiorize primitivity into the modern personality as the theoretical id from which we *differentiate* our egos. By the close of the nineteenth century, concern with the primitive, indivisible from its roots in colonialist expansion and racism, was rapidly being assimilated, or incorporated, even consumed, into the foundational understanding of the modern self as its (repressed) driving force.

Not surprisingly, then, ten years after *Ubu Roi*, what was antithetical to art was already being fully assimilated into high art. The modern was being expressed in and through the primitive. By 1907, the year of *Les Demoiselles d'Avignon*, Picasso and others were mimicking the artifactual fetishes which they observed in the Trocadero and collected in their studios. Ultimately the savage object and the explicit physical detail would no longer be antithetical to the inner psyche as they had been for the Symbolists, but would, by the time of the Surrealists, in fact *come to represent it* – the inner psyche as the dark unruly continent of the modern unconscious.

DADA'S BIG DRUM: PRIMITIVISM AND THE PERFORMATIVE

In many respects, Dadaists, in the midst of World War I, were working against the storm of "progress." That storm not only brought the inanity of war, but was solidly blowing primitive fetishes into glass displays, the Snow White caskets of aestheticization, under the authorizing auspices of Western authority. Though Carl Einstein was a Dadaist who applauded the aestheticization of artifact as respectful of African aesthetic sensibilities, in general "aesthetic sensibility" was the target "NoNo" of early Dada. Rather, early Dadaists arguably sought to employ primitivism in an effort to wrest art away from museumification, into the realm of ritual or everyday experience. They wanted "aesthetics" to come out from behind the mask of transcendence, to acknowledge the ritual properties of display, and to reignite an active engagement in art as practice.

Looking to confront tenets of distanced aestheticization, Dadaists turned to performance. In terms of primitivism there remained a big difference between studio art and performative art. If primitivist painting had crossed into "high art," primitivist ritual practice had not. Studio art, such as painting, is arguably a medium more tailored to the tenets of aesthetic distance than "performance art," a medium in which the artist's body is intimately implicated in the scene and in which the spectator bears a present complicity in the "act."[30] In performance, the savage or barbarian body and allusion to ritual practice were not so easily assimilable into the institution of "decided" art as were the formal properties of the primitive artifact – they retained an element of scandal and danger.

Twenty years after *Ubu*, in the midst of World War I, expatriate artists gathered in Zurich – the "neutral" eye of a storm. The artists who collected at the Café Voltaire – among them Hugo Ball, Emmy Hennings, and Richard

Huelsenbeck from Germany, Tristan Tzara, Georges and Marcel Janco from Romania, Hans Arp, an Alsatian with German citizenship who had been living in Paris – pushed themselves as far as they could in raucous evenings of performance, poetry, and manifesto. Ball wrote in his diary the first year:

> April 14, 1916: Our Cabaret is a gesture. Every word that is spoken says at least this one thing: that this humiliating age has not succeeded in winning our respect. What could be respectable and impressive about it? Its cannons? Our big drum drowns them.

> October 6, 1916: The false structure is collapsing. Move away as far as possible, into tradition, into strangeness, into the supernatural; then you will not get hit.
> (1974:61, 82)

In anger and defiance Dadaism became an act of nihilism, where artists expressed anti-war and anti-humanist sentiments by being, expressly, anti-art (Burger 1984:51f.). They pushed "into tradition" as one would push a fist into a face, resolutely drumming "negro rhythms," drumming "into strangeness, into the supernatural" – underscoring and utilizing contemporary racisms by which the "negro" continued to signal a threat to the bases of civilization, especially aestheticism. Again, the institutionalized tenets of art were interrogated through an insistent primitivism, but Dadaist primitivism was aligned more with Jarry's riotous performance than with Picasso's canvases.

Dadaist live performance of "pseudo-Africanisms" worked to drive home the movement's anti-art credo.[31] The only pictorial record of those first Dada soirées is Arp's 1916 painting *Cabaret Voltaire* in which an oversized African-like face mask hangs on the café wall behind the core Dada performers – the mask leers out at the audience closely packed around café tables. Under the mascot of the mask, rejection of aesthetic distance took place at Café Voltaire in the form of the "big drum," "tomtom," and "negro rhythms"; dada dances with "dread masks of primitive peoples"; Tzara's African-gibberish plays; and Hugo Ball's witch-doctor/Bishop trance performance. Through rejecting the "unutterable horror of the times" by rejecting art, Dadaists accused aesthetic ways of knowing and habits of vision of complicity in the debacle of fratricide that was World War I. On a 1916 poster announcing a Dadaist event, Marcel Janco drew naked, black-skinned "primitives" dancing on an almost perspectival grid to represent the Dadaist anti-art agenda (Plate 5.3).

Dadaist rejection of aesthetics, especially studio art, relied on primitivism employed performatively. The pseudo-African masks and drum rhythms accompanied manifesto statements like the following, linking primitivism to performance and by extention to anti-aesthetics:

MUSICIANS SMASH YOUR INSTRUMENTS
BLIND MEN take the stage . . .
Art is a PRETENSION warmed by the
TIMIDITY of the urinary basin, the *hysteria* born
in THE STUDIO

Plate 5.3 Marcel Janco, *Invitation to a Dada Evening*, 1916. Courtesy of Kunsthaus Zürich. Photo by Walter Drayer.

We are in search of
the force that is direct pure sober
UNIQUE we are in search of NOTHING
we affirm the VITALITY of every IN-
STANT.

(Tzara in Motherwell 1951:82)

Dadaist insistence on "the vitality of every instant" invoked a *performative* art and admonished a static studio art. The invocation of "blindness" in this manifesto is worth noting, suggesting that Dada's anti-art was also antiocular. This invocation is in keeping with the notion of the primitive or feminized as blind, unable to see back, as discussed in Chapter 3, but it also suggests an anti-perspectivalism embedded in Dada's project to call into question the institution of art. Importantly, the search for an anti-art of vitality versus alienation again found its force in scatological allusions to bodily function, found its commentary on the corrupt institution of aesthetic "value" through a valorization of "waste," and found its critique of the Western status quo in a mimesis of tribal practice. The performative practice of primitivism was a practice of binary terrorism, linked in Dadaist thinking to both primal nature and natural disaster – above all it invoked the danger of life as opposed to the static complacency of "socially organized" art:

We are like a raging wind that rips up the clothes of clouds and prayers, we are preparing the great spectacle of disaster, conflagration and decomposition . . . I destroy the drawers of the brain, and those of social organization: to sow demoralization everywhere, and throw heaven's hand into hell, hell's eyes into heaven, to reinstate the fertile wheel of a universal circus in the Powers of reality, and the fantasy of every individual . . . DADA, DADA, DADA; – the roar of contorted pains, the interweaving of contraries and of all contradictions, freaks, and irrelevancies: LIFE.

(Tzara manifesto in Gordon 1987:47, 51)

With the end of World War I, as the Zurich ex-patriates made their various ways home, Dada transmogrified, becoming Surrealism in France and Berlin Dada in Germany. In its Surrealist manifestation, impulses from Zurich Dada were wed to psychoanalysis and, arguably, regained the aesthetic distance Zurich Dada had aimed to sabotage – in part through a return to tenets of vision (Jay 1994:237). In France, as André Breton took over from Tristan Tzara, Dadaist primitivism reconnected with the primitivism evident in *Les Demoiselles d'Avignon* where the impulse toward African and Oceanic "fetish" had found a neat double in the discourse of sexology at the time – the primitivity of the female body. Indeed, as Rosalind Krauss has written, woman became "the obsessional subject" of Surrealist practice, especially photography, though Susan Rubin Suleiman has countered with a correction: self was the subject and woman the "obsessional object" of Surrealist experimentation (Krauss 1985:70; Suleiman 1990:16). Obsession with the female body doubled with remarkable ease with the primitive fetish, underscoring the ongoing realignment of the meaning of "fetishism" from primitive religious animism to, explicitly, male sexual desire – a realignment begun in the 1890s during the golden age of contemporary sexology (Nye 1993:13).

With the Surrealist lifting of the Dadaist ban on studio art and with the reinstitution of aesthetic distance (and also with the migration of tribal artifact into the mainstream category of formally acceptable art), allusions to primitive fetish no longer automatically flashed as anti-aesthetic. Instead, they became mascots of a new symbolic landscape, linked to the fledgling science of the interior of the modern psyche – repressed desire, dream, wish. What once had confronted Symbolism as Jarry's ribald literality was now corralled into the service of a symbolism of the unconscious.

HARD PRIMITIVISM, BASE MATTER, AND THE BLIND SPOT

To the extent that Knowledge takes itself for an end, it founders upon the blind spot.

Georges Bataille

Even Surrealism's symbology – the landscape of the unconscious – was vulnerable to confrontational excess, and that excess found itself again coagulating around the issue of the savage body. Reminiscent of Jarry's "savage god" affront to Symbolism, a number of dissident Surrealists, notably Georges Bataille, Michel Leiris, Roger Caillois, Andre Masson, and Antonin Artaud (whose theater was named Théâtre Alfred Jarry), crossed the line of tolerability and found themselves excommunicated from the Surrealist ranks. For quite a few of these dissidents the central issue of the rift concerned the significance to art of ethnological artifact and narrative in terms of transgressive social practice versus aesthetic or formal properties.[32] This dissident affront to what might be called "high" Surrealism was staged, yet again, by exploiting the conjunction of primitive expression with base physicality and the transgressive properties of the sexual or scatological detail – prompting Breton, arbiter of "appropriate" Surrealism, to condemn Bataille as an "excremental philosopher" (Breton 1969:184; see also Stoekl 1985). Generally speaking, at issue across sides in the debate was the positioning of the explicit body and primitive practice so as either to reconstitute Western art-canonical tenets of vision and formal aesthetic distance or to interrogate and disrupt those tenets.

Of course, acceptable Surrealist art (passed by Breton) employed tribal artifact and the explicit body in close conjunction, but as aesthetically removed, as symbolic rather than literal landscapes, always under the auspices of contemporary understandings of the unconscious – that is, as a way of reading modernist dreamscapes, not puncturing them (see Plate 5.4). Theirs was generally a primitivism Rosalind Krauss has referred to as soft primitivism, "a primitivism gone formal and therefore gutless," part of the general "art for art's sake" aestheticizing discourse on the primitive. To this Krauss contrasts the dissident group's "hard primitivism," which sought in the primitive a kind of "primal vandalism" (1988:51, 52, 54). For dissidents surrounding Bataille and the journals *Documents* and *Acephale*, mimesis of primitive expression was a means

Plate 5.4 Man Ray, *Noire et blanche*. 1926. Silver print on tissue, 8⅝" × 10⅞" (21.9 × 27.7 cm). © 1996 Artists' Rights Society (ARS), New York/ADAGP/Man Ray Trust, Paris.

of triggering a deep critique of positivist, "civil" identity. Hard primitivism was not a means of expanding the "marvelous" domain of Western aesthetic sensibilities but was a way of transgressing that domain in order to expose its veiled but ever-present "sadistic" underbelly.

It is important to note that though the Collège de Sociologie critiqued positivist identity, they nevertheless struggled to burst beyond modern anomie into "the sacred" without completely losing sight of scientific objectivity or critical distance. Like scientists who wanted to commit suicide in order to come back and expose, observe, and chronicle death, their work struggled to lay bare, self-dissect, self-wound, self-implicate. It was their conviction that through resolute exposure of the transgressed personal detail – the "anus," the "bitten buttock," the "bleeding navel," the "bloody wrist"[33] – one could access a blindspot like a portal to the "real," and seeing through that blindspot one could puncture the dreamscape of modern anomie to achieve, in Leiris's words, "vital fulfillment" (in Blanchot 1992:151). To enter into the hidden, horrific detail (to shine the light where the sun don't shine – to expose the "solar anus") or to tell the untellable truth of private perversion in public would, as Leiris put it, somehow invoke the fear inspired by the *torero*'s art and "introduce even the shadow of a bull's horn" into our efforts to understand ourselves (Leiris 1984:157). The body made explicit – the anus for Bataille or the wound for Leiris – provided a profane portal to a sacral hidden interiority that, recognized, could collapse aesthetic distance and make literature and art evident as "an act," as performative (Leiris 1984:164). Such exposure could "contribute to the liber-ation of all men" (Leiris), or could at least "illuminate the night for an instant"

(Bataille) – an instant, like Benjamin's "flash in a moment of danger," in which critical inquiry could take place.[34] For the Collège de Sociologie, the body made explicit was conjoined to racist paradigms of primitivism: the transgressive potential of "savage" practices that "unites gatherings of blacks," especially human sacrifice and cannibalism. Fascinatingly, the body confessed, or made explicit, and the mimetic *practice* of savagery were decidedly aimed at exposing socially inscribed blindspots in dominant ways of seeing.[35]

Like Jarry and the Dadaists, the Collège's "hard primitivism" and its inherent threat of literality in the face of symbolic or aesthetic remove, reverberates with some of the work of contemporary feminist performance artists of the explicit body. Though the Collège, unlike contemporary explicit body artists, employed primitivism without ultimately critiquing its sexist and racist premises, nevertheless some of the properties of the Collège's dissidence ghosts contemporary confrontative practice. As J.B. Pontalis has written, "The confusion of subject and object," endemic to the writings of Leiris and Bataille in particular but also to Artaud, "abolishes the minimal distance without which there is not even a gaze" (1992:128). Bataille situated his dissident primitivism relative to his general theory of "alteration," the ambivalence which runs like a crack through the center of all signification, threatening at all times to erupt and destroy the "minimal distance" between symbolic sign and literal signified. This crack in the seeming interdependency of binary terms fed the central obsessive fire heating up the Collège de Sociologie: the violence at the heart of all sacred acts, the sacred moment at the center of sadism. In its conjunction with the explicit body, mimesis of (hard) primitivity was inexorably linked with sadism in that it was seen as inherently opposed to the humanism and idealism of Western civilization. Thus, practice of primitivity, like practice of transgressive sexuality, could function as a "crack in the system" disrupting humanist and idealist unities and aspirations through the suggestion or practice of erotic taboos, exposure to pornography, or the practice of primitive rituals of human sacrifice.[36] For Bataille, the primitivity of the explicit body functioned like a pothole in a sidewalk wreaking violent slippage in upright, or upward-reaching, secularizing systems of meaning (1985:20–3).

Alteration, the slippage in signification from one meaning to another to another, is illustrated in Bataille's *Story of the Eye* in which an eyeball becomes a saucer of milk becomes a testicle becomes the sun becomes an eyeball again. Such alteration or slippage of signs in a nervous network of correspondence works precisely in the ambivalent and fertile middle space between signs and their supposedly fixed referents. Roland Barthes's reading of *Story of the Eye* would have it that Bataille's slippage of detail continually services metaphor – that Bataille's slipping into and out of concrete particulars trips up the fixity of any meaning so that "any term is never anything but the signifier of a neighboring term" (Barthes 1963:195–6). I think this reading misses Bataille's point, however, in that it bleeds meaning away from its effects. I would argue that the crux of Bataille's alteration of repetitive and corresponding details lies not in the result that any term is "never anything but" its neighbor, but much more in the terror that any term is *always also* its neighbor – that what goes around comes around through a nervous system of sensuous correspondences in which acts, words, ideas actually imprint, impact, and have literal effect upon an entire neighborhood, indeed a nervous universe of corresponding details in which we are always already implicated – complicit, not removed.[37]

For Bataille, signs are never bonded, fixed, or bound to their referents, and yet nor is the relation of sign to literal referent free floating, detached or completely arbitrary. Rather, meaning operates with a slippery kind of Benjaminian sensuous correspondence[38] by which the symbolic "alters" with that which it pretends to supersede: the literal – in much the same way as an eyeball alters with a saucer, testicles, the sun in *Story of the Eye*. Indeed the very notion of detached or arbitrary or "accidental" correspondence is a ruse of the market, linked in Bataille's thinking as well as Benjamin's to the secret of commodities: the ruses of the "homogeneity" of capital (Bataille 1985:137–8) and the social structure of bourgeois modernism (Benjamin 1986:324). For Bataille, the contradiction, or sensuous "heterogeneity" implied in alteration does not resolve, Hegel-like, into any progressive synthesis, or reach, as Breton desired, any Icarian "point" of congruence and communion where antinomies "cease being perceived contradictorily" (Breton 1969). Rather, the alteration between symbolic and literal refuses to resolve but dances in a kind of frenzied contradiction around a volatile crack – a "blindspot."

In fact, the "blindspot" is key in understanding Bataille's hard primitivism. Like the Surrealist soft primitivists, Bataille was intent upon prying open the eyelids to get at that which exceeded appropriate (civil) vision. While for Breton that which exceeded normative, quotidian vision was linked to the "marvelous" symbolism of the unconscious, for Bataille that which exceeded appropriate vision was linked to the demise of symbolic structuring – to the fearful potential of base, literal matter to implode upon any and all symbolism. Bataille saw "Hegel's immense fatigue" as "linked to the horror of the blind spot" (Bataille in Richman 1982:67). In Bataillean formulation the blindspot is the point at which the literal detail exceeds the symbol, exceeds the foundational or rationalized system given to contain it. He found this excess in laughter, ecstasy, violence, death, and combinations of the above in which the erotic, explicit body was the most accessible for the modern. The blindspot is the crack through which duality overflows, exceeding its own distinctions – for instance, where something is *both heimlich and unheimlich*, familiar and strange – not without contradiction, but inexorably *in* contradiction, or "alteration." Again, however, very importantly, the blindspot was not a high-flying site of transcendence or an "Icarian adventure" such as he accused the Surrealists of seeking. Rather, Bataille articulated this site, this blindspot, as where "laughter no longer laughs and tears no longer cry, where the divine and the horrible, the poetic and the repugnant, the erotic and the funereal coincide," saying, this is *"not a point of the spirit"* (Bataille in Richman 1982:68).

The irony and the horror in Bataille is that this blindspot is an insistently base and material instant in which symbolic constructs encounter their own inversion in concrete particular, in *literal*, "disgusting," bodily detail – such as "menstrual blood, bodily putrefaction" (Bataille 1988:106, 111). This (blinding) point of excess coagulates in matter and becomes not a site of spirit, but rather a site of terror at which dream or symbol defecates, is literalized. Looking back at the viewer, the blindspot of excessive literality, the explicit body, the overly real, the resolutely possible, disallows symbolic remove, disallows the space between a sign and its referent, and in collapsing that space it "castrates" the eye.[39] Bataille appears to court that castration, advocating a "recognition" of the terror protecting socially inscribed, indeed "civilized" blindspots. As he wrote, "I believe nothing is more important for us than that we recognize that we are bound and sworn to that which horrifies us most, that which provokes our most intense disgust" (1988:114).

Of course, as mentioned above, Bataille employed primitivism without ultimately critiquing its premises. Bataille never located the patriarchal foundations, the sexism and racism inscribing bodily markings with anxiety, "terror," and "disgust" – rather he saw such terror and disgust as "essential," even universal. But his interest in "recognition," and his articulation of recognition as relative to the social institution of blindspots regarding literal, exigent bodies is a project that can be read as related to contemporary feminist investigations of the explicit body, especially in its inherent "dissidence" with art-canonical practice. In Bataille's excremental philosophy, the blindspot is a fearful space of collapse in the distance needed to maintain a distinction between the symbolic and the literal. The matter of the literal detail, as a flipside of the symbolic, points up the blindspot – that which a symbolic system cannot allow to be seen. In this sense, as explored in Chapter 3, the *view of* the explicitly marked body and the *view from* the marked body come into explicit contact as symbolic expectation slaps against literal realization – as eyeball meets the secret's blinded eye which sees back. This is a material moment of exchange marked by the Surrealist dissidents as illuminating yet horrifying and remarked by contemporary feminist dissidents as illuminating and *promising*. The prerogatives of disinterested perspectival vision get turned belly up by the wound at the vanishing point rendered *literal*, the blindspot rendered sighted, the secret made explicit – explicated – refusing to vanish.

> Bandage any part of your body . . .
> If people forget about it, remind
> them of it and keep telling.
> Do not talk about anything else.
> Yoko Ono (1970)

LITERAL PRIMITIVES

Mimetic allusion to the savage savage in modernist arts of confrontation, such as Jarry's *Ubu*, Dada's big drum, and the "sacrifices" of the Collège de Sociologie, bear relevance to contemporary feminist manipulations of the explicit body. The confrontation of the literal detail in the space of transcendent symbolic practice is key. Remember Kandinsky's metaphor in which he conquers the "chaste virgin" of his canvas like a "European colonist." In making their bodies their canvases – Schneemann smearing her body with paint or Karen Finley smearing her body with viscous substances or Sprinkle explicating her make-up as whore – feminist artists of the explicit body might be rendering literal Kandinsky's "symbolic equivalence" (to borrow Freud's phrase). She becomes the canvas literally, under-scoring the impact of perhaps more symbolic "colonization" in the modern imagination. In rendering the symbolic literal, such artists make explicit the ways implicit patriarchal signifying systems have been maintained through the repeated iconic deployment of bodies marked for gender and race.

In a coagulation of modernist fears and desires, female bodies and primitive artifacts were constructed to embrace as strange doubles of the unconscious. They were conjoined to stare back at the modern civil (male) subject from inside his primitivized psyche as insignia not of Western colonial and patriarchal social oppressions, but as insignia of interior psychic repressions. The woman and the primitive came to symbolize the terrible wink of the modern's inner eye – the gatekeepers guarding the secret – that which civil man does not let himself see. As we struggle to understand ourselves as postcolonial, the iconography of the colonial and "savage" sexual body – the black body, the gendered body of explicit physical markings and implicit hidden agendas, and the body of "transgressive" sexual practice such as the body deemed homoerotic – still circulates as that which unsettles civil identity.

Though many claim the avant-garde is defunct, that "transgression" carries no weight in the consumptive landscape of postmodernism, it would be short-sighted to claim that the explicit body no longer agitates socially "appropriate" sensibilities. Charting soft and hard primitivism from Surrealism through to the present day is a project in need of closer examination than space allows in this study. Does reading and recognizing the fascination with the primitive and the prostitute that was so much at the foundation of modernist expression take us "beyond" the thrall? In what ways, and for whom, are we beyond the fears and obsessions with primitivism and prostitution in our postcoloniality, our post-modernisms? The "Ubu" of the last turning century shocked at a time when colonialism – the question of who dis-covers, who governs, who medicalizes, who anthropologizes, who *controls the production* of the colonial other – was of pressing concern. Today's Ubus, an exposed black penis in a polyester suit photographed by Mapplethorpe, or Sprinkle's insistent cervix, continue to wield the explicitly marked body as social confrontation. It is no coincidence that the body of genital detail should confront at a time when Americans are embattled over the issue of *control of reproduction* – concerned about control of the reproductive rights of women and anxious about the population growth of people of color. An early '90s cover of *Time* magazine was telling in its boldfaced query: "The Browning of America: What Color America in the Year 2000?"

And yet, today's Ubus are significantly different from yesterday's in at least one important respect, marking a significant shift in the use of the shock of the savage body in performative confrontation. Today, it is mostly women, artists of color, and gay and lesbian artists who, rather than utilizing shock for shock's sake, are interrogating the social properties of that shock – interrogating the markings of "disgust" and "terror" by asking precisely who is disgusted and terrorized and across whose body has that disgust been inscribed? The terms of savagery and prostitution in the art gallery have become more literal than metaphoric – it is the "primitivized," the "prostituted," and the "perverse" themselves who now manipulate the frames around their primitivization. They are not mimetically alluded to but have, though hardly to the degree that Hilton Kramer feared, "taken over the museums." The "barbarians" themselves are reflexively re-presenting the primitivizing process, pointing the finger at primitivism by exposing it as inscribed in a patriarchal vocabulary of differentiation, historically mapped upon their own specific physical markings – their explicit bodies.

Contemporary explicit body performers wrestle with the patriarchal premises of terror and disgust that have marked them. In the preceding chapters we have examined how some artists explicate the explicit sexuality that marks them as the terrain of infinite recession and insatiable desire. How have feminist artists explicated primitivism and its racist tenets in relation to gender? Ahead of her time in many ways, Berlin Dadaist Hannah Höch created images in the late 1920s and early 1930s which illustrate explicitly the "feminine" in tension with the "primitive." In a series of unsettling photomontages which appear to look back at the viewer, Höch collapses the distinction between "primitive" and "woman," utilizing, very often, an alarming single eye (Plate 5.5). Keenly attentive to the dynamics of woman as "fetish object on display," Maud Lavin has suggested that Höch was drawing an equation between "the store mannequin as bearer of commodity fetishes and the museum mannequin as bearer of tribal fetishes" (1993:168, 179). In general Höch diverged from the primitivism of her contemporaries – especially the Expressionists – in her focus on Western representation of racial difference and its application to gender politics. She did not, unlike more contemporary explicit body artists, generally use her own body as scene, but the degree to which her primitivism differs from the "soft primitivism" of her contemporaries, such as in Man Ray's *Noire et blanche* (1926), is worth noting. Höch's single-eyed montages are haunting and unmistakably suggestive of the aim to "see back through" primitivization and feminization – the view from the blindspot.

In the following chapter I will look closely at a contemporary troupe, Spiderwoman Theater, who wrestle with primitivization and its complex imbrication with commodity fetishism across their own bodies. In the process of exploring Spiderwoman's tandem critique of and search for an "authentic" identity unmarked by Western commodity culture, I bump up against problems of reading "the body" at all and find myself wrestling on a more personal plane with more *literal* ghosts – explicitly invisible bodies.

Plate 5.5 Hannah Höch, *Die Süsse*, from the series From an Ethnographical Museum, 1926. Collage 11⅞ × 6⅛ (30 × 15.5 cm). Courtesy of Eva-Maria and Heinrich Rössner, Tubingen-Lustnau, Germany.

6 Seeing the big show

It's coming! It's coming! I hear it! It's coming! I'm scared! I'm not ready yet! I know something is there – . . . oh . . . oh . . . It's going! It's going . . . I didn't see it. I didn't see it! Coyote saw it. The birds saw it. The trees whispered . . . I didn't see it.

from Reverb-ber-ber-rations[1]

Spiderwoman has a show called *Reverb-ber-ber-rations* in which the three Native American sisters who make up the company – Lisa Mayo, Gloria Miguel, and Muriel Miguel – drum memories and counter-memories onto the stage, layered and folded over upon each other, repetitive, hysterical, rich. Stories are inter-woven from before birth to after death, from an experience at a Taos corn dance to the time Muriel was possessed by Uncle George. Now the sisters are in Panama City surveying a military parade after the US invasion (their Cuna father was born in the San Blas Islands). Now they sit at a table having tea and discussing their shows. Now they are in a backyard in Brooklyn. Now they are mothers, now they are children, now they are grandmothers, now tea again, now a backyard, now a Sun Dance, now Panama among the dead and wounded (see Plate 6.1). Gloria listens to a tape of Indian singing and coyote calling. "I hear it! It's coming! . . . " Muriel tells about the time she was possessed by her grandmother. They sing Cole Porter: "Like the beat beat beat of the tom tom . . . Night and Day." And they talk, again, about their shows: "Just what did you tell those people?"

FIRST, A STORY ABOUT DOUBT THAT INCLUDES A REVERBERATION

The search for descent is not the erecting of foundations: on the contrary, it disturbs what was previously considered immobile; it fragments what was thought unified; it shows the heterogeneity of what was imagined consistent with itself. What convictions and, far more decisively, what knowledge can resist it? . . . Descent attaches itself to the body. It inscribes itself in the nervous system.

Michel Foucault (1977:147)

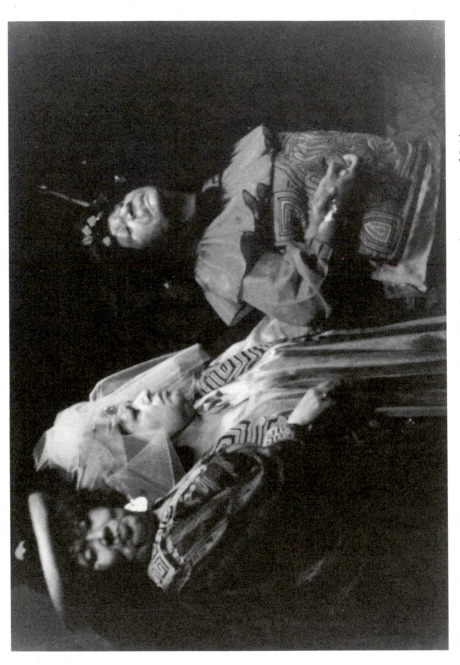

Plate 6.1 Spiderwoman Theater during a performance of *Reverb-ber-ber-rations*. Photo courtesy of Spiderwoman.

No matter how narrativized and progress-oriented the portrayal of history, in reality there is always a point in relation to our own circumstances in history when the steps in the story crack open . . . Like the Nervous System, this seismological method of Benjamin's and the hope it contains is based on the notion that History forms no structural whole but is made to appear as if it does, and as such is empowered.

Michael Taussig (1989:59)

And my grandmother stepped into my head
And my grandmother stepped into my head
Behind my eyes
Behind my eyes
My grandmother was stepping into my head
from *Reverb-ber-ber-rations*

In attempting to explore Spiderwoman's work in terms of the explicit body I encountered, again, the problem of *thinking* the body at all. It seemed that, inevitably, "the body," taken as some kind of whole, whether as a visceral stage or as a conceptual notion, became bogusly separated from details and markings, hues and shades of particular – literal – bodies. Once articulated, once explicated in any way, "the body" was made appropriate, congealed, accessible and therefore safe – immediately removed from the "inappropriate" body, a body resisting boundaries and definitives which my feminism instructed me to champion. Working and thinking about "the body" too easily located it, somehow, outside over there – an object at safe distance from a subject. Perhaps, I told myself, my work on gender and representation had simply become awkwardly split from my own body. Perhaps I had lost an intimacy with my own work. This concern with my own body erupted, troublingly, just as I was beginning to think, specifically, about women of color in explicit body practice.

But there was no returning to "my body" as a safe place. As though through a crack in the steps, doubt had seeped into my inquiry, staining the space between a *theory* of bodily literality and a practice – a more literal, perhaps inappropriate experience. And that doubt, I realized, was visceral – felt in my belly, bones, and nerves as much as in my head. Significantly, the doubt surfaced most palpably as I approached writing on the racially marked body. I felt more comfortable writing on the body inscribed as sexual – as a "woman" I myself bore the visible markings culturally inscribed femininity. But as a white woman, I bore the visible markings of the Euro-American cultural "privilege" to be invisible, seemingly racially unmarked. As I approached writing about Spiderwoman,[2] I wondered if it would be better, more "appropriate," to write about performers who make their whiteness explicit – such as Sandra Bernhard's *Without You I'm Nothing* (1988) – thus writing about other white women. I would then be writing from a position of sameness, whereas writing across difference I would risk the myriad problematics of appropriation even as I attempted to write about the myriad problematics of appropriation.

One thing my doubt or fear repeated upon me was an old question: how can a white woman begin to write about a Native American performance group in a way that grapples honestly and productively with the tangle of issues involved across race? How can a white woman write about people of color without appropriating, yet again, the markings of difference? Yes, I could ante up in the realm of identity politics and proclaim my whiteness from the start, acknowledging and underscoring my social privilege. But was there something beyond the acknowledgment of that gulf? As opposed to the gulf, should I look for and could I find an intimacy with "racially marked work"[3] despite or even *because* of the breach of race? And how to write an intimacy of difference? Is an intimacy of difference radically different from the intimacy of same which so often informs academic feminist associations with women artists? Fifteen-year-old words knocked at the door of my project: "The failure of the academic feminists to recognize difference as a crucial strength . . . " (Lorde 1981b:100). The beat of Audre Lorde's words in my mind. "The failure of academic feminists to recognize difference" . . . the failure . . . the failure. Shut up, I said to my doubt. But its silence was more alarming than its voice.

So I went to bed.

Scratch, glitch, break.

The following story is about a sensual memory, perhaps a bodily memory, which is to say, I remembered something I had never known. I remembered something differently, something that started me thinking about difference in a more conflicted and intimate way. Because of the following experience I began to think more rigorously about history in-bodied, inscribed not only across visible markings, but as accessible in the invisible or disguised traces, in visceral (inappropriate) counter-memories of gender, race, and class. Thinking of history in-bodied, I thought about the past as tactile, differently accessible in the material senses of a body, in reverberations across viscera – not only across bloodlines, but across nervous systems, the networks of synapses between social structures and the experiences those structures often serve to veil.

The story: As I lay in bed I was visited by a ghost.

I didn't think of it at the time of the visitation, but I later remembered that Foucault used the word "apparition" while arguing for another way of apprehending the past, one less patriarchally linear, one which includes ruptures and breaks, one situated in bodies. Walter Benjamin, too, wrote of another history retained in physical "flashes."[4] My ghost, however, was making no academic claims. In fact, there was no body to be situated. Absent, invisible, she stood quietly by my computer. She stood beside a poster of Spiderwoman I had hung on my wall.

An invisible body makes a strange impression – especially to an academic preoccupied by theories of bodies made explicit. I had no idea who this absent presence was. I had no idea what she wanted. I felt I must be overtired, stressed out. I tried to ignore her, ignore my fear, and sleep. But then as suddenly as I'd become aware of her presence, I became aware of her identity – scratch, glitch – she was my mother's father's mother. Now, as my inquiry trips and falls into personal narrative, I ask my reader to bear with my attempt to steer a critical course through personal experience. First, it's important to know that no one in my family knew anything about my mother's father or his side of the family – a divorce had completely wiped them out of the lineage. We only knew that they were Ozark mountain people – "hillbillies" – a major reason that side of the family had disappeared from the map of lineage. For the sake of class purity in narrative line, family history had conveniently erased the details of genealogy.

Visibly but not viscerally erased, I thought, because here was this presence in my bedroom.

Unable to deal with the invisible body, I decided to go downstairs, watch TV, and get real.

What appeared on the screen was a PBS documentary about Ozark mountain women.

I went back to bed. What do you want?

The ghost told me to keep working. Then she was gone.

The next day I called my mother on the phone wanting any information she might have on this great-grandmother. Surprised, she told me that she, too, had been visited in a dream. But, she said, her dream was more far-fetched than my encounter. In her dream the woman had appeared as a Native American and had spoken of certain Indian diseases. Isn't that strange, she said. And we silently agreed to forget about it.

Perhaps you have guessed where this is headed. The visitation occurred in February 1990. In March 1990 I saw *Reverb-ber-ber-rations*. In July 1990, my mother did some genealogical investigation and uncovered an aunt in Missouri. "Did you know," the new-found old aunt asked, "that your grandmother was an American Indian? Her name was Elzina but she signed her name with an X."

For me, something profound had occurred: I had remembered something differently. I felt elated at first. I felt I had overcome a kind of social erasure – tapped a kind of counter-memory. I even felt hopeful: perhaps Difference is always already a personal geography, experienced intimately, and fear that demarcates an "other" can be glimpsed as inscribed, palimpsestuous, across the veiled face of the Same.

> *I urge each one of us here to reach down into that deep place of knowledge inside herself and touch that terror and loathing of any difference that lives there. See whose face it wears.*
>
> (Lorde 1981b:101, Lorde's italics)

And yet, other specters soon raised themselves when I considered how to incorporate this visceral memory – or even the idea of bodily experience – into a materialist-informed inquiry into "the body" in white male patriarchy.

The notion of knowledge IN a body smacks of essentialism. The absurd idea that I might understand Spiderwoman because of some buried bloodline smacks of colonialist nostalgia. Though interrupting my space of doubt, the invisible body had simultaneously immensely complicated my project – I had allowed myself (my story) to become awkwardly and even perhaps indulgently tangled in the complexities of desire and fear surrounding difference. I knew that for many Native Americans, including Spiderwoman, a "Cherokee grandmother" is a problematic symbol of white nostalgia, a symbol of the general unwillingness of whites to acknowledge difference as strength without appropriating some part of it.

> Two weeks ago that woman was nothing but a plain old white woman. After taking one swig of our Yataholay Indian snake oil, she now has a Cherokee grandmother![5]

Still, my experience with the invisible body sat relentlessly in the middle of my efforts to write about Spiderwoman – indeed my efforts to write about the explicit body at all. What to do with that visit – that explicitly disembodied body? What to do with the reverberations? With the counter-memories of miscegenations forgotten, buried in bodies and cultures – miscegenations that knock on the neat door marked difference? My family is also related by blood to Booker T. Washington. A slave-owning ancestor named Taliaferro (the "T." of Washington's middle name) had "owned" and impregnated Booker's black mother. I am the "recognized," "legitimate" or "decided" offspring of that slave-holder, just as my unrecognized relatives of color (whom I have never met – what would such a meeting be like?) are his "illegitimate" heirs. Disavowed miscegenations or buried genealogies of rape trouble the neatnesses of narrative line and threaten to dismember, if not disembody, carefully crafted lineages of sameness.

I returned to my familiar "body" of theory as a way of apprehending the strange disembodiment of my great-grandmother literally present as absent in my room – invisible in my space, and invisible in my white skin. Following Nietzsche, Foucault proposed a methodology, a practice based upon attention to details, accidents, and errors – to bodies erased by history. As against the sweeping narrative tradition of historical analysis, he suggested the posture of critical retrospection that Nietzsche called genealogy, not only because, opposed to the search for origins, genealogy can find "something altogether different" from dominant practice, but because it approaches bodies as landscapes of counter-memory situated in and affected by that narrative (Foucault 1977:142).

> The body manifests the stigmata of past experience and so gives rise to desires, failings, and errors . . . Genealogy, as an analysis of descent, is thus situated within the articulation of the body and history. Its task is to expose a body totally imprinted by history and the process of history's destruction of the body.
>
> (1977:148)

Of course, one of history's destructions of the specific, the particular body is the active forgetting, the disavowal of exchanges and the fear of recognitions across difference (see Bhabha 1984:125–33). In place of the body erased, disavowed, forgotten, or rendered illegitimate, a body of "authenticity" is constructed which diverts attention from the fraught terrain of exchange (see Minh-Ha 1986/86).

The presence of the absence of my forgotten great-grandparent underscored for me the notion that implicit in the visibility of my "whiteness" and Spider-woman's "color" is a host of invisible bodies – a host of counter-memories that reverberate between us. And yet it is very important to emphasize that those counter-memories would reverberate *regardless of a Cherokee grandmother*. Aporias in the dominant narratives of colonialism, oppression, and exchange belong to all of us, caught nervously in the synapses of our shared social nervous system, surging intimately if invisibly between and through our differences regardless of bloodlines – like a public secret (Taussig 1992). Acknowledged or unacknowledged, a social genealogy continues to reverberate in the tangled spaces between our race, gender, age, and class identities – available at any moment to be, to quote Lorde again quoting Mary Daly, "re-membered" differently (1981a:96).

Re-membering, re-embodying, is precisely what Spiderwoman does, though not in a way that fixates upon the past as outside over there. Rather, the sisters flash their memories across the present, slicing through the myriad fears and desires that surround the issue of neo-colonial identity. Spiderwoman's theatrical re-membering is a bold counter-practice, aimed at the creation of the "authentic" and "primitive" Native American and doubling back upon that creation with counter-memory in the form of counter-mimicry.

WHITE NOSTALGIA, AUTHENTICITY, AND THE SPLIT SUBJECT

> Today, planned authenticity is rife; as a product of hegemony and a remark-able counterpart of hegemony and universal standardization, it constitutes an efficacious means of silencing the cry of racial oppression . . . On the one hand, i play into the Savior's hands by concentrating on authenticity, for my attention is numbed by it and diverted from other, important issues; on the other hand, i do feel the necessity to return to my so-called roots, since they are the fount of my strength, the guiding arrow to which i constantly refer before heading for a new direction.
>
> Trinh T. Minh-Ha (1986/87)

"I used to be a white woman," says Muriel Miguel. She pulls a coquettish, WASP-miming smile at the audience as though she were doing an ad for Spic 'n' Span or Tammy's Tanning Parlor. In fact, Muriel is spinning a parody on the increasing number of whites who think they can simply become native by uncovering long lost relatives or being bequeathed an Indian name. In *Winnetou's Snake Oil Show from Wigwam City*, Spiderwoman enact a mock weekend workshop in which, for $3,000 a head, they turn white people into Indians with their amazing "Yataholay Indian Snake Oil." They are spoofing the New Age trend they call "plastic shamanism."

As part of the gimmick to sell their oil, Spiderwoman present a series of mimed Indian rope, knife, and horse tricks in a send up of Wild West sideshows. At moments between the acts, they occasionally pause to intimate another experience – an experience of cultural identity that resists the spoof and touches sometimes on a notion of grace, even sanctity, and often pain. I will return to these interludes later, but the acts themselves are pointedly banal. "Mother Moon Face," played by Hortensia Colorado,[6] is "an equestrian from the Ponderosa" who dares to "change horses mid-gallop!" The horses are two mops Colorado rides around the stage, simply crossing them over each other as she "gallops." Lisa Mayo, Princess Pissy Willow of the Mish Mash Tribe, makes an elaborate show of shooting balloons out of an audience member's hands. When she says "pow" the balloon is popped with a tack. Muriel Miguel is Ethel Christian Christianson. She uses a rope "so fine that it can't be seen by the naked eye." After lassoing Gloria and Hortensia with the invisible rope, she has herself tied up for a "psychic" rope trick. She goes into a trance to deliver a "message from the other side." The message, which she speaks in a low and laboriously slow trance voice, is "I have hemorrhoids." The solution, of course: "Buy Snake Oil."

While exposing the complicated collusion of "Indian" identity with commodity culture, Spiderwoman repeatedly and purposefully foul their material with allusions to base bodily function, provocatively resisting the more common attempt to counter commodification by alluding to an "essential spirituality" of natives or native experience. At one point in the *Winnetou* show, the women all stand around a cauldron, mixing their Yataholay brew. The lights dim, as they dim for more serious moments in the interludes in which the company invokes ancestors, leaving the audience somewhat unsure of the line between satire and seriousness, sanctity and sacrilege:

> What shall this concoction be?
> Pure white cat, daughter of a pure white mother
> Porcupine piss
> Velvet antlers of a well-hung moose (find a left hind leg and
>   suck out the marrow)
> Bull turd
> Bat shit
> Yum yum from a bum
> Toenails of a lounge lizard
> Skunk cum
> What shall this concoction cure?
> Running asshole
> Constipation
> Half-breeditis . . .

The banality of the recipe is obvious, but nonetheless the presentation is somehow ambiguous, leaving unclear the fine line between the sacred and the profane and making the audience suddenly unsure of the appropriateness of laughter. When the lights come back up one can no longer be secure in the conviction that Spiderwoman's spoof is unqualifiedly funny. Having mixed their brew, the sisters are now raucously in the business of *making* natives. One "swig" of their oil and a member of the audience, picked by Gloria – anyone who buys a ticket for the "show" is susceptible – inherits a tribe and picks a name from a list that includes "Olddogeyedick" and "Two Dogs Fucking." The audience member, a white man both times I saw the show, is then given a xeroxed photo of a "real" Indian's face circa 1900 and told to hold it in front of his face for the rest of his life. He is sent back to his seat – transformed.

Such moments of bogus transformation stand in strange relation to the interludes in which the spoof is dropped. In one such moment, a member of the company holds a large bone up into the light of a movie projector which is casting a silent black and white image of natives dancing in full-feathered regalia onto a screen at the back of the stage. The silence is prolonged as the image flickers over the bone and across the back of the woman. Then come words, slowly articulated: "This is the bone of our ancestors. This is the bone of our relations. Digging, digging, digging for bones . . . " It is in relation to such moments that Spiderwoman's parody gathers the kind of punch that knocks the wind out of a spectator.

Laughing, Spiderwoman is sending up something extremely serious. Who are the "primitives" that have been created by white nostalgia? Much of Spiderwoman's work is related to the issue of "Indianness," adroitly played in the painful space between the need to claim an "authentic" native identity and their awareness of the appropriation and the historical commodification of the signs of that authenticity. Their material falls in the interstices where their autobiographies meet popular and aesthetic constructions of the "primitive," specifically the primitivized American Indian. In fact, Spiderwoman Theater shows up the split subjectivity that ensues from the encounter between these two – their autobiographies and cultural history – the doubled image that creates the terrain of their senses of self. Restaging antic Snake Oil sideshows, they explore and explode the business of being exotic. Showing the Indian Other as Show, they display as much about white-man's Indian (the big drum "beat beat beat of the tom tom") as about native identity until the two are seen as impossibly intertwined.

This sense of split subjectivity is poignantly expressed in *Sun, Moon, Feather*, a performance piece woven from childhood memories which deals explicitly with multiple layers of identity. Cuna on their father's side and Rappahannock on their mother's, the sisters are also Brooklynites who played "Indian Love Call" in their backyard as kids, acting out the parts from the 1938 MGM musical *Girl of the Golden West* and fighting over who got to be Jeannette MacDonald and who had to settle for Nelson Eddy. First performed at the Newfoundland Theater on West 18th Street in 1981 and later made into a film, *Sun, Moon, Feather* combines storytelling with silent filmclips of family outings and snake oil shows, as well as clips from *Girl of the Golden West*.

Gloria Every once in a while our family would go to a pow wow or a snake oil show.
Lisa Brooklyn.

Gloria We were part of the circus.

Lisa And one of the sideshows was my family's snake oil show.

Gloria Here we had an Indian village with teepees and children running around and people eating and so forth.

Lisa I looked up one day and I saw this whole bunch of people, you know, tourists. And they said "Hey – come here, come here, come here, come here! Look! Look at the Indians eating!"

[A slide is projected of an Indian with a hot dog.]

Gloria My father and a man named Sam Blowsnake –

Lisa – the Winnebago guy –

Gloria – were the two big chiefs there and they would go out in the street and around the circus there –

Lisa To get the people in – Ballyhoo. We'd go outside: "OK – all the Indians out." We'd all be dressed up.

Gloria Screaming Cheedebeecho! Cheedebeecho! Cheedebeecho!

Lisa And we'd give them like a little taste of what the show would be like on the inside, you see.

[Silent film clip of many Indians on an outdoor platform dancing together]

Gloria Well, years later I met this Winnebago woman and we were talking and I said, "You know, I know some words in Winnebago." And she said, "Yeah? What are they?"

"Cheedebeecho."

She said, "Cheedebeecho? That's not Winnebago."

I said, "It isn't?"

And she said, "No, I never heard Cheedebeecho. Uh-uh, that's not Winnebago."

I said, "Sure, Sam and my father used to ballyhoo and they'd go out front and call people in and say Cheedebeecho!"

She said, "That's not Winnebago."

You know, this is like after many many years. I say this over to myself slowly: Cheedebeecho . . . Cheedebeecho . . . hee de bee cho . . . Seedebeeshow . . . See the big show! See the big show! That's what they were calling out! See the big show!

The embattled search for the "authentic" Indian frequently uncovers, for Spiderwoman, the Symbolic Order of the white colonial. Too often, behind the painted-face of the authentic is the "wanna-bee."[7] Too often the authentic Indian becomes the one stuck, stuffed for a museum, not allowed to step beyond the boundaries of a tradition frozen in a moment of colonization as "primitive" or "savage." As Lisa Mayo told me in 1989, the authentic Indian is a dead Indian around whom white nostalgia for "better days" can congeal: "What the white search for the shaman misses is the reality of the Native American here and now. They're not interested in that. Really for them it would be a lot easier if we would disappear, all die of alcoholism, and then they could take over and talk about what we had been." This attitude can be insidious. For example, in 1990,

Taxi, a popular fashion magazine, featured an article entitled "Keeping the Faith" about native performers and "art built on the balance of old and new" (Bloom 1990:104–9). While the article was hip to Spiderwoman's message, nevertheless the photographs the magazine published to accompany the text were treated to resemble faded tin-types, tattered at the edges, stained, and weathered – as though the subjects pictured, including the Spiderwoman company, all belonged to a dead and lost generation, circa 1900 (Figure 6.2).

Determined to break beyond the boundaries of a potentially crippling authenticity, Spiderwoman "doubles back" upon white culture the problem of their own authentication – showing the show, spoofing the gaze of the white. Thus their stories are counter-memories, and though often humorous, their work is painful. They stand defiantly where a white tin-typifying gaze meets Spiderwoman's own desire for the authentic – to express their experience free from the pressure of a commodity culture repeatedly fueled by modernist nostalgia for the "noble savage." Lisa talks of technique, of sending up the authentic only to double back and insist upon the reality of the effects of that authentication: "People are laughing. Then – POW! – we get them with the real stuff" (in Burns and Hurlbutt 1992).

SPIDERWOMAN: THE EARLY DAYS

> For our types in the mainstream there was the maid and the mother or there was the mother and the maid – or you could paste on an accent and be Mrs. Sanchez. In our own theater we could do anything we wanted: be skinny, do Juliet – anything.
>
> Muriel Miguel (interview with author, 1990)

These are big, strong women. These are grandmothers, dressed in outrageous filigree and wielding a sharp reflexivity. There may be a feather in someone's hair, but there is also loud lamé, glitter, and, especially in *Winnetou*, a purposeful polyester sheen (Plate 6.2). Working against the expectations that surround "native performance," Spiderwoman enter the stage fully aware of the complexities in the identifications they are weaving. They are also studiously amateur in their style, their work intricately and consummately flawed: Spider Grandmother Woman, their namesake, always wove an error into her designs to allow her spirit to find its way out and be free.

The sisters began working together in New York in 1976. Muriel was the one to start it. Youngest of the three, she had been a member of Joseph Chaikin's Open Theater in the early 1970s. She had worked with Megan Terry, Sam Shepard, and Alwin Nikolai, but had gotten tired of being endlessly typecast as "the Indian." When a woman director, Gilda Russo, cast Muriel in a successful piece called *The Three Marias* only to bump her for an "uptown actress" when the show moved closer to Broadway, telling her she was just too fat, Muriel discovered that "you can be just as disappointed in a female director." It was this disappointment that made her realize that if she didn't

Plate 6.2 Lisa Mayo of Spiderwoman during a performance of *Lysistrata Numbah*.
Photo by Martin S. Selway. Courtesy of Spiderwoman.

make the appropriate-body problem explicit herself, nothing would change. As she says: "If you don't shake it yourself, nothing will shake."[8]

Muriel Miguel started Womanspace with two white women, Carol Grossberg and Laura Foner, and soon found herself involved in something that was as much a consciousness-raising group as a theater. She had never felt that her opinions were worth much at the Open Theater, but Womanspace gave her confidence. At first she was not at all sure that she wanted to "disclose herself" to white women, but eventually talking with other women and answering questions about herself felt like the "sun shining in on a new interior." Out of the consciousness-raising, Womanspace created *Cycles*, an autobiographical piece in which Laura Foner came out as a lesbian. The group won a CAPS fellowship but was already breaking up under the stress of internal competition.

Muriel started another group – this time with "lots of women." Awarded a grant to do a piece on violence, Muriel felt that she needed both of her sisters to work with her. At this point, however, her sisters would have "nothing to do with her." Gloria was living in Oberlin, Ohio, the wife of a faculty member. But it was Lisa, an accomplished singer studying "serious" acting at HB studio, who was the most reluctant:

> I liked her work, but it was too scroungy. They did everything on the floor [she laughs]. I just couldn't see myself doing it that way. I was an actress; I had a very good technique; working with Uta Hagen. I was also a classical singer, a mezzo soprano . . . And she asked me to lay on the floor, and do all these scroungy things and talk about orgasms. "Oh God," I thought.
>
> (in Burns and Hurlbutt 1992)

But Muriel was persistent and eventually brought Lisa and Gloria together with Lois Weaver (white), Pam Verge (white), Nadia Bay (black), and Brandy Pen ("part Asian and part WASP"). They named themselves Spiderwoman after Spider Grandmother Woman, a familiar household god of the Hopi who was the first to create designs and teach her people to weave.

Developing a working technique called "storyweaving," the group kept to a no-holds-barred philosophy. The only thing set at the beginning of any project was the performance date. But no-holds-barred was relatively easy – because their racial mix and body types were already outside of the bounds of normative theater, the group found itself automatically free from the pressure of expectation. Even within most feminist theater at that time the notion of the appropriate body held firm: "You still had to be blonde and blue-eyed – or you could be black and thin." Spiderwoman found this *a priori* freedom from the appropriate exhilarating, and built upon that freedom as the cornerstone of their identity:

CHALLENGING THE "ONE-SIZE-FITS-ALL" VIEW OF FEMINISM, THIS SEVEN WOMAN COMPANY USES THEIR DIVERSE EXPERIENCES AS WOMEN, AS AMERICAN INDIAN WOMEN, AS LESBIANS, AS SCORPIOS, AS WOMEN OVER FIFTY AND WOMEN UNDER TWENTY-FIVE AS, SISTERS

AND MOTHERS AND GRANDMOTHERS TO DEFY SUCH OLD GENERAL-
IZATIONS AS: "ALL BLONDES HAVE MORE FUN," AND "ALL WOMEN'S
THEATER IS THE SAME." [9]

Women and Violence, their first piece, performed in 1976 at the Washington
Square Methodist Church, wove stories from members' own lives around a
central story of a well-known revolutionary leader in the 1970s American Indian
movement who saw no discrepancy between his fight for native rights and
his own brutality toward women. Already the slapstick style and hysterical
behavior around extremely serious topics was in full swing. Vigilently batting
at the gadfly of the "appropriate," the show closed with the women throwing
popcorn and pies at each other. In-jokes were there as well: Lisa had joined the
troupe but disguised herself as a white woman. She was de-wigged and exposed
at the finale, when, says Lisa, "they insisted that I throw the pie in my own face
because I was such a perfect lady."[10]

After *Women and Violence* came other shows – *Trilogy*, *Cabaret: An Evening of
Disgusting Songs and Pukey Images* (see Plate 6.3), *Lysistrata Numbah*, and *The
Fittin' Room* – but the stress of special interests within the group began to take
a toll. Difference, one of the group's original strong points, began to present
difficulties. "White ways" began to clash with "native ways," lesbian issues with
heterosexual ones. I asked the sisters about the 1981 break up of the original
Spiderwoman into two separate performing troupes – Spiderwoman and Split
Britches:

Gloria Some of the women who were lesbian wanted to make Spiderwoman
an all-lesbian group . . . and – over our dead bodies.
Lisa Well, you can't become a lesbian if you're not a lesbian. I mean, do we
all have to be the same?
Muriel That was the exciting thing about Spiderwoman at that time. We
were young, we were old, we were black, we were Indian, we were gay, we
were straight, fat, skinny, short. It was really exciting. It was really sad when
it broke up. My feeling was that the pressure of the white women in the
group got too much for me. The pressure was: you do things this way, you
don't do things this way. You know –
Gloria – "this is the white way" –
Muriel, Lisa, and Gloria (laughing) – but they didn't say that.
Muriel And involved in all that was the getting grants and everything. And
there was always the "right" way to do these things. Also, in the beginning we
had wanted it to be that there would be more nonwhite than white women in
the group, but a lot of white women ended up coming in, somehow. The stage
managers, the costumers, the business manager – they all came and they were
white. And there was also the feeling that "the sisters get a lot of attention
because they're Indians." It wasn't easy then. There were hard feelings.
Lisa Well that was a long time ago and now everyone's doing well. In 1981
we got a grant which we split between *Sun, Moon, Feather* – our show – and
Split Britches with Lois Weaver, Peggy Shaw, and Deborah Margolin.[11] After

Plate 6.3 Spiderwoman Theater in the late 1970s performing *An Evening of Disgusting Songs and Pukey Images.* Left to right: Gloria Miguel, Pam Verge, Nadja Beye, Lisa Mayo, Peggy Shaw, Muriel Miguel, Lois Weaver. Photo by Antonio Sferlazzo. Courtesy of Spiderwoman.

that Split Britches became their own company, we stayed on as Spiderwoman, and the amazing thing is –
Lisa, Gloria, and Muriel – we're all still here![12]

VIGILANT REPETITIONS, THE COMIC TURN, AND COUNTER-MIMICRY

1990. Theater for the New City. We sit in the dark waiting for *Reverb-ber-ber-rations* to begin. A loud, very loud, drumming assaults us and continues in the dark for some time. There is also a scuffling of feet. When the lights come up we see that the drum is a garbage can. Spiderwoman had been clumsily stumbling around in the dark. "I gotta pee!" says Muriel. The sisters Broadway belt Cole Porter: "Like the beat beat beat of the tom tom when the jungle shadows fall . . . " What stands between the drum, the tom tom, and the trash can? Does the space between them generate a counter-memory?

Natalie Zemon Davis and Peter Starn define counter-memory as the "residual or resistant strains that withstand official versions of historical continuity" (1989:2). Foucault's translator defines counter-memory as the name of an "action that defines itself, that recognizes itself in words – in the multiplication of meaning through the practice of vigilant repetitions" (Bouchard in Foucault 1977:9). Can counter-memory be an action that defines not only in words, but in the vigilant repetitions of a body or an object, as in the visceral "words" of a performer's gesture or the violent vibrations of a drum which repeats itself, doubling as both trash-can and tom tom?

Vigilant repetitions. The dark drumming and the trash-can scene are repeated later in the show. So are the jokes and ribald humor. So are the knife-in-the-heart stories of loss. So are the reflexive tea scenes. So are the women themselves as the features of one sister can be seen, almost the same but not quite, on the body of another sister. "Just what did you tell those people?" they ask each other again.

Since 1981, Lisa Mayo, Gloria Miguel, and Muriel Miguel have been the core of Spiderwoman. Theater for the New City[13] and the American Indian Community House, both on the Lower East Side of Manhattan, generally host Spiderwoman's work before they tour. *Sun, Moon, Feather* (1981) was followed by *The Three Sisters From Here to There* (1982) – a take-off on Chekhov; *3 Up, 3 Down* (1987); *Winnetou's Snake Oil Show from Wigwam City* (1988); and finally, *Reverb-ber-ber-rations* (1990). Surprisingly, however, the differences celebrated in the original Spiderwoman have not disappeared but have grown in complexity. There is a depth to Spiderwoman's exploration of identity – the differences they explore, like the realities they explore, are rarely limited to the strictly visible ones. In fact, things that "ought" to be different – such as a trash can and a tom tom – are constantly bombarded against each other and against audience expectations. More often than not it is the "appropriate" which is challenged. In a segment of *Reverb-ber-ber-rations* titled "Vincent," Lisa Mayo enters the stage chanting: "Hey, hey, dooten day, dooten day, hey, hey, dooten day, dooten day." Suddenly she weaves into her chant the lyrics from a pop tune – "Starry, Starry Night" – and her words become impossibly intertwined, miscegenated, with the popular Don Maclean lyrics about Van Gogh.

> The world of the five senses in the world of illusion. Reality cannot be seen with the physical eye. With the eyes that watch the world and can't forget strangers that they've met.
>
> Starry, starry night. The responsibility of creators; people who make things, build, mold, and shape things, is to interpenetrate the layers, bring information between the layers.
>
> Starry, starry night! Going back into the before to use for the future.
>
> Starry, starry night. Portraits hung in empty halls. Ragged men in ragged clothes. How you tried to set them free. They would not – They did not know how. Perhaps they'll listen now.
>
> Starry, starry night. Hey, hey, dooten day dooten day.[14]

What to make of such syncretism, such hybrid perspective in which categories of difference lose their clean edges, their appropriate delineations? Cultivating "details and accidents," counter-memory, closely linked to the notion of genealogy, always already "attaches itself to the body" (Foucault 1977:148–9). But *the* body? Here problems proliferate like rashes, grammatical blemishes, slips of the tongue. What is "the" body to which the details and accidents of counter-memory attach – especially when redoubled in such a tumult of blatant and insistent syncretism? The beat of Audre Lorde's words: *See whose face it wears.* In the blindspots of the abluted body of the "appropriate," the inappropriate reverberates in a concatenation of resemblances, a circle of "almost the same but not quite" (Bhabha 1984:126), always, it seems, just beyond the field of appropriation. And yet the challenge demands a recognition of terror: *See whose face it wears. See whose face it wears. See whose face it wears.*

Spiderwoman practice double vision. "Turning" a white into a native and marking that identity across the body by means of a photograph held in front of the face, they turn upon a mimicry that has colonized, fixed, commodified and natural-historified Indian identity as a product of colonial representational practices. They make explicit the ways their bodies have been staged, framed by colonial representational practices, and delimited. Here, they turn upon that historical representation of the native, upon colonial mimicry of native identity, with what might be called counter-mimicry.

Exploring the historical mechanisms of colonial power, Homi Bhabha uncovered what he called a comic turn. The colonizers constructed their colonial subject through representation which presented the colonial project as noble by presenting the native as ignoble, or more to the point, as deficient, partial, or incomplete. The "nobility" of the civilizing mission was erected through the "primitivizing" of the Other, and that primitive was produced through mimicry – textual effects which split that subject into both "human and not wholly human," into almost the same but not quite. Thus the self-proclaimed noble intentions of the colonizer's construction of the colonial subject ironically hinged upon the ignoble literary effects of repetition, mimicry, and farce to create the colonial subject's deficiency. This literary flip which creates nobility through creating deficiency is what Bhabha calls the "comic turn" of colonialism.[15] As Bhabha notes, historically, white recognition of a member of another race as human was always already insidiously coupled with a disavowal of that Other as "wholly human." Through the coupling of recognition with disavowal, that Other emerged as a split subject – a "partial subject" – not wholly human in the eyes of colonizers – "almost the same but not white." The Other exists then in a strange space of ambiguity, oddly doubled with him/herself: both the same *and* different, subject and object at once. Bhabha defines mimicry as a complex strategy of representation, repeating or doubling the image of the Other in a shroud of the authentic, continually producing and delimiting difference through a strategy which "'appropriates' the Other as it visualizes power" (Bhabha 1984:126).

But mimicry has an edge. If mimicry can be articulated as the disciplining gaze which doubles its subjects, then the menace of mimicry is in fact the potential return or ricochet of that gaze. As Bhabha puts it: "The menace of mimicry is its double vision which in disclosing the ambivalence of colonial discourse also disrupts its authority." Thus, "the reforming, civilizing mission is threatened by the displacing gaze of its disciplinary double" (1984:128). The view from the blindspot. In this displacing gaze, the tables are turned on the "appropriate," showing the mimicry inherent in its construction. Under the stress of double vision, "the body" appropriate becomes a scrim. Making that body explicit as scrim can throw into relief the concealment or erasure of other bodies – specific, detailed, and multiple.

Counter-mimicry. In *Sun, Moon, Feather* Gloria and Lisa play "Indian Love Call" in their living room. But they don't act out the Indian parts – the virulent, near-naked, dancing brave or the dark Indian Princess – they fight over who gets to be be-ringleted, vaseline-over-the-lens Jeanette MacDonald and who has to play stalwart, straight-backed Canadian Mountie Nelson Eddy. They are not re-playing, re-membering, or re-claiming native images, but counter-appropriating the appropriate. They sing beautifully: "When I'm calling you-ooo-ooo." Lisa is Nelson. She wears a low-cut slip and a wide-brimmed hat. Gloria stands on a chair as Jeanette. They gaze into each other's eyes as they sing. Silent clips from the movie are interwoven with their scene so that the mouths of MacDonald and Eddy seem to lip-synch the lilting voices of Lisa and Gloria, whose bodies repeat upon the Hollywood lovers, doubling back.

Doubling-back, myriad "appropriates" are recognized as they are disrupted.[16] The inappropriate bodies of Lisa and Gloria appropriate the bodies of Jeanette and Nelson and expose a hot-bed of error. First, the lovers Nelson and Jeanette are supposed to be male and female, not female and female. Nelson isn't supposed to wear a slip that exposes a healthy cleavage. Second, in a Wild West fantasy whites aren't supposed to be non-whites (though Native Americans have been played by whites in ruddy make-up, one doesn't find "real" natives playing whites in pancake). Third, and importantly, heavy women aren't supposed to be so clearly free and comfortable with their bodies. And fourth, a native performance troupe isn't supposed to mirror "mainstream" performance traditions, though the mainstream can mimic native traditions (the native dances in *Girl of the Golden West* itself a case in point). A native troupe is expected to chase after a vanishing point marked as "loss," the "authentic" rendered by colonialist nostalgia as stuck in time, dislocated, pre-contact.

Another example of counter-mimicry occurs in *Winnetou's Snake Oil Show from Wigwam City*. The show opens with a skit about a German explorer's "discovery" of Indian ways circa 1860. Hortensia Colorado plays a scurvy guide. Lisa plays Gunther, a German explorer visiting the Wild West for the first time. Gloria plays a vicious bear killed by Gunther with a toy hatchet – the dime-store variety that squeaks on impact. When the bear is dead (after a drawn-out Swan Lake-type death), Gloria reappears as an ugly, smelly "Injun" who looks like "a horse walked all over his face." Seeing the dead bear, the Injun raises his arms and begins to chant. At this moment Muriel enters as Great Chief Winnetou, wise and noble savage, brilliant and strong. At Winnetou's entrance the skit becomes a full-fledged opera. Winnetou introduces himself in Wagnerian splendor singing: "I am Winnetou." An operatic medley follows in which Winnetou invites the German to become his blood brother and smoke the peace pipe. The sisters bellow operatically and bump into one another while dancing a circle dance with token "Indian" gestures. The point here is that the German meets Winnetou through the medium of grand opera, making explicit the European construction of the "noble savage" and counter-mimicking the high ideals of European form.

Yet, if the colonial project turned from "high ideals" to its "low mimetic literary effect," as Bhabha would have it, Spiderwoman conversely turns from the low mimetic effect to a searing critique. "People are laughing. Then – POW! – we get them with the real stuff." In fact, if Spiderwoman did not incorporate another turn from the parody of counter-mimicry to the "hit" of "real-stuff" – or rather, if they did not make explicit the reality effects of mimicry – then the bite of their critique might slide into a whirlpool of mimesis for mimesis' sake, re-enacted without critical commentary across their own bodies. The seemingly endless concatenation of resemblances and counter-resemblances, in which mimesis repeats again and again and again, is interrupted by Spiderwoman by something they insist on as "real." Here, the re-doubling of representation does not erect a Baudrillardian hall of mirrors in which others mimic others mimicking others till the Different supposedly collapses with the Same under the label "representation is all." Instead Spiderwoman insist upon an interruption: "POW! – we get them with the real stuff." The punch of the literal in the face of the symbolic.

But what is the "real stuff" that interrupts? What is the literal which exceeds the boundaries of its service to the Symbolic Order? Gloria and Lisa are not doubling back over Jeanette and Nelson to lose themselves in an endless con-catenation of mimicry. In fact, something more strikingly heretical is occurring: they are telling a story about real effects on real lives and they have an agenda pitched toward change. They are "going back into the before to use for the future."[17] Their doubling back in fact bears a double meaning. On the one hand, it is a repetition of the technique of mimesis upon the dominant culture that has mimicked them (as if to say, you've doubled me now I'll double you back). But, on the other hand, it is a significant historical counter-analysis, a doubling back as in a retracing of steps to expose something secreted, erased, silenced along the way. The audience laughs with the sisters at their antic re-membering of the double, but in the next instant find that we rub up against the silenced side of the double – the "real stuff." Stories of their father's alcoholism, his violence and his death, sober stories of their mother's embattled Christianity, and stories of their deep, deep anger repeat upon the spoof of the authentic. In one moment the "authentic" is distanced, exposed as corrupted by colonialist nostalgia, but in the next it (painfully) "alters," becomes a detail, a vital memory, a *literal* reality – their mother, themselves, their grandmother – very much alive in literal reverberations across their daily experience.

Reverb-ber-ber-rations closes with a straightforward statement. Muriel Miguel faces her audience in dim light and speaks simply and quietly. Her words echo against all that went before:

> I am an Indian woman.
> I am proud of the women that came before me.
> I am a woman with two daughters.
> I am a woman with a woman lover.
> A woman that is claiming the wisdom
> of the women in my family.
> I am here now.
> I am saying this now because to deny these events
> about me and my life
> would be denying my children.

THE IRRUPTION OF "REAL STUFF" AND THE POLITIC OF SACRALITY

Counter-mimicry, vigilant repetition, and the painful irruption of "real stuff." All of this tremors and repeats with other feminist explicit body performance art in obvious and fundamental ways. The insistence upon *literal* effects of symbolic systems is integral to and powerful in Spiderwoman's work. These performers play back legacies of symbolic identity across their literal bodies, counter-appropriating the "appropriate" as Jeanette and Nelson embrace between sisters, and mimicking the ways natives have been mimicked. Their bodies are the literal ground of the "real stuff." But their stories, too, carry the weight of the real that Benjamin marked as overly possible, "wreckage upon wreckage" (see Chapter 4). Yet Spiderwoman's insistent "real stuff" extends not only to the too often dismissed social details of alcoholism and abuse intimated earlier, nor to just a literality tied to explicit materiality, but into a reverberating realm of the sacred – to the *real* stuff of the *spirit* world.

By doubling their parodies with serious interlude segments, as in *Winnetou,* that beckon toward sacred experience, by folding their criticisms of nostalgia over upon their own invocations of ghosts, Spiderwoman unleash multiple and seemingly conflicting reverberations into the space between performer and spectator. An invocation of ghosts that does not succumb to the logic of an insatiable and inaccessible vanishing point is an invocation which fully expects the ghosts to respond as present (in terms of both time and space). The real is not lost, just as *loss is very "real stuff"* – not displaced but accessible, ready to be enountered as a blindspot that is not blind. Here, neither "real stuff" nor "dream stuff" is dictated by insatiability, marked as impossible to access. Rather "real" and "dream" are every bit as tangible, exigent, sensual, and accessible as ghosts of ancestors.

In considering the politic of the sacred in Spiderwoman's work – for indeed, in their work, the "political" and "sacred" are not mutually exclusive – it is important to note that Spiderwoman's invocation of the sacred functions as theatrical interruption, tightly woven into the fabric of the parodic.[18] The sacred is embedded in the parodic, both standing in distinction to the comic turn, the doubling back, *and* part and parcel of that parody. As interruptions, such moments of serious invocation present a challenge to the audience. These "sacred" moments interrupt the profanity of parody as if to cast cracks into the criticism (or weave errors into the fabric) through which another vision, another experience might breathe. Brecht used interruptions in order to add critical distance, to point to or underscore the social gest of a situation. While Spiderwoman's interruptions may not add distance in precisely a Brechtian manner, they do ask the viewer to "think again" – to take a second look, like second sight, into the deeper complexities at work in their parodies. Here, the beauty of the interludes invoking ancestors – "digging, digging, digging for bones" – provide the audience with the recognition of the layer upon layer of sediment (and sentiment) stirred up by the storm of Spiderwoman's own parodic critique.

THE IRRUPTION OF GRANDMOTHERS AND THE REALITY OF DREAMS

Spiderwoman explicates modernist primitivism and commodity fetishism across their literal bodies, replaying white fetishization of natives by counter-appropriating the appropriate. Dominant culture reserves its dramas of desirability for, in Spiderwoman's words, "young, thin blondes with cute little noses," while near-naked Indian braves and their adoring native princesses dance and sweat as sexualized displacements. In the Jeanette and Nelson replay in *Sun, Moon, Feather* it is precisely the issue of "primitive" bodies appropriated for the sexualization of "civilized" identities that Spiderwoman bring to critical visibility. If, as Richard Dyer suggests, "it is white women who have been positioned as the apotheosis of desirability, all that a man could want, yet nothing that can be had, nor anything that a woman can be" (1988:64), then people of color, like Olympia's servant, have historically been more often representative of acquisition: everything that a man can have, yet nothing that he will recognize.

In *Sally's Rape*, African-American performance artist Robbie McCauley doubles back over primitivism, sexuality, and commodification in their most blatant terms. On stage, McCauley strips naked and stands on a bench. A white woman, Jeannie Hutchins, tells McCauley's audience that the bench is an auction block and she instructs spectators to join together in the chant "Bid em in, bid em in ... Bid em in, bid em in ... " As the chanting continues, McCauley becomes her great-great-grandmother in the process of being exchanged among slave holders as a piece of property. The link between race, gender, and commodification could not be more blatant. The scene is simple and straightforward and devastating. As if history itself had invisible fingers, McCauley is probed (she flinches) and poked (she winces). She is asked to turn around slowly. She tells us:

> On the auction block, they put
> their hands all down yr body
> the men smell ya, feel ya
> That's what they brought us here for
> (in Whyte 1993:278)

McCauley tells her audience that she dreams of her grandmother, and in her dreams she is her grandmother. In performance, she plays her grandmother back across her body, feeling the tightness in her own thighs as her grandmother is raped repeatedly "in the chickens." The subtitle of *Sally's Rape* is telling: *The Whole Story – The Past Becomes the Present in this Portrait of Survival within Today's Plantation Culture*. Like Spiderwoman, McCauley doubles back to mine the residue, the wreckage, that speaks across our own bodies in fitful historical counter-memories. Such memories do not exist in the past, but rather are part and parcel of the present, and they repeat across our social nervous system until we find a way to acknowledge their bones, to re-member.

As a spectator chanting "Bid em in" at The Kitchen in 1991, in the midst of a mostly white audience, I wanted to choke. Repeating those words over and over again before the spectacle of McCauley's body made explicit as stage, or more literally, *as aution block* – I had to fight to keep the words crawling out of my mouth because they felt heavy and hard against my tongue like material possessions regurgitated, or like my own guts turned to stone and spat out. I knew that we were witnessing here – an active spectating more akin to ritual than entertainment. And I knew that the experience through performance of a collective, embodied acknowledgment of such a history as present, in the room, at all times, was empowering. But it was perhaps because of such knowledge that my words, our words, the sea of "bid em ins" lapping over each other seemed to slap against the side of McCauley's face as she opened her mouth to have her teeth checked by some invisible slaveholder, my grandfather, returned from the dead – no, not returned, acknowledged as having never left, as always already with us, among us, here, digging at *my* bones.

I found myself grappling not with safe residue or inert traces of history removed from the present, but with a vital, visceral plumb-line of historical ghostings questioning neatly marked categories of difference. Rather than stark dividing lines, McCauley and Spiderwoman present the hybrids of complicity – audience members, chanting as McCauley is sold, are reminded of participation. Spectators are not disembodied, dislocated viewers, but very much a part of the scene as history becomes personal present narrative. Here, "desire" is a smoke screen hiding the deeper machinations of "private" property, appropriation, and exchange. Dreams become literal visitations – not dislocated wish fulfillments suited to the displacements of capitalist desire. Rather dreams are already actual encounters irrupting onto the scene like disavowed grandmothers: blindspotted "real stuff." As ancestors are re-membered differently, *other* histories, shared across the present pulse of a social nervous system as across the complicit space between performer and spectator, are thrown into sudden and violent relief.

What is old is new again.
We all have the same gift.
Every person has the gift
but may not always listen to the messages.
           from *Reverb-ber-ber-rations*

Epilog: returning from the dead

A writer – by which I mean . . . the subject of a praxis – must have the persistence of the watcher who stands at the crossroads of all other discourses, in a position that is *trivial in respect to purity* of doctrine (trivialis is the etymological attribute of the prostitute who waits at the intersection of three roads.)

> Tania Modleski quoting Shoshana Feldman quoting
> Roland Barthes (1991:52)

Though a commodity may at first sight appear to be "a very *trivial* thing, and easily understood . . . it is, in reality, a very queer thing, abounding in metaphysical subtleties and theological niceties."

> Luce Irigaray quoting Karl Marx (1985a:182)

If, as Irigaray cites Marx, the commodity appears trivial on "first sight," what is the "second sight" we might employ to re-mark our relations between subjects within the visual field and without? It is the "trivialized" or impure view from the blindspot of the prostituted, the primitivized, the commodified, that this exegesis on explicit body artists has hoped to address. In this book I have explored how feminist performers use their bodies beside themselves, as if for a second time, as a means of making explicit the historical staging of that body. As such, these performers interrogate the apprehensions of perspectival vision, the inscribed insatiability of the object of desire, and the constructed "savagery" of the body marked for race and gender.

But once apprehension is apprehended – its terms made literal, embodied – what then? What replaces *apprehension*, in the twin sense of fear and acquisition of the object, as we attempt to see otherwise, standing beside our historical inscriptions to see for a second time? Second sight might signal a Brechtian distancing by which the familiar is looked at again, made strange, and opened for critical inquiry. But second sight might also beckon the occluded eyes of the intuitive, psychic, superstitious, or ascientific reflexes of a feared vision, an intuition or embodied knowledge aligned with the fear of women. If second sight generally refers to the ability to see into the future, to foresee events before they unfold, what is a second sight that looks back? Entering into our fears – in the sense of excavating our modes of apprehension – can be a first step. But when modes of apprehension are unpacked for patriarchal fear and anxiety, what then? What is the second step?

If we only did away with perspective, with point of view as modus operandi of knowing, and devised an all-inclusive vision born of multiplicity, might we achieve a true universally inclusive way of knowing? Such a utopian endeavor would be, as Susan Bordo has pointed out, an impossible "view from nowhere," or conversely, a "dream of everywhere." In her essay "Feminism, Postmodernism, and Gender Skepticism," Bordo argues that we "need to guard against the view from nowhere supposition that if we only employ the right method we can avoid ethnocentrism, totalizing constructions, and false universalizations." Bordo goes on, however, to assert, with Nietzsche, that perspectivalism is, thus, the "only" way to see:

> [It] is an inescapable fact of human embodiment, as Nietzsche was the first to point out: "The eye . . . in which the active and interpreting forces, through which alone seeing becomes seeing something, are supposed to be lacking [is] an absurdity and a nonsense. There is only a perspectival seeing, *only* a perspectival knowing."
>
> (1993: 222)

Bordo reminds her readers that vision always bears social, political, and personal investments, "even in the desire to do justice to heterogeneity" (1993:223). And she is right. But her assumption that without perspectivalism we have only the absurdly utopian vacancy of "nowhere" is perhaps short sighted. Are there no other options?

In 1949 Simone de Beauvoir may have offered an alarmingly simple answer to this question. What perspectival models of vision based on surveillance and apprehension of the object cannot allow, she suggested, is the notion of reciprocity between subject and object. Reciprocity between subject and object is ultimately disavowed in traditional, Hegelian modes of apprehension. The disavowal of reciprocity – of mutual exchange between subject and object (which would become subject and subject, or object and object) – maintains the structural blindspots which prop insatiability and loss as modus operandi of exchange. In the fight for recognition that, for Hegel, "makes" man man, de Beauvoir asked: "How is it then, that reciprocity has not been recognized?"[1]

Reciprocity? It is arguably the current project of postcolonial and cultural critical studies to ask: What can reciprocity look like? How can we *do* it? How do we access this reciprocity in our approach to alterity, our approach to "objects" of study as well as our approach to our "selves"?[2] Reciprocity suggests a two-way street, but it does not necessarily reconstitute the delimiting binaries which feminists and postcolonial theorists have been fighting to undermine. Binaries such as subject and object, male and female, have been erected according to a hierarchical, oppositional structure. In 1986, excited by potential crossroads between feminism and deconstruction, Susan Suleiman argued that contemporary feminism should attempt to "get beyond, not only the number one – the number that determines unity of body or of self – but also to get beyond the number two, which determines difference, antagonism, and exchange." Looking beyond the number two, Suleiman turned to deconstruction and Derrida's "incalculable choreographies" to find, perhaps, the end of gender in an infinite range of possibility and combination, an "endless complication" and a "dizzying accumulation" (1986:24–5). But it is crucial to remember that the notion of infinite was instituted in relation to the prerogatives of the unitary perspective point, and, in league with commodity culture, successful in promoting the very dizzying insatiability of accumulation we experience in late capitalism, by which the "real" is always already insatiably lost.

If the number two is jettisoned in favor of the infinite, might we be missing a valuable site of reconceiving difference? Suleiman cites "two" as determining "antagonism." But this is painfully reminiscent of Hegel's premise that recognition must always involve a battle to the death – only one can be recognized when two are involved. But is antagonism the *only* mode of conceiving of difference between one and one? Or is there something imaginable as satiable in a mutual gaze, double vision, a hybrid pass, a two-way street, or even a "trivialis"? Performance, a medium of mimesis and exchange, has become a terrain well suited to this exploration because performance acknowledges the present moment of exchange between embodied participants, embedded in cultural codes.

Embedded in cultural codes. As I run the "subjects" of this book back across my mind, I think again about glitches and breaks. I watch for mutuality, reciprocity, complicity in the act of watching a woman writhing on a bed – writing performance artist Schneemann on the bed of her own film, in the frame of art, getting laid.

I write: Scratch, glitch, break.

And I watch for an access to the exchange between my viewing, my writing "self" and the artist/subject who writ(h)es before me, embedded in her own creation. But regardless of savvy in any positioning I can conjure, and regardless of the textual effort that stretches behind me and before me about the mechanisms of meaning and secrecy ghosting and informing the significances of any woman on any bed, my eyes continue to inhabit the familiar place of the lens, my mind infests the vacated space of these words, like the camera, the flash, doubling over the apparatus, standing in. Watching.

On comes the knee-jerk spasm of reflexivity, the habit of critical *hope* in locating myself in the scene. I take the predictable flight of the thinking viewer out of her immediate body to see herself seeing, hoping, again, that reflexivity might lead, somehow, to an acknowledgment of habitually disavowed reciprocity. If I can locate myself I might locate my relation to my object, laying the ground for something that might be called a two-way street.

Having fledged my wings on poststructuralism, I've taken this flight before. I see the back of my head in silhouette against the screen of my subject – the screened image of Schneemann on her bed with her lover – then, of course, I see myself seeing that silhouette – and then comes the rushing multiplication of alienated shadow selves sucking their essences away from the moment of sight, seeing themselves seeing themselves seeing themselves seeing in a concatenation of visuality, creating that by-now-familiar postmodern hall of mirrors with the reflections of Schneemann's lovemaking glowing in my thousand shadowy eyes, infinitely recessing.

As seeing selves multiply into and out of themselves, I sense the rush – a Barthesian *jouissance* – the exuberant death throes of the author, denouncing authority even as she attempts to locate herself. This reflexive flight is still a one-way attempt to see myself seeing, as I find myself ecstatically recessing from a simultaneously recessing, increasingly unattainable object. Endless desire. Impossible, insatiable love.

Impossible love? Insatiable desire? I have to stop and think: the scene of the commodity and the thrall to the vanishing point appear to reappear now in my very attempts to locate my viewing reflexively and I am left with the sense that reflexivity alone cannot insure reciprocal exchange. Reflexivity as an infinite flight away from the scene of viewing creates a thrall with the viewing self that is twin to the displacement of that self onto the viewed object in classic paradigms of perspective. To quote Judith Butler again: "The phallogocentric mode of signifying the female sex perpetually reproduces phantasms of its own self-amplifying desire" (1990b:12–13). Reflexivity is a one-way street running away from an intersection and, alone, it only re-marks reciprocity as impossible.

Slavoj Zizek refers to this dynamic of reflexivity as "lethal." As it is postulated in Lacanian psychoanalytic theory, reflexivity bears the potential of coming to know "too much," at the conclusion of which "terrifying experience . . . we may lose our very being:"

> [T]he subject can pay for such a [reflexive] reflection with the loss of his [sic] very ontological consistency. It is in this sense that the knowledge which we approach through psychoanalysis is impossible-real: we are on dangerous ground; in getting too close to it we observe suddenly how our consistency, our positivity, is dissolving itself . . . In other words, to abolish the mis-recognition [of the self and the object] means at the same time to abolish, to dissolve, the 'substance' which was supposed to hide itself behind the form-illusion of misrecognition.
>
> (1989:68)

In Lacanian theory, while the infinite recession of reflexivity purports to display the inevitable corruption of self-hood and its endless misrecognitions, it also threatens to abort any "real" or reciprocal exchange between subject and object. However illusory, misrecognized, or desire-ridden that subject and object appear to have been and to be, they are caught in a continual dissolve which results (and resulted in critical thought by the 1960s) in the general poststructural death of the author, death of the subject, the loss of "our very being."

The "terrifying experience" which Zizek extracts from Lacan leaves us with a subject who reflexively dissolves from subjecthood in direct relation to an infinitely recessing (impossible, misrecognized) object of desire. It leaves us squarely saddled with loss. As suggested in Chapter 4, poststructuralist and psychoanalytic impulses to dissolve the subject in the face of incessant mis-recognition of the object can be seen as relative to the socio-cultural scene of the subject and object in late capitalism, dependent upon the perpetual displacement of desire and the dynamics of a misrecognition posited as inevitable. The historical materialist intervention in this scene of corresponding dissolves is to suggest that we take a second look – a double take – at such habits of loss to see our thrall to loss as imbricated in a scene of historical–social–cultural–political–economic habituation, to see our thrall to misrecognition as socially inscribed. The result of this second look is, in Hal Foster's terms, a second death, or a second burial in that "the death of the subject is now dead in its turn" – by necessity, "the subject has returned" (1993:7).

This issue of the "return" of the subject, for a second time, after death, is key. In a late modernist conundrum of corresponding dissolves – the deaths of the subject and object – the political drive toward voice and agency became mired in a perpetually phantasmic dance of insatiable desire and repetitive loss. The question – the same question which had motivated Frankfurt School examinations of the space between Marx and Freud and which had influenced Fanon's inflections on Lacan – rises again *vis-à-vis* Lacanian feminism: Can the effort to speak to the dynamic of misrecognition move from one of self-perpetuating loss of the subject and object to one of political gain? Is the return from the lethal flight of reflexivity a return to the subject's body, reinhabiting that body with critical distance as it sits in classic apprehension of its object?

It seems to me that these questions pivot on a materialist point of distancing versus dissolve, criticism versus nostalgia. Privileging nostalgia, we double back over a scene of misrecognition to reinhabit the dynamic for the modernist, Eliotic purpose of "know[ing] it for the *first* time,"[3] finding an originary, constituting moment, thus repeating the whole scene as though for the first time, again and again, infinitely, in an ecstatic Nietzschean Eternal Return of the Same. Privileging critical analysis, we double back to know the scene for the *second* time, *in difference*, after death, as if beside the scene. The dead subject returns to interrupt the thrall to loss, interrupt the self-reflexive search for a transcendental self-same subject by introducing a juxtaposition, a "genealogy," of self-difference.[4]

To return to Foster's phrasing: "the death of the subject is now dead in its turn: the subject has returned." What can we make of this return from the dead? I would submit that the subject returns for a second time in direct relation to its own death, as if beside itself. Referring obliquely to postcolonialism, feminism, and queer theory, Foster writes that the subject returns "in the guise of a politics of new, ignored, and different subjectivities, sexualities, and ethnicities" (1993:7, 11, n13). Importantly, though he makes nothing of it, Foster uses the phrase "in the guise" of new subjectivities. This phrasing is important. The subject returns from its recessive poststructuralist death, but it returns removed, counter-mimetic, not as originary. The subject returns *as a subject's guise*, indeed *performative*, like a ghost in a body-suit, donned and wielded in a show of social and political significances, manipulating and bent on exposing the historical mechanisms of a social drama which has parsed its players, by bodily markings, into subjects and objects.

In an effort to understand the significance of this doubling back, this return from the dead, or this re-cognition of the dead as present, Foster examines the historical institution and differentiation of subject and object as one of "correct distancing." Charting the development of Western cultural concepts of self from Lacan's revisions of Freud in the 1930s through the poststructural death of the self in the 1960s and on to the present critical return of the self in its new intercultural or postcolonial constellation, Foster finds that throughout both anthropology and its domestic twin psychoanalysis the distance between self and other has been orchestrated and traversed solely from the perspective of the Western "self" in an attempt to delineate a difference from "others." Foster cites Franz Fanon with the admonition that never did a negotiation of "correct distance" come *in the other's terms* and Foster returns to Fanon to suggest that the current postcolonial return of the subject is one in which the subject returns as one who *has-been-other*, as one who has been the object of misrecognition as well as one who misrecognizes. That is, the subject returns as a subject subjected, conscious of complicity in the drama of othering. And yet, like the whore at the crossroads who is not a "proper" woman, this returning subject is not a proper subject at all, but precisely an improper, inappropriate subject, in the "guise" of subjectivity – making that subjectivity explicit as, literally, guise.

I began this exegesis on the subject's ghost – inspired at least in part by the literal ghost I encountered in my work on Spiderwoman – by returning to the subject of Chapter 1, a woman on a bed. Now, in the wake of poststructuralist dissolves, I try another return, boomeranglike, to the tactility of my own body, undissolved, embodied before the scene. Where am I? When I "saw" the absent presence of the ghost that led to my thoughts on Spiderwoman, I was in my own bed. Unseen by me, yet seen as unseen, the ghost provoked an encounter. But where am I when I sit before performance artists who employ excessive visibility? – the over-exposure of Sprinkle's cervix, the eye/body of Schneemann, the penis/baby of Freud/Finley?

Seated before *Fuses*, I watch Schneemann in her own bed in her film. I am, supposedly, unseen by Schneemann, who writhes with passion in the filmic traces of 1964. Watching in 1996, I'm a ghost from the future, looking in on the filmic traces of the past. Returning to my body in the scene of viewing I find myself sitting, unseen by Schneemann – yet anticipated, seen perhaps as unseen – a second time, afterwards – sensate, sentient, marked, and rapt before the image of Schneemann's body, wrapped against that of her lover, making art.

The personal, signaled by any return to "my" body, is not essential, hardly originary, never redemptive. It is not triumphant. Indeed the positing of "my" body is rather like the acknowledgment of your eyes, reader, upon this text – you, a ghost from the future. There is an audacity in such a citing, such a sighting, such a siting. There is the intersection of different routes leading to the same spot at a trivialis, and the smell of self-indulgence, that sometime ur-evil of academe. The interruptive, self-referential citing of "my body" – as if body bore weight here as a ghost – appears to trivialize, worse, to essentialize. Certainly to cast the inappropriate literal into the space of symbols between us. It is also to retread a well-worn road cut by years of feminist endeavor, dedicated to interrogating the terrors at the heart of our habits of knowledge.

Speaking of the space between reader and read – to suggest that in watching Schneemann on the bed in her film I am *not* as removed as "aesthetic distance" would hope, suggests that I am implicated as much as the future is foreseen by the past, or the past is *foreseen* by the future – as it stretches before me as scene of my inquiry. Such a suggestion summons all the creepy crawly ghost-inferences of "second sight" at the same time that it heralds the critical potential of seeing again, differently. Second sight threatens any neat, linear distinction between times and spaces, even as it insists on historical context and precise location. The problematics of "my body," therefore, is an attempt to acknowledge the effort at reciprocity which struggles against the grain of text, against the grain of how we habitually write and read to mean. Of course the question arises: do we re-turn to something as problematical and essentialist as body writing – "feminine writing" – as libidinal as slippage and antinarrative – as fraught as unintelligibility? Or can we conceive of ghost writing? Perhaps the summoning of "body" is to summon and wrestle with the legacies of subjectivity and objectivity which, having marked bodies in social relation, continue to haunt us. Perhaps summoning the body is an effort to make disembodiment take form before us – to struggle with the cloak of the text itself that continues to *assume* disembodiment.

The material body of the viewing subject (or the subject of the body) is performative – nested in context, in time, in habits of apprehension. Yet to "return" to that which can never have left is oxymoronic. It is the troubled re-turn of the seeing subject to find "himself" relentlessly marked. When the subject throws off his thrall to disembodiment, as if returning from the dead, he finds himself precisely, inexorably, relentlessly in historical context. "He" returns to find his supposedly disinterested gaze always already attached to his privilege and his privilege attached to his mode of apprehension – his "perspective." Perhaps the writer returns to discover that he is countenanced, as written as that which he writes about. Perhaps he finds that he is she, that she is white, and that these things bear weight, impact even as he resists the essentialism such weight threatens to assume. The subject returns recognizing that the "guise" of authority has been the cloak of subjectivity, and that that cloak has afforded him *the privilege to assume invisibility*. The subject returns with his baggage, his author-ity exposed as guise. He totes his worn-out cloak, his outmoded veil which lies across his arm. He is facing something now as troubling as his own body facing other bodies – and when he cannot recognize his own, he trembles. His has been, after all, the privilege of misrecognition, even as he assumed he was misrecognizing only the "other." His has been the troubled privilege to refuse reciprocity, to refuse, quoting Audre Lorde again, "to *recognize* difference as a crucial strength" (1981b:100).

I return, then, to find myself sitting, again, before my material – Schneemann's explicit lovemaking, Sprinkle's winking cervix, Finley's overt literality, Mendieta's embodied erasure, Spiderwoman's political sacrality. I am surprised (and a little dismayed) to find myself toting the guise of a subject, returned from the dead. I examine the worn-out cloak, the privilege to misrecognize. Pressing his vision through blood-stained sockets, the bedraggled Western Man in his Tragic Drama of Selfhood, his tragedy of misrecognition attributed to "fate" . . .

A woman on a bed. Misrecognized.
A drama at the intersection of roads.

A misreading, picking out a particular, re-dressing a ghost: Oedipus saw an ur-blindspot – maternal pleasure – and, seeing that he had seen, he blinded himself. When he recognized misrecognition and saw that his lover was his mother, that his mother was his lover, he had seen "too much." His literal blinding was a physical concretizing of the blindness he had previously maintained through misrecognition. As such, his self-blinding was a literal rendering of a blindness he had already known. In the Oedipal sense, blindness is akin to vision as misrecognition, and as such it keeps us from acknowledging that which must not be seen or that which can, remembering Schneemann, "hardly be seen."

Significantly for feminist inquiry, the drama of Western cultural loss and misrecognition has been played out across the stage of the body and its ultimate disavowal. It is a drama based on the tired mandate that coagulates the bodily as the literal detail, the literal as the terrifyingly finite, the penetrated, the feminized. It is a drama which has scripted a moral injunction, outlined by Irigaray: "Neither as mother nor as virgin nor as prostitute has woman any right to her own pleasure" (1985a:186). We can conjecture: Oedipus' crime was/is that he saw/sees his mother's sexual pleasure – or, that his *mother* knows the power of her own pleasure. This, of course, among other crimes, but this, of course, as base (at least for modern appropriations of the myth). The agency of mature women (whether or not we are biological mothers), and explicitly our active satiability, our finitude, has been, as we have explored, a site of anxiety in representation, linked with racisms of primitivity, excesses of prostitution, castration, and death by blinding. Taboos on recognizing maternal satisfaction – and especially on seeing that a "mother" can *know/see/remark* her own pleasure (in representation) – ghost the scene of a body marked female. Importantly, this taboo on satiate, embodied maternal pleasure doubles as a taboo on mental productivity/textual pleasure of mature women. Even Sade, who was not known for a lack of imagination, could not imagine committing the ur-taboo – the taboo of conceiving of mothers as "philosophers" (see Gallop 1988:3; Irigaray 1985a:198–204; Modleski 1991:48). Indeed, Sade's entire host of committed sins arguably served to epiphanize modernity's emergent primary taboo: *mother-philosophy* as the ultimately uncommittable transgression, the holiest of holy blindspots.

It is into such sacred blindspots, as into the patriarchally unimaginable, that feminist inquiry continues to press. What is the terror that marks this unimaginable? *See whose face it wears. See whose face it wears. See whose face it wears* (Lorde 1981b:101). When we bust out of the given habits of vision, given modes of apprehension, we collapse a terror-marked host of symbolic signposts. We find ourselves straddling the divide between the symbolic order and the literal renderings that it disavows, disallows, blinds and secret(e)s. Thus we invoke a certain psychosis, a hysteria certainly – an encounter with the "unnatural" as we press ourselves into an inspection of the cracks (Buck-Morss 1989:290). For women, figured historically as always already different, aberrant, cracked, this project is deeply unsettling in its classic double bind. Figured as already aberrant, different, we potentially illustrate and prop that inscription by courting aberrance, difference – by promoting cracks. Explicating *while* illustrating this double bind is the project of feminist performance artists of the explicit body who present their bodies as stretched across this paradox like canvases across the framework of the Symbolic Order.

After all, the historical materialist has stood separately from the object and asked how to "invest" it with a gaze which looks back (Benjamin 1973:148). But the *marked* materialist feels the slap of this question (see Martin 1990). The materialist marked with the presumptions of, say, gender – the "female" materialist facing a feminized "object" – does not bear as easily the (dubious) privilege of standing separately, even as she stands beside her representation to take a second look. She is asking this question of her own object status, the representation which precedes her. Her standing separately from that object, her critical distance, is as distant as one ever gets from one's own shadow, which is to say, not distant at all – even as it is, deeply, critical. The object that is "invested" with vision will be an object in which she is deeply invested. That we must explicate our "investments" for hosts of blindspots propping privileges, for imbrications of race, ethnicity, and class as well as gender, is to insist on ushering a complex host of ghosts who had been relegated to the wings out onto the stage, again and again. For the feminist materialist "reciprocity" becomes a project of recognizing the ricochet of gazes, and the histories of who-gets-to-see-what-where. The invested object will be, to some degree, *both* separate from *and* relative to herself in her general struggle with historical legacies of disembodiment – paradoxical and impossible as she is, being, herself, the previously unimaginable: philosopher *and* mother, prostitute *and* historical materialist, in one.

One which is, of course, not one. Never only one.

Notes

1 BINARY TERROR AND THE BODY MADE EXPLICIT

1 See Steven C. Dubin, *Arresting Images: Impolitic Art and Uncivil Actions* (New York: Routledge, 1992): 159–96; Peggy Phelan, "Money Talks," *The Drama Review* (Spring 1990): 4–15, and "Money Talks, Again," *The Drama Review* (Fall 1991): 131–42; Carol S. Vance, "The War on Culture," *Art in America* (September 1989): 39–45, and "Misunderstanding Obscenity," *Art in America* (May 1990): 49–55; Elizabeth Hess, "Backing Down: Behind Closed Doors at the NEA," *Village Voice*, 25 September 1991: 37; and C. Carr, "War on Art," *Village Voice*, 5 June 1990: 25–8.

2 Feminist debates about pornography are wide-ranging. See the collection *Take Back the Night: Women On Pornography*, ed. Laura Lederer (New York: Morrow, 1980), which includes all the important documents from the first wave of anti-porn feminism. See *Pleasure and Danger: Exploring Female Sexuality*, ed. Carole S. Vance (Boston: Routledge and Kegan Paul, 1983) for a collection of early essays complicating the anti-porn position. See *Women Against Censorship*, ed. Varda Burstyn (Vancouver: Douglas and McIntyre, 1985), and a special issue of *Social Text* (Winter 1993), ed. Anne McClintock, exploring the sex trade. See also Gail Pheterson, ed., *A Vindication of the Rights of Whores* (Seattle: Seal Press, 1989) and Frederique Delacoste and Priscilla Alexander, eds, *Sex Work: Writings By Women in the Sex Industry* (San Francisco: Cleis Press, 1987).

3 Theodor Adorno writes on the forcefield of antimonies in *Prisms* (London: Neville Spearman, 1967). See also Susan Buck-Morss, *The Origin of Negative Dialectics: Theodor Adorno, Walter Benjamin, and the Frankfurt Institute* (New York: The Free Press, 1977): 49; and Martin Jay, *The Dialectical Imagination* (Boston: Little, Brown, and Company, 1973): 69.

4 "The best way I can think to carry out this idea of danger on stage is the . . . unexpected transition from a mental image to a real image." Antonin Artaud, from "The Theater and Its Double", in *Antonin Artaud: Selected Writings* (Berkeley: University of California Press, 1988): 235–6. On Frankfurt School fascination with the space between mind and matter see Susan Buck-Morss, *The Origin of Negative Dialectics: Theodor Adorno, Walter Benjamin, and the Frankfurt Institute*, (New York: The Free Press, 1977): 43–110, especially pp. 85–8.

5 The following quote from Theodor Adorno is relevant to this discussion of frame and form: "Works of art do not lie; what they say is literally true. Their reality however lies in the fact that they are answers to questions brought before them from outside. The tension in art therefore has meaning only in relation to the tension outside. The fundamental layers of artistic experience are akin to the objective world from which art recoils. The unresolved antagonisms of reality appear in art in the guise of immanent problems of artistic form." Adorno goes on to say that debates

about form, and not content, define art's relationship to society. Form is the site of debate not because it can be distinguished from content, but because it shapes, frames, molds, and "decides" content according to social formations. *Aesthetic Theory* (New York: Routledge and Kegan Paul, 1984): 8.

6   On the shift from modernist avant-garde art modes of "transgression" to postmodern modes of interrogation which investigate "the processes and apparatuses" of art forms, see Hal Foster, "For a Concept of the Political in Contemporary Art," *Recodings: Art, Spectacle, Cultural Politics* (Port Townsend, WA: Bay Press, 1985): 153. I have used the term "interrogate" here. Foster uses the term "resist" in distinction to modernism's "transgress," but does not claim that all postmodern art promotes resistant readings. See his distinction between reactionary and resistant postmodernism in *The Anti-Aesthetic* (Port Townsend, WA: Bay Press 1983): xii.

7   See Kobena Mercer, "Looking for Trouble," *Transition* 51 (1991):184–97 and "Reading Racial Fetishism: The Photographs of Robert Mapplethorpe," *Fetishism as Cultural Discourse* (Ithaca: Cornell University Press, 1993). I use the "mimesis" here with some caution, not wanting to suggest that the pleasure is "fake" or "false" as much as to suggest that it is lexical, imbricated in a signifying discourse of pleasure. The expression is so standard and legible that it is as much a controlled reference to female *jouissance* (interestingly posited by Lacan as that which must escape signification, perhaps another reason for the social taboo on porn), as it is to the lexical structure that contains that expression – that is, a lexical reference to the venue of porn.

8   See Judith Williamson "Images of Woman," *Screen* 24 (November 1983); Abigail Solomon-Godeau, "Suitable for Framing: The Critical Recasting of Cindy Sherman," *Parkett* no. 29 (1991); Peggy Phelan *Unmarked* (New York: Routledge, 1993): 60–70; and *Cindy Sherman: 1975–1993* (New York: Rizzoli, 1993).

9   Theodor Adorno, *Aesthetic Theory* (New York: Routledge, 1984): 29. Adorno states (p. 31) succinctly that the phenomenon of this thrall is "a historical product. In its original economic setting, novelty is that characteristic of consumer goods . . . The new in art is the aesthetic counterpart to the expanding reproduction of capital in society. Both hold out the promise of undiminished plenitude."

10 The term "reality effects" is taken from Roland Barthes, "The Reality Effect," *The Rustle of Language* (Berkeley: University of California Press, 1989). I use the term, however, in an inversion of Barthes's usage. Barthes was explicating textual effects of the detail, utilized in naturalist texts to speak of the real. I use the term to indicate the way in which the perception of the real is indeed effected through the historical accumulation of cultural texting. I also use the term to refer to the way text and image bear effect on persons in a cultural complex of mimesis and alterity. Writing on gender Klaus Theweleit has used the phrase "reality production," culled from Deleuze and Guattari. See Theweleit, *Male Fantasies* (Minneapolis: University of Minnesota Press, 1987). I prefer the term "effect" to "product" for, while it loses some allusion to capitalist machinations, it nonetheless retains a sense of impact and concrete, visceral immediacy – in a sense, the effect of the production of the real.

11 The long-standing modern privilege afforded vision and visual perspective – or better, the instituting of a one-way modality for visuality – has propped the supremacy of objectification as the prime Western cultural mode of knowledge, contributing to the dynamics maintaining "others" and "selves." Though there are many debates on when and whether Cartesian perspectival ocularcentrism has been outmoded or whether it persists, albeit reconfigured to meet the pressures of modernization, the fact remains that the trope of perspective and the disinterest it promotes are extremely important ingredients of Western culture. See Martin Jay, *Downcast Eyes* (Berkeley: University of California Press, 1993) for an argument on the demise of perspectivalism and Jonathan Crary's *Techniques of the Observer* (Cambridge, MA: MIT Press, 1991), for an argument on its reconfiguration. There is a very large body of work on

perspective historically, including Panovsky's *Perspective as Symbolic Form* (New York: Zone Books, 1991). For some contemporary treatments generally, see Hal Foster, ed., *Vision and Visuality* (Seattle: Bay Press, 1988); Evelyn Fox Keller and Christine Grontkowski, "The Mind's Eye," *Discovering Reality: Feminist Perspectives on Epistemology, Metaphysics, Methodology, and Philosophy of Science* (Dordrecht: D. Reidel, 1983). As a result of critiques of perspectivalism across the twentieth century, a host of alternatives has been suggested. Anthropology, for example, has seen emphases placed on sensual perception other than vision explicitly to offset the "antipersonalist orientation of visualism" (Fabian in Emily Martin, "Science and Women's Bodies: Forms of Anthropological Knowledge," *Body/Politics* (New York: Routledge, 1990): 69, such as Ong's emphasis on the aural, Clifford's later emphasis on "discursive " or vocal and gestic expression, and Taussig's exploration of tactility, including tactility in vision. See Taussig, "Physiognomic Aspects of Visual Worlds," *Visualizing Theory* (New York: Routledge, 1994). However, the legacy of perspectivalism can be traced even into alternative modes, such as visual tactility, and we have to caution repeatedly against our ready desire to jettison ourselves beyond our histories, as if those histories could not continue to ghost and inform our "new" ways of viewing, inscribing, knowing bodies in social, cultural, and political space.

12 Deborah Tannen, "Markers: Wears Jump Suit, Sensible Shoes, Uses Husband's Last Name," *New York Times Magazine*, 20 June 1993. Peggy Phelan, *Unmarked: The Politics of Performance* (New York: Routledge, 1993). In *Unmarked*, Phelan is so sensitive to the problematic of passing from visibility that she argues against the grain of the effort to "see" at all, advocating an active vanishing and suggesting a feminist anti-perspective born of the generative force of blindness.

13 For an analysis of the intersection between formalism and modern science see Paul C. Vitz and Arnold B. Glimcher *Modern Art and Modern Science: The Parallel Analysis of Vision* (New York: Praeger, 1984). On the science-inspired, social Darwinist bases of naturalism, see Emile Zola's treatises "The Experimental Novel" and "Naturalism in the Theater," in Becker, ed., *Documents of Modern Literary Realism* (Princeton, NJ: Princeton University Press, 1963).

14 See Linda Nochlin, *Realism* (New York: Penguin, 1971). See Marianna Torgovnick, *Gone Primitive* (Chicago: University of Chicago Press, 1990); Hal Foster "The 'Primitive' Unconscious in Modern Art," *October* 34 (1985); Susan Hiller, ed., *The Myth of Primitivism* (New York: Routledge, 1991); and William Rubin, ed., *"Primitivism" in 20th-Century Art* (New York: Museum of Modern Art, 1984). See especially Rosalind Krauss, "No More Play" in *The Originality of the Avant-Garde and Other Modernist Myths* (Cambridge, MA: MIT Press, 1988).

15 Also of interest regarding Olympia's non-agency is the feminist attempt to "find" the woman, Victorine Meurent, who posed for Manet's rendering. See the novel/art history/autobiography *Alias Olympia*, by Eunice Lipton (New York: Charles Scribner's Sons, 1992).

16 On the double nature inscribed to women see Sandra Gilbert and Susan Gubar, *Madwoman in the Attic: The Woman Writer and the Nineteenth-Century Literary Imagination* (New Haven: Yale University Press, 1979); Luce Irigaray, *This Sex Which Is Not One* (Ithaca, NY: Cornell University Press, 1985). On women of color as already "fallen" see Patricia Hill Collins, *Black Feminist Thought: Knowledge, Consciousness, and the Politics of Empowerment* (New York: Routledge, 1990): 170–1; bell hooks, *Black Looks: Race and Representation* (Boston: South End Press, 1992):160; Lauren Berlant, "National Brands/National Body," *Comparative American Identities: Race, Sex, and Nationality in the Modern Text*, ed. Hortense J. Spillers (New York: Routledge, 1991).

17 There is no positive female-identified correlative for the word "virile" which aligns masculine sexuality with positive, powerful creativity. According to Webster's Ninth New Collegiate Dictionary, to be virile is to be energetic, vigorous, forceful and to

be "capable of functioning as a male in copulation." I have chosen the word passion, though it is clearly inadequate to convey the notion of a positive and powerful woman-identified sexual force.

18 We can look to 1963 as a watershed point at which a number of women began loudly to defy the structural impossibility of being both women *and* artists. See Sally Banes's *Greenwich Village 1963: Avant-Garde Performance and the Effervescent Body* (Durham, NC: Duke University Press, 1993) which posits 1963 as a general watershed year in the arts at the intersection between modernism and postmodernism.

19 Schneemann, interview with author, February 1996.

20 In the later years of the 1950s and the early 1960s, art practice was actively mingling with the performative under the general formalist rubric of "actions" in Happenings, Events, and Fluxus. Direct precedents were the early 1950s action paintings of Jackson Pollock, James Waring's dance, and John Cage's music and collaborative work. Cage had organized the important multimedia event at Black Mountain College in 1952, at which painter Robert Rauschenberg, dancer Merce Cunningham, and others joined together for collaborative experimentation in repetition, alogical structures, simultaneous events, and the material of the quotidian world. The examples set by these experiments would prove foundational to American experimentation in the blurring of aesthetic forms. Also influential were the Gutai group, originated in 1951 in Osaka, Japan, by Jiro Yoshihara, devoted to the actualization of spirit in matter. Images were generated, for example, by rolling around in mud or shooting canvases with arrows. This work directly influenced Allan Kaprow, who had studied with John Cage and who, in 1959, inaugurated American Happenings. Kaprow published images of Gutai work in *Assemblage, Environments, and Happenings* (New York: Abrams, 1966). See also Kirby, *Happenings* (New York: Dutton, 1965); and Martin Duberman, *Black Mountain: An Exploration in Community* (New York: Doubleday, Anchor Books, 1973): 370–9. Dick Higgins coined the phrase "intermedia" with his influential essay "Intermedia" on Fluxus in 1966. See Mariellen Sandford, ed., *Happenings and Other Acts* (New York: Routledge, 1995) for a collection of primary documents.

Of course, the history of performance art can be traced further back than the 1950s. Precedents are numerous and complex and include Russian Constructivists, Italian Futurists, and Zurich Dadaists in the early part of the twentieth century. The "place" of women as it was articulated and then historicized in these movements has always been tenuous. Highly influential women were relegated to the status of "spouse" or "lover" or "muse" or "try-hard." See Susan Rubin Suleiman, *Subversive Intent: Gender, Politics, and the Avant-Garde* (Cambridge, MA: Harvard University Press, 1990) on the influence, status, and erasure of women in the historical avant-garde.

21 The major visual art movement of the 1940s and 1950s, Abstract Expressionism, which effectively shifted the center of the avant-garde to New York City, was made up virtually entirely of male artists. Its most successful direct descendants in the 1960s, Minimalism and Pop Art, were also male dominated, with only one or two female members counted among participants. See the lists of recognized members in Diana Crane, *Transformation of the Avant-Garde* (Chicago: University of Chicago Press, 1987): 153–7, and pp. 28–9, 40, 57. Schneemann's sense of being a "cunt mascot" in a male clique was not directed at Judson Church which was largely composed of dancers in a medium with a heritage of female involvement. Her anger was directed at the art circles of Fluxus and Happenings that surrounded Judson. Fluxus, a neo-Dada movement, performances of which date between 1962 and 1970, was actually more inclusive of women than avant-garde movements preceding it, yet the demarcations of appropriate and inappropriate expression often corresponded to explicit gender coding.

22 Schneemann actually wanted to make her status as image interrogate the authority of any image maker, almost to the point of disavowing her position as artist in favor

of her active object status. She wrote in *Cezanne, She was a Great Painter*, a 1975 self-published book, that she was an "image, but not an Image-Maker" because she was "creating my own self-image."

23 See Elin Diamond, "Realism and Hysteria: Toward a Feminist Mimesis," *Discourse* 13, no. 1 (1990/91): 59–92. See the provocative collection *The Hysterical Male: New Feminist Theory*, edited by Arthur and Marilouise Kroker (New York: St. Martins Press, 1991). See Mady Schutzman, "The Aesthetics of Hysteria: Performance, Pathology, and Advertising" (Ph.D. dissertation, New York University, 1994).

24 Schneemann, *More Than Meat Joy*. 52. Though she had been involved in the inception of Fluxus in New York, she was officially excommunicated by Fluxus's founder George Maciunus for "expressionist tendencies" which he considered messy. Schneemann has written that George Maciunus found her to be a "terrifying female" and banished her to the Happenings realm, only paradoxically to admit Wolf Vostell and Claus Oldenburg (equally "messy") as welcome guests. Maciunus printed a note officially excommunicating Schneemann in the dense Flux papers. In Europe, Schneemann's work was always treated as Flux-inclusive, but in America she found herself consistently excluded. To this day Schneemann still considers some of her work "Flux-affiliated," which is to say, if not pure Fluxus, then "based within and configuring the community aesthetic – projects, editions, collaborations, performances." From letter to Liz Armstrong, Walker Art Museum, June 1992, Schneemann personal archives. See also Kristine Stiles, "Between Water and Stone," *In the Spirit of Fluxus*. 98, n80.

25 The cultural alignment of active/passive along gender lines has been amply explored. Freud himself attempted to unpack the alignment in his essay "Femininity," *New Introductory Lectures on Psychoanalysis* (New York: W.W. Norton, 1965). In 1975 Laura Mulvey took up the issue in her extremely influential essay "Visual Pleasure and Narrative Cinema" in which she analyzed that alignment relative to paradigms of spectatorship and representation (*Screen* 16, no. 3).

26 On paint-brush-as-phallus see Carol Duncan, "The Aesthetics of Power in Modern Erotic Art," *Feminist Art Criticism* (New York: Icon Editions, 1988): 62. "The actors were all men," comes from Norman O. Brown, prime wielder of the "pen as phallus" metaphor, who cites Levi-Strauss on the primacy of the male as active agent in *Love's Body* (New York: Random House, 1966): 23. See Mary Ann Doane on the split "mode of entry" between narcissism and transvestitism classically established for women relative to representation of the female body. "The 'Woman's Film': Possession and Address," *Revision: Essays in Feminist Film Criticism* (Los Angeles: The American Film Institute, 1984). Doane writes of this split relative to women as spectators, but the same can be argued relative to women as authors/artists, the most influential treatment of this being Sandra M. Gilbert and Susan Gubar's *The Madwoman in the Attic* (New Haven: Yale University Press, 1979).

27 Judy Chicago's *Red Flag* (1971) is a lithograph depicting an extreme close-up of part of a hand, a thigh, and a dark pubic shadow. "It was an image of a woman's hand pulling a bloody Tampax out of her vagina. I tried to make the image as overt as I could, and even then some people interpreted the Tampax as a bloody penis, a testament to the damage done to our perceptual powers by the absence of images of female reality." Judy Chicago, *Through the Flower: My Struggles as a Woman Artist* (New York: Penguin Books, 1993 [1975]): 135–6.

2 LOGIC OF THE TWISTER, EYE OF THE STORM

1 See Walter Benjamin, *Charles Baudelaire: A Lyric Poet in the Era of High Capitalism* (London: New Left Books, 1973). See also George Bataille, "The Pineal Eye," on his effort to recognize himself "in the virulence of his own phantasms," *Visions of*

Excess (Minneapolis: University of Minnesota Press, 1985): 80. Of course, this sense of waking into the dream has also been utilized by psychoanalytic feminists. Though in a nearly inverse fashion from Benjamin, Lacan points to the way awakening from a dream means waking to the fact that one has been dreaming simultaneously as we wake to reality, and the "real" is thus oddly constituted, "enveloped," by the dream. Unlike Benjamin, Lacan is speaking of the dreaming subject versus the dreamscapes of the modernist collective, but the commonality is compelling. The real, for Lacan then, is relative to the dreamscape, hidden by it. He writes: "How can we fail to see that awakening works in two directions – and that the awakening that re-situates us in a constituted and represented reality carries out two tasks? The real has to be sought beyond the dream – in what the dream has enveloped, hidden from us, behind the lack of representation of which there is only one representative" (*Four Fundamental Concepts of Psychoanalysis* (New York: W.W.Norton, 1981): 60). For Benjamin, after Marx, waking to the dream will afford a glimpse of the way capitalist reality is *constructed*, the way the real is brought into its effects through dreamscapes. For Benjamin the "real" is apprehendable, therefore, as that which is effected, secrete-ed, by the ruses of social dreamscapes. Lacan's concern, after Freud, was with the subject and his desire, rather than collective dreamscapes informing and instituting said subjects and desires. In extreme distinction to Benjamin, then, the real is always relative to the subject and can only be apprehended as missing, as lack – apprehension of any real is always already apprehension in terms of fear, and anxiety thus dictates that the real is an encounter always missed, deferred, occluded. The real then falls by the wayside as impossible, whereas for historical materialist Benjamin the real actually accumulates, like dust, as only too possible. Despite these differences, however, the sense of awakening to the dream, either through the materialist or the psychoanalytic agenda, has deeply influenced feminist inquiry.

2 Lynda Hart has explored this "awakening" in terms of acknowledging the terms and terrains of "hallucination." She writes: "If the Symbolic Order is the social order of a masculine imaginary, within its terms lesbian identities are hallucinations. When they nonetheless appear they indicate that the Symbolic Order is itself a fantasy construction" ("Identity and Seduction: Lesbians in the Mainstream," *Acting Out: Feminist Performances* (Ann Arbor: University of Michigan Press, 1993): 135).

3 In line with the structural veilings of dreamscapes, Irigaray explicated the ways in which the ban on homosexual expression and the compulsory dictates of hetero-sexuality veil the "hom(m)osexual" workings of an economic and political system which privileges same sex engagement, a hom(m)osociality of men, *homme*, or "man" (*This Sex Which Is Not One* (Ithaca, NY: Cornell University Press, 1985):192–4).

4 For an analysis of the transition from "transgression" to "resistance" as political strategy in contemporary art see Hal Foster "For a Concept of the Political in Contemporary Art," *Recodings: Art, Spectacle, Cultural Politics* (Port Townsend, WA: Bay Press, 1985).

5 See Teresa de Lauretis, *Technologies of Gender* (Bloomington: Indiana University Press, 1987): 3. Bestiality may imply an unsettling of gender coding from sexuality as it is strictly marked upon the human body, but a significant amount of work has been done on the ways in which animals are feminized in human discourse, closely linked to the status of woman as more primitive, more animal, than man. See Donna Haraway, *Primate Visions: Gender, Race, and Nature in the World of Modern Science* (New York: Routledge, 1989), and Suzanne Kappeler's "Why Look at Women," building on John Berger's "Why Look at Animals" in *The Pornography of Representation* (Cambridge: Polity Press, 1986). See Hazel V. Carby on the delineations of animality across racial distinctions vis-à-vis women of color, *Reconstructing Womanhood* (New York: Oxford University Press, 1987). Writing on the differing ways black women and white women are constructed in heterosexual pornography, Patricia Hill Collins writes: "As objects white women become creations

of culture – in this case, the mind of white men – using the materials of nature – in this case, uncontrolled female sexuality. In contrast, as animals Black women receive no such redeeming dose of culture and remain open to the type or exploitation visited on nature overall." Collins is quoted in Kate Davy's important essay "Outing Whiteness: A Feminist/Lesbian Project," *Theater Journal* 47, no.2 (May 1995): 195. Schneemann's bestiality in the frame of art can be said to beckon toward a deeper reading of gender and animality (or primitivity).

6 Interview with author, June 1992.

7 See Slavoj Zizek on this foreclosure and resultant symptomatology in Lacanian analysis, in *The Sublime Object of Ideology* (New York: Verso, 1989): 73–5. See also Lynda Hart on hallucination, or "the return of the real that has never been signified," in "Identity and Seduction: Lesbians in the Mainstream," *Acting Out* (New York: Routledge, 1993).

8 This condition of "women" as a function of patriarchal representation is the historical legacy of women being "killed into art." See Gilbert and Gubar, *Madwoman in the Attic* (New Haven: Yale University Press, 1979): 14–17. See also Laurie A. Finke "Painting Women: Images of Femininity in Jacobean Tragedy," *Performing Feminisms* (Baltimore: Johns Hopkins Press, 1990); and Elizabeth Bronfen, *Over Her Dead Body* (New York: Routledge, 1992).

9 It cannot be insignificant that it is just as women and people of color increasingly gained access to spheres of production after 1968 that Baudrillard-identified postmodernism claimed the death of modern foundational distinctions between "sex" and "work." See *Simulacra and Simulation* (Ann Arbor: University of Michigan Press, 1994): 18. Also proclaimed defunct were distinctions betweeen production and consumption, public and private, active and passive (p. 31), "real" and "imaginary" (p. 12) – even the "end of perspectival and panoptic space" which is, supposedly, an end to "power" (pp. 30, 19). Baudrillard is exemplary of a general postmodern valorization of feminine negativity, a valorization which simply recapitulates the old equation of the feminine with lack, reinscribing the feminine at the now championed (now subversive) vanishing point of meaning. Upholding the logic of the vanishing point *as gendered*, Baudrillard thus reinscribes perspectivalism even as he attempts to declare its death. See Jane Gallop, "French Theory and the Seduction of Feminism," *Men in Feminism*, ed. A Jardine and P. Smith (New York: Routledge, 1989): 113; Judith Butler, "Contingent Foundations: Feminism and the Question of 'Postmodernism,'" *Praxis International* 11, no. 2 (July 1991): 150–7; Teresa de Lauretis, *Technologies of Gender* (Bloomington: Indiana University Press, 1987): 23. Baudrillard might be read as representative of an anxiety born of women's entry into realms of production. As "she" strays across realms of distinction between production and consumption, she apparently destroys the distinction between the categories themselves, illustrating the intensity of her service as lynchpin. This destruction can be promising and ultimately empowering (Butler 1990b), or it can signal a broadly based vacating of empowerment as possible at all (Baudrillard 1981).

10 *The Prometheus Project* was extremely influential for Sprinkle. Though Sprinkle had appeared in an art venue at the Furnace in *Deep Inside Porn Stars* (see Chapter 1), her performance in *The Prometheus Project* set the stage for her one-woman show. Richard Schechner has said that he "discovered" Sprinkle while on a field trip with NYU Performance Studies graduate students to Times Square where she was performing her Nurse Sprinkle routine in a burlesque house. Schechner asked her to bring her Nurse act to his downtown "art" project. She did. In Schechner's *Prometheus*, Sprinkle played Io as well as Nurse Sprinkle. As Nurse Sprinkle she walked about the audience and handed a magnifying glass to spectators in their seats (mostly men) and asked them to inspect her genitalia. The magnifying glass set the stage for the "Public Cervix Announcement," a phrase Sprinkle adopted in

1989 after C. Carr coined it in a review of *Post Porn Modernism* (Carr 1993: 176).

11 See Lacan on the gaze, *Four Fundamental Concepts of Psychoanalysis* (New York: W.W. Norton, 1981): 67–119. See Sartre's essay "The Look," which constitutes the gaze as the agent of authority relative to the "shame" of an object, implicitly marking the gaze not only as phallic but decidedly subject to anxiety, in *Being and Nothingness* (New York: Pocket Books, 1966). Lacan and Sartre were both building on Kojève's reading of Hegel's master/slave narrative and are arguably delimited by Hegel's paradigm of selfhood. Hegel articulates the anxious battle of the gaze as a battle for selfhood, but delimits selfhood to a paradigm which cannot admit *reciprocity between* subject and object, but only a shame-driven struggle for domination. (Alexandre Kojève, *Introduction to the Reading of Hegel* (Ithaca, NY: Cornell University Press, 1969).)

3   PERMISSION TO SEE

1 Some scholars have theorized photography as a breakdown of perspectivalism due to its temporality and the flattening of space. See John Berger, *Ways of Seeing* (New York: Penguin Books, 1972): 18; Paul C. Vitz and Arnold B. Glimcher, *Modern Art and Modern Science: The Parallel Analysis of Vision* (New York: Praeger, 1984): 50; Martin Jay, *Downcast Eyes: The Denigration of Vision in Twentieth-Century Thought* (Berkeley: University of California Press, 1993): 137. It is possible to argue, however, that in some important ways photography has not broken with perspectival tradition, but leaves us still in its thrall. The meanings and effects of the camera obscura, the apparatus at the roots of photography, are inherently related to perspective, if not synonymous with it; see Jonathan Crary, *Techniques of the Observer* (Cambrige, MA: MIT Press, 1991): 33–4. Crary writes of the camera obscura as "decorporialized" vision: "The camera obscura a priori prevents the observer from seeing his or her position as part of the representation" (1991:41). Crary argues that later developments in science and photography generated the corporealization of the viewer, and thus broke with the camera obscura model of an absent observer. In the nineteenth century, vision was increasingly approached as physiological, and thus the image before the viewer became an image "which now belongs to the eye." Yet, the locating of vision in the eye, and Crary's resultant corporealization of the viewer, can be seen in at least one respect as continuous with a perspectival model in that the image remains subservient to the eye, indeed now entirely subject to its conditions. Though the viewer may be corporealized, unlike the veiled perspectival or camera obscura viewer, the *viewed* continues to have no agency in interaction. See Susan Sontag on photography as extending the dissociated, voyeuristic eye of the "flaneur," a way of seeing linked to perspectivalism, in *On Photography* (New York: Farrar, Straus, and Giroux, 1977): 55.

2 On the deeply ingrained link between habits of vision and habits of verbalization see Michael Argyle and Mark Cook, *Gaze and Mutual Gaze* (Cambridge: Cambridge University Press, 1976): 88–9. See Teresa de Lauretis on the gendering of narrative structure, "Desire in Narrative," in *Alice Doesn't* (Bloomington: Indiana University Press, 1985).

3 The heterosexual imperative is actually, in Luce Irigaray's terms, a ruse of the more "hom(m)osexual" imperative of the market by which women are insignia of desire exchanged fundamentally between men. See *This Sex Which Is Not One* (Ithaca, NY: Cornell University Press, 1985): 170–97.

4 A concern with the dynamics of perspectival vision is one of the predominant concerns of modernity: predating Panovsky's famous critique of perspective is Heidegger's notion of perspectivalism's complicity with a subject's will to mastery,

Sartre's analysis of subject/object relations as generated by the terms of the "look," Lacan's exploration of the phallic paranoia of vision, Fanon's critique of perspective (in terms of Hegelian "recognition") relative to the colonial subject, and de Beauvoir's critique relative to the gendered subject. See Foster, ed., *Vision and Visuality*, (Dia Art Foundation Discussions in Contemporary Culture, No. 2., Seattle: Bay Press, 1988): xiv. Hegel's analysis of the dynamics of mastery is germinal here, built on the trope of vision – the master-subject's impossible, self-defeating drive for recognition from the slave-object he has metaphorically blinded (in an arguably perspectival model). See Kojève, *Introduction to the Reading of Hegel* (Ithaca, NY: Cornell University Press, 1969).

5 Jay cites, among many others, Bataille's antiocular discourse as participant in the "denigration" of vision he envisions. In my opinion, however, Jay misreads Bataille's emphasis on blindness to mean the end of vision and thus an end to ocularcentrism. On the contrary, Bataille is investigating the way ocularcentrism is propped atop blindness, institutes blindness, and is perpetuated by fear of blindness/fear of castration. Bataille is working within the terms of perspectivalism to explore its realm from the underside up. He is not jettisoning himself beyond the tenets of perspectivalism, beyond vision as it were, but is delving into its secrets, and thus cannot be said to herald the "end" of anything. See Georges Bataille, *Visions of Excess: Selected Writings, 1927–1939* (Minneapolis: University of Minnesota Press, 1985).

6 As mentioned above, Theodor Adorno refers to the particular modernist cult of the new, by which, as Crary puts it after Gianni Vattimo, "the continual production of the new is what allows things to stay the same." See Crary 1991:4–11. Crary refers to Vattimo, *The End of Modernity* (Baltimore: Johns Hopkins University Press, 1988): 7–8. Given the imbrication of the "new" with the maintenance of dominant modernist paradigms, it is not surprising that it was politically invested artists who orchestrated a shift away from the "new vision" of formalist abstraction, toward quoting and mimicking seemingly outmoded forms of figuration and referentiality in the arts, as if to double back over the "old" paradigm of perspectivalism, to reinhabit that paradigm for the purposes of interrogation and critical inquiry.

7 Conservatives, as Crary points out, use an unbroken lineage of perspectivalism to pose an "account of ever-increasing progress toward verisimilitude in representation in which Renaissance perspective and photography are part of the same quest for a fully objective equivalent of a 'natural vision.'" Radical historians likewise use perspective and cinema as bound up in a "single enduring apparatus of political and social power, elaborated over several centuries, that continues to discipline and regulate the status of the observer." See Crary 1991:26.

8 Ibid.:137–50. Similarly, Crary provocatively suggests that abstraction in the arts is not such a radical break with the drive to realism as might be presumed. As Crary argues, "some of the most pervasive means of producing 'realistic' effects in mass visual culture, such as the stereoscope, were in fact based on a radical abstraction and reconstruction of optical experience." That effects of the real are based on abstraction of optical experience might have inspired abstract painters who sought what Clement Greenberg called the "conditions of vision," linking abstraction more with the positivist tenets of naturalism than with its demise.

9 Following Foucault, Crary writes, "The subjective vision affirmed by Goethe and Schopenhauer that endowed the observer with a new perceptual autonomy also coincided with the making of the observer into a subject of new knowledge and new techniques of power . . . It was the discovery that knowledge was conditioned by the physical and anatomical functioning of the body, and perhaps most importantly, of the eyes. Yet physiology, as a science of life, equally signals the appearance if new methods of power" (Crary 1991:80).

10 Panovsky, *Perspective as Symbolic Form* (New York: Zone Books, 1991): 57. Though point of view was stable in early modern perspectivalism as opposed to its dislocation

in later capitalism, a dislocation linked interestingly to the poststructural dislocation of subjectivity itself, there is nevertheless a lineage of perspectival detachment and, perhaps less reconfigured, a lineage of the crucial notion of infinite. In the later modern model of dislocation, the infinite is no longer strictly relative to the vanishing point within the scopic field but becomes, as well, a property of the viewing subject in his infinite deferral. Implicit in this analysis, articulated in Crary's work, is the suggestion that this infinity is enhanced by the submission of both subject and object to the increasingly dislocating terms of the phantasmic commodity and its relentlessly desire-deferring opticality.

11 "[T]he 'object' is not as massive, as resistant, as one might wish to believe. And her possession by a 'subject,' a subject's desire to appropriate her, is yet another of his vertiginous failures. For where he projects a something to absorb, to take, to see, to possess . . . as well as a patch of ground to stand upon, a mirror to catch his reflection, he is already faced by another specularization. Whose twisted character is her inability to say what she represents. The quest for the 'object' becomes a game of Chinese boxes. Infinitely receding."

12 For Lacan, men and women exist always already in language, and that language institutes women as the negative term (man is not woman, woman, therefore, is "not"). Relative to Lacan's larger critique of the "subject-presumed-to-know" as situated always already in language, woman, as the negative term of language, in part escapes the Symbolic Order. Her *jouissance* exceeds the phallus, and exceeds language. But because knowledge, or the presumption of knowledge, is situated in language, woman cannot know that very negativity she is presumed to possess. Thus, she can have her jouissance, figured as excess or "something more" than phallic, but cannot know her own *jouissance*. See "God and the *Jouissance* of the Woman" in Lacan's *Feminine Sexuality* (New York: W.W. Norton and Company, 1982). This, however, continues the mystification of woman that Lacan simultaneously attempts to expose.

13 This paradigm is suited to the "fourth wall" aims of naturalism, linked to nineteenth-century scientific positivism (see Emile Zola, "Naturalism in Theatre," in George J. Becker, ed., *Documents of Modern Literary Realism*, (Princeton: Princeton University Press, 1963)). We still function largely under the auspices of naturalism today as, in a direct lineage, the major tenets of mainstream Hollywood cinema generate a "slice of life," "as if" that life were not under observation – as if actors, far more than in previous styles of theatrical representation, did not know they were being watched. On the practical lineage from naturalism to mainstream American cinema, see Paul Gray, "Stanislavski and America: A Critical Chronology," *The Drama Review* 9, no. 2 (1964): 21–60.

14 Baudrillard reads this documentary as indicative of the end of perspectivalism and panoptic surveillance. He suggests that the viewing of "real" life implies that the scene is presented as if the viewer were there, *in* the scene. "You no longer watch TV, it watches you (live)" – equating the Louds with "you," the viewer. See *Simulacra and Simulation* (Ann Arbor: University of Michigan Press 1994): 28. But rather than opposed to perspective, this is a precise equation of the vanishing point, by which the viewer is in geometral relation to the viewed, with the perspectival equation that he who sees is that which he sees, he who sees appropriates what he sees to himself.

15 Woman is symbolic of private life. The concept of private as opposed to public is historically (and legally) linked to notions of private property, and women, within patriarchy, have been the emblematic item of property exchange between men. See Gayle Rubin, "The Traffic in Women: Notes on the 'Political Economy' of Sex," *Toward an Anthropology of Women* (New York: Monthly Review Press, 1975). See also Michelle Rosaldo, "Women, Culture, and Society," *The Bonds of Womanhood* (New Haven: Yale University Press, 1977); and Seyla Benhabib, "The Generalized

and the Concrete Other," *Feminism as Critique* (Minneapolis: University of Minnesota Press, 1987). See also Traian Stoianovich, "Gender and Family: Myths, Models and Ideologies," *The History Teacher* 15, no. 1 (November 1981).

16 For a helpful articulation of the terms of this "fray," see Linda J. Nicholson, ed., *Feminism/Postmodernism* (New York: Routledge Press, 1990), especially the essay by Andreas Huyssen, "Mapping the Postmodern."

17 The phrase is taken from a 1971 flyer announcing a showing of *Fuses* in London (Schneemann archives). Schneemann made the film between 1964 and 1965 in large part in response to avant-garde film-maker Stan Brakhage's representation of Schneemann's sexuality in his films *Loving* and *Cat's Cradle*. Like Brakhage, Schneemann aimed to cross the dangerous line between art and "real" life. *Fuses*, however, contradicted Brakhage's mode of formal, aesthetic detachment from the documented real. Where Brakhage suggested a kind of aesthetic remove in the formal properties of everyday life, Schneemann aimed to present the flavor of visceral everyday life as infusing, muddying, and erotically cacophonizing any formal remove. See David E. James, *Allegories of Cinema: American Film in the Sixties* (Princeton, NJ: Princeton University Press, 1989): 317–18.

18 Of course, this "labyrinthine" organization is marked "feminine" in the classic paradigm of the feminine "riddle" as well. Again, Norman O. Brown's formulation can stand as exemplary: "A woman penetrated is a labyrinth. You emerge into another world inside the woman. The penis is the bridge; the passage to another world is coitus; the other world is a womb-cave" (Brown, *Love's Body* (New York: Random House, 1966)). What Schneemann disavows relative to the classic inscription of the feminine labyrinth is the penis, or phallic eye, as bridge. Still, the anti-narrative strategy of such cultural feminist works stands in distinction to later materialist works which struggled to work within narrative to expose, using the tools of narrative, the gender implications of woman as labyrinth/anti-narrative/womb/cave. See de Lauretis, *Alice Doesn't* (Bloomington: University of Indiana Press, 1985). The labyrinthine organization of Schneemann's montage is, arguably, less disruptive of the classic inscription of the feminine than is her straddling of the subject/object divide in the position of viewer and viewed.

19 The film won critical recognition, winning an award in 1969 at Cannes and in 1972 at the Yale Film Festival. But despite these awards, Schneemann backs up James with her claim that *Fuses* was never widely shown in art circles and was constantly canceled from showings. Schneemann tells the story of forty men "going berserk" in the audience at Cannes to the point where they tore up the seats in the theater. She recounts other stories of audience fights and censorship struggles in an interview with Scott MacDonald in *Critical Cinema: Interviews with Independent Filmmakers* (Berkeley: University of California Press, 1988): 134–51.

20 When she was first showing the film Schneemann suspected that much of her audience "anxiety" resulted from the "lack of predictable pornographic narrative sequencing" (Scott MacDonald 1988:141). The lack of predictable porn sequencing confused the borders between porn and art in the same way that the bodies of the lovers within the film demonstrated "equitable interchange," refusing to resolve, as Schneemann put it in 1975, into readable "subject and object" positions marked by bodily difference (Schneemann, *Cezanne, She was a Great Painter* (New Paltz, NY: Tresspuss Press, 1975)).

21 See Maria Pramaggiore on the ways in which Karen Finley, as well, exceeds and critiques the framework of pornography. ("Resisting/Performing/Femininity: Words, Flesh, and Feminism in Karen Finley's *The Constant State of Desire*," *Theater Journal* 44, no.3 (1992): 282–7).

22 See also Steven Marcus 1974; Kendrick 1987; Lears 1994. Gertrude Koch, writing on film pornography, notes that pornographic cinema emerged at the end of a developmental process in a society of specialization and differentiation, and anxiety

about differentiation is evident in the regulations of porn according to categories of "pornographic understanding" – categories constructed, we should add, relative to socio-cultural anxieties about the regulation of sexuality vis-à-vis consumption. "The differentiation of pornography as a product parallels developments in society as producers speculate on the consumer's current and projected needs and taboos. Male homosexuality doesn't turn up in a heterosexual porn house and vice versa, anal eroticism only takes place between men and women, and the only way a man comes close to another man is when a woman, who lies between them, is entered both vaginally and anally. Lesbian sex does not appear either; when women caress each other, it is only because they are waiting for a man or performing for a male voyeur" (Koch, "The Body's Shadow Realm," *October* 50 (Fall 1989): 19). See also Patricia Hill Collins, *Black Feminist Thought: Knowledge, Consciousness, and the Politics of Empowerment* (New York: Routledge, 1990): 170, on the carefully constricted roles of black women and white women in heterosexual pornography which play out dominant constructs of race.

23 Jonathan Crary's charting of the demise of the stereoscope – an apparatus designed on the principle of binocular vision – is fascinating, especially *vis-à-vis* the ways in which binocular vision was declared inherently pornographic. The single-pointed perspective of the camera obscura was threatened by the *double optic* of the stereoscope, which, by juxtaposing and blending two dissimilar images, added depth of field to the flattened space of the photograph. The stereoscope became quickly obsolete because doubled vision was, Crary argues, a threat to the habit of perpectivalism that continued to spur the success of photography, and in part because "the simulation of a tangible three-dimensionality hovers uneasily at the limits of acceptable verisimilitude." Crary suggests that it is no coincidence that the stereoscope and its binocular vision, by which the relation of observer to image is no longer relative to a single point of view but rather "to two dissimilar images whose position simulates the anatomical structure of the observer's body," became synonymous with pornography. As a means of representation, based on double versus single perspective and relative to the observer's body, it was "inherently obscene, in the most literal sense. It shattered the scenic relationship between viewer and object that was intrinsic to the fundamentally theatrical setup of the camera obscura" (Crary 1991:127). The stereoscope suggested a complicity that denied the detached dislocation of the observer, just as pornography, in its blatant appeal to bodily function, aims overtly to involve a spectator libidinally. The fact that the apparatus of the stereoscope was so tangible – requiring hands-on manipulation by each individual viewer – similarly denied the dislocation of the viewer, which may be another reason it was abandoned in favor of optical devices more phantasmagoric and effaced in their operation (1991:132–3).

24 Indeed, the link between spheres of consumption and the dangers of "uncanny" ambivalence is interesting to theorize. A recurrent social anxiety in the nineteenth and early twentieth centuries concerned the potential of consumption to rage out of control, damaging the abilities of production to regulate consumer desires and damaging the ability of consumers to be responsible citizens in a decent capitalist society. According to historian Jackson Lears, "the fundamental fear [was . . .] that without proper boundaries consumption could undermine self control" (Lears, *Fables of Abundance* (New York: Basic Books, 1994): 73). As women were given to be the primary consumers, and men the singular producers, this threatening potential of consumption to rage out of control was a fear associated with the "imagined voracity of woman" (1994:120) – her capacity to revolt beyond the bounds of regulation.

25 "In short, the point of the gaze always participates in the ambiguity of the jewel" (Lacan, *Four Fundamental Concepts* (New York: W.W. Norton, 1981): 96). Lacan explored the inherent ambiguity in "geometral" vision, in his examination of

anamorphosis, the inversion of perspective. See *Four Fundamental Concepts*: 79–90. See also Rosalind Krauss, "Gleams and Reflections," *Cindy Sherman: 1975–1993* (New York: Rizzoli, 1993b). Panovsky, too, wrote of ambivalence at the heart of perspectival vision: "Perspective is a two-edged sword: it creates room for bodies to expand plastically and move gesturally, and yet at the same time it enables light to spread out in space and in a painterly way dissolve the body. Perspective creates distance between human beings and things . . . but then in turn it abolishes this distance . . . drawing this world of things, an autonomous world confronting the individual, into the eye" (Panovsky 1991:67).

26 Interesting in this regard is Deleuze and Guattari's suggestion that desire is not based on lack but instead on an overdetermined fear of lack, or an anxiety of a lack always deferred, displaced, or secreted. Desire as an "abject fear of lacking something" is, they suggest, a "process of production, of 'industrial' production" (Deleuze and Guattari, *Anti-Oedipus: Capitalism and Schizophrenia*, (Minneapolis: University of Minnesota Press, 1983): 26–7).

27 See Bataille's essay "The Pineal Eye" in which he writes, "The Pineal eye, detaching itself from the horizontal system of normal ocular vision, appears in a kind of nimbus of tears, like the eye of a tree, or, perhaps like a human tree. At the same time this ocular tree is only a giant (ignoble) pink penis, drunk with the sun and suggesting of soliciting a nauseous malaise, the sickening despair of vertigo. In this transfiguration of nature . . . vision itself is torn out and torn apart . . . Immense nature breaks its chains and collapses into the limitless void. A severed penis, soft and bloody, is substituted for the habitual order of things" (Bataille, *Visions of Excess* (Minneapolis: University of Minnesota Press, 1985): 84).

Michel Leiris's *Manhood*, closely linked to Bataille's work and written in the same year as Duchamp painted *Etant donnés*, provides as a further example of the horror/thrall of the enucleated eyeball conceived as always already vulvic:

> You blindfold the one who is "it" and tell him you're going to make him "put someone's eye out." You lead him, index finger extended, toward the supposed victim, who is holding in front of his eye an egg cup filled with moistened bread crumbs. At the moment the forefinger penetrates the sticky mess, the supposed victim screams.
>
> I was "it" and my sister the victim. My horror was indescribable.
>
> The significance of "eye put out" is very deep for me. Today I often tend to regard the female organ as something dirty, or as a wound, no less attractive for that, but dangerous in itself, like everything bloody, mucous, and contaminated.
>
> Michel Leiris, *Manhood* (San Francisco: North Point Press, 1946 [1984]): 46

28 See Teresa de Lauretis on "space-off" in *Technologies of Gender*: 26.

29 Lacan theorized a way in which the seen object "looks back" from *within* the scopic field to catch the viewer viewing. Yet here it is not the object as subject which looks back with any kind of reciprocity or mutually acknowledged vision. Rather, the object rebounds out of the scopic field as a screen of signifiers which bombard the viewer. In Lacan's model, anxiety remains the modus operandi of exchange as the viewer's gaze is "persecuted" by the screen of signifiers which cast a terror, or as Norman Bryson put it, a "shadow of death" over the viewer (Bryson, "The Gaze in the Expanded Field," *Vision and Visuality*, ed. by Hal Foster (Seattle: Bay Press, 1988): 92). Sartre theorized a gaze which can catch the perspectival viewer viewing, rendering him visible as viewer. However, that gaze does not come from within the feminized domain of the perspectival scopic field but from the viewer's blinded sides, from that which is not countenanced within the scope of his perspective. In Sartre's model, the perspectival viewer can be caught, surprised, and shamed by a paternal interruption – a phallic gaze which catches him at his keyhole, catching him from

outside the scope of his vision, rendering him both embodied and blind. Interestingly, Sartre writes that the effect of being caught viewing and returned to one's body as an object of another's gaze is that one is forced to become aware of one's "self" and aware that that self is "of the world," relative to other bodies, other objects, time and space. "Here the self comes to haunt the unreflective consciousness." The "self in the world" implodes upon the disembodied viewer when that viewer is rendered embodied as an object by an interrupting gaze, but that "self" takes the form of a ghost – *haunting* the viewer caught viewing: "This means that all of a sudden I am conscious of myself as escaping myself . . . I have a foundation ouside myself. I am for myself only as I am a pure reference to the Other" (Jean-Paul Sartre, *Being and Nothingness* (New York: Pocket Books, 1966): 349).

30 For a feminist psychoanalytic reading of Pandora see Laura Mulvey, "Pandora: Topographies of the Mask and Curiosity," *Sexuality and Space*, ed. by Beatriz Colomina (New York: Princeton Architectural Press, 1992). See Sylvia Bovenschen for a historical materialist treatment of myth in "The Contemporary Witch, the Historical Witch and the Witch Myth: The Witch, Subject of the Appropriation of Nature and Object of the Domination of Nature," *New German Critique* 15 (Fall 1978): 93. See also Dora and Erwin Panovsky, *Pandora's Box; The Changing Aspects of a Mythical Symbol* (New York: Pantheon Books, 1956).

4 THE SECRET'S EYE

1 As Rosalind Williams has put it, the dislocation in perspective or flaneur-like vision creates an "aesthetic distance between the onlooker and the distant scenery [that] reflects the social distance between production and consumption which has become pervasive since the industrial revolution" (Williams, *Dream Worlds: Mass Consumption in Late 19th-Century France (Berkeley: University of California Press, 1982): 187).* See also Raymond Williams, *The Country and The City* (New York: Oxford University Press, 1973): 121; and Martin Jay, *Downcast Eyes: The Denigration of Vision in Twentieth-Century Thought* (Berkeley: University of California Press, 1993): 57–9. There is, of course, an irony in the gendered separation of realms of consumption from realms of production in that women become both the primary consumer and the primarily consumed. See Jackson Lears, *Fables of Abundance* (New York: Basic Books, 1994): 17–39. Feminist inquiry into this irony has focused attention of the split subjectivity that results in women as consumer (maculinized viewer) of her own image which she is given to consume. Irigaray has focused on the image of woman as the "product of man's labor" – she is the product she consumes (Irigaray, *This Sex Which Is Not One* (Ithaca: Cornell University Press, 1985): 175).

2 A great deal has been written on images of women in advertising. See especially Judith Williamson, "Woman is an Island: Femininity and Colonization," *Studies in Entertainment: Critical Approaches to Mass Culture*, (Bloomington: University of Indiana Press, 1986b); Susan Bordo, *Unbearable Weight: Feminism, Western Culture, and the Body* (Berkeley: University of California Press, 1993). Micheline Wandor has noted that images of women employed in advertising are generally divided into two categories: "the pre-marital, sexily available female" and "the various versions of the post-sexual wife and mother." Wandor notes that ad images swing between a wild and insatiable, wanton and passionate desire on the one hand and a ultimate control as imaged and embodied in the wife/mother on the other. The trajectory in terms of age and status of the women in the ads outlines a trajectory for women in society in general: "Woman as sexual object must be tamed because female sexuality is seen as somehow dangerous and uncontainable" (Wandor, *Carry On, Understudies* (New York: Routledge, 1986): 30). That danger and uncontainability is arguably scripted by the needs of the market which wants to promote passionate

and wanton spending. The domesticated wife/mother is also an icon which serves the market as woman, as domesticated consumer, serves as iconic marker of the distinction between public/private, spheres of production and spheres of consumption. See Betty Friedan, *The Feminine Mystique* (New York: Dell, 1963): 206–32. The juxtaposition of these two images across ad-scapes places women's sexuality on a continuum that leads from sexual availability to controlled domestic reproduction. She is doubled in that continuum as both that which is consumed (desired) and ultimately that which consumes, augmenting the female status as primary domestic consumer, delimited to spheres of consumption. Male bodies presented as commodities, or emblems of sexual desire, are traditionally taboo. While male beefcake imagery is on the rise in the 1990s, it is still highly curtailed relative to female sexual iconicity. Luce Irigaray (1985a) writes on the taboo on images of men as commodities as relative to the social secret of a "hom(m)osexual" economy by which wealth and women are exchanged between men. Michael Bronski, too, writes on the taboo of male to male desire in advertising, but his analysis stands in a certain distinction to Irigaray's (*Culture Clash: The Making of a Gay Sensibility* (Boston: South End Press, 1984): 209–10).

3 Slavoj Zizek has provocatively linked the structural insatiability of the commodity to the institution and practice of "blindness" toward the real, imbricated in commodity exchange. Zizek's analysis suggests that the structure of commodity capitalism is founded on an Oedipal anxiety where to achieve satisfaction is to "know too much." To know too much, to acknowledge the "real," would result in the blinding dissolve of the dreamscape, the demise of the commodity structure itself (Zizek, *The Sublime Object of Ideology* (New York: Verso, 1989): 16–21).

4 The relationship of the structure of commodity logic to Western imperialism and the construction and display of the "exotic" other, outside-over-there, often labeled "primitive," is also key, and linked to the dynamics of femininity. See Judith Williamson, "Woman is an Island: Femininity and Colonization," *Studies in Entertainment: Critical Approaches to Mass Culture* (Bloomington: University of Indiana Press, 1986). Timothy Mitchell has discussed how colonial exhibitions aided the capitalist tenet of the "real" as relative to and dictated by commodity dreamscapes: "the real world, as at the exhibition, was something created in the representations of its commodities" (Mitchell, *Colonising Egypt* (New York: Cambridge University Press, 1988): 11).

5 Markings of race and age relative to the female body are also extremely significant. See Sander L. Gilman on the ways the black female body in the nineteenth century was particularly marked for primitive sexual insatiability. The black body, often in the form of male or female servants, served iconically in representation to sexualize the white female body which, in distinction to the black, was marked for purity, or potential deflowerment, whereas the black was always already deflowered, marked by inherent primitivity. Gilman also explicates the link between black females, prostitutes, and lesbians in nineteenth-century iconography ("Black Bodies, White Bodies: Toward an Iconography of Female Sexuality in Late Nineteenth-Century Art, Medicine, and Literature," *"Race," Writing, and Difference* (Chicago: University of Chicago Press, 1985)). See also Lauren Berlant 1991, Richard Dyer 1988, Anne McClintock 1995, Susan Bordo 1993, Jackson Lears 1994, Marilyn Kern-Foxworth 1994, Patricia Hill Collins 1990.

6 See Friedan 1963; Lears 1994; Marchand 1985:164–205; Goldman 1992:107–29; McClintock 1995:207–31.

7 We see this changing in the later 1980s and 1990s as more "beefcake" advertisements include a sexualized masculine form and as "multiculturalism" broadens the spectrum of race representation on the market. See William Sonnega, "Morphing Borders: The Remanence of MTV," *The Drama Review* 39, no. 1 (1995): 45–61. The beefcake mode for men is increasing in the ad-scape, especially in fragrance ads.

This suggests that Irigaray's (1988) analysis of the prohibition on the male body presented as a commodity (a prohibition which props the gender division of the market, privileging men as producers) may be altering. Still, close inspection of these beefcake ads in mainstram magazines reveals some definite distinctions between female "cheesecake" and male "beefcake." Most interesting is the fact that very rarely, when the male body is given to be seen as site of sexual desire, are the model's eyes shown. A male model scantily clad *and* looking at the viewer seductively, as so many young women are given to do, is as yet "too much."

8 See Marshall Berman, *All That is Solid Melts into Air: The Experience of Modernity* (New York: Simon and Schuster, 1982): 99. See also Mady Schutzman, "The Aesthetics of Hysteria: Performance, Pathology, and Advertising" (Ph.D. dissertation, New York University, 1994). See also Joan Copjec, "Flavit et Dissipati Sunt" on the images of hysterics as "all under the sign of irony, of deception, that what seems, what appears, *is* not" (*October* 18 (1981): 20–40). See also Marianna Torgovnick, *Gone Primitive: Savage Intellects, Modern Lives* (Chicago: University of Chicago Press, 1990).

9 Yoko Ono's 1962 score for an "action" titled "Conversation Piece." Kristine Stiles draws an interesting lineage from Ono to Karen Finley in "Survival Ethos and Destruction Art," *Discourse* 14, no. 2 (1992): 74–102.

10 I am indebted to Michael Taussig for the phrase "capitalist mimetics" in a lecture delivered at New York University, 1991.

11 See Naomi Schor on the particular need for "irony" in feminist strategic manipulations of the dynamics of capitalist mimetics, specifically fetishism ("Fetishism and Its Ironies," *Fetishism as Cultural Discourse* (Ithaca, NY: Cornell University Press, 1993): 92–100).

12 That women have been obsessively represented in modernist art does not imply that their bodies signified "women" at all. Susan Rubin Suleiman has written on the need to rethink modernist avant-garde "obsession" with woman as the subject of work. Writing specifically of Surrealist photography, she notes that the female body is invariably the obsessive object of the work, while "women" as practicing subjects are marginalized. "To call woman the obsessional subject . . . is misleading" also because, as Suleiman follows Gauthier to show, whether Surrealists "idealized the female body and their love of it, as they did in their poetry, or attacked it and dismembered it, as they did in their paintings, the male Surrealists . . . were essentially using the women to work out their rebellion against the Father." Thus the obsession, figuratively worked out across female bodies, was arguably not "about" women at all. Thus performance artists today "talk back" to the staging of their bodies as obsessional terrain for displaced, or secreted, agendas (*Subversive Intent: Gender, Politics, and the Avant-Garde* (Cambridge: Harvard University Press, 1989): 18–19).

13 See Julia Kristeva, "The True-Real," *The Kristeva Reader* (New York: Columbia University Press, 1986); and Elin Diamond's "Mimesis, Mimicry, and the True-Real," *Modern Drama* 32, no. 1 (1989): 58–72. See also Tania Modleski's *Feminism Without Women* (New York: Routledge, 1991). Also of interest is Klaus Theweleit, *Male Fantasies*, vol. 1. (Minneapolis: University of Minnesota Press, 1987): 220–2. Making the tangled politic between socio-cultural fantasy and the reality effects of those fantasies particularly evident, Theweleit examines the gender fantasies at the base of twentieth-century fascism to find the particular oppressive patriarchal fantasy of gendering manifested in mimetic relations between family and state.

14 Note that this is not the anti-porn position which fears that fantasy *leads to* reality. On the contrary, the notion that fantasy is real teeters at the edges of incomprehensibility. Though it leads to threatening extremes such as Camille Paglia's condoning of snuff films in *Time* (because what is the distinction between reality and fantasy?), such threats to dominant systems of comprehensibility have been a strategy of feminist criticism and performance. See Teresa de Lauretis on non-sense and narrative in

"Desire in Narrative," *Alice Doesn't* (Bloomington: Indiana University Press, 1985): 103–57; as well as her "Strategies of Coherence," *Technologies of Gender* (Bloomington: Indiana University Press, 1987): 107–26. See also Suzanne Kappeler, "Fact and Fiction," *The Pornography of Representation* (Cambridge: Polity Press, 1986).

15 Freud, of course, can be credited with this proclamation as well, though in his abdication of the implications of his own seduction theory of hysteria in favor of his Oedipal theory, he arguably re-stacked his cards to privilege the terms of desire, naturalizing desire over "reality" and relegating reality effects of this naturalized desire to a secondary, nostalgic or displaced status. Where psychoanalysis retains a distinction between fantasy and reality at its foundation, Bright provokes a binary terrorism by completely collapsing this distinction *in entirety.*

16 See bell hooks on Madonna's crotch grabbing as an unacknowledged appropriation of "phallic black masculinity" which she reads as envy and an appropriation designed to assert power "along very traditional, white supremacist, capitalistic, patriarchal lines" (hooks, *Black Looks* (Boston: South End Press, 1992): 161–3). See also Susan Bordo, *Unbearable Weight* (Berkeley: University of California Press, 1993): 265–75.

17 Quoted as promotional on the back cover of Bright's *Sexual Reality* (San Francisco: Cleis Press, 1992).

18 This is a critique Butler herself echoes in Liz Kotz's "The Body You Want: An Interview with Judith Butler," *Artforum* (November 1992): 82–9. While it would be a misreading to assume that Butler completely ignores historical exigencies and effects of engenderment in *Gender Trouble* (New York: Routledge, 1990), Butler herself acknowledges that her treatment of reality effects is overshadowed by her political and hopeful choice to emphasize masquerade.

19 That the streetwalker might be biologically male or female is not as significant as it might seem. The feminization of commodity objects works in either case, sometimes with horrifying results. See Peggy Phelan on the murder of male transvestite prostitute Venus Xtravaganza in *Unmarked: The Politics of Performance*, (New York: Routledge, 1993): 111.

20 Some feminist scholars have difficulty with Finley's unwillingness to make her seemingly inappropriate rantings more understandable, or appropriate, by way of explanation. See Catherine Schuler, "Spectator Response and Comprehension: The Problem of Karen Finley's *Constant State of Desire*," *The Drama Review* 32, no. 1 (1990): 131–45. See the more complex and in-depth analysis of the subject in Lynda Hart, "Reconsidering Homophobia: Karen Finley's Indiscretions," *Fatal Women: Lesbian Sexuality and the Mark of Aggression* (New York: Routledge, 1994): 89–103. See also Hart, "Motherhood According to Finley: The Theory of Total Blame," *The Drama Review* 36, no. 1 (1992). See Jeanie Forte, "Women's Performance Art: Feminism and Postmodernism," *Theater Journal* 40 (May 1988), and "Focus on the Body: Pain, Praxis, and Pleaure in Feminist Performance," *Critical Theory and Performance* (Ann Arbor: University of Michigan Press, 1992). See also the excellent essay by Maria Pramaggiore, "Resisting/Performing/Femininity: Words, Flesh, and Feminism in Karen Finley's *Constant State of Desire*," *Theater Journal* 44 (1992): 269–90. I have previously written on Finley's literalization of Freud in "See the Big Show," *Acting Out: Feminist Performances* (Ann Arbor: University of Michigan Press, 1993): 250–1.

21 Taken from an April 28, 1995, performance of *A Certain Level of Denial* at Northampton Center for the Arts, Northampton, MA.

22 See Elaine Showalter, "Feminism and Hysteria," *The Female Malady* (New York: Penguin Books, 1985): 159–64. See Mady Schutzman, "The Aesthetics of Hysteria: Performance, Pathology, and Advertising" (1994). Lynda Hart has posited a fundamental difference between hysteria and hallucination, positing that heterosexual aberration is marked as hysterical – a return of the Real which has been repressed in

signification – while lesbianism is given to be nonexistent, more hallucinatory than hysterical – a "return of the Real that has never been signified." This is a provocative distinction. Reading for hysteria in lesbian works, Hart seems to suggest, may be limited, inscribing discourse particular to the terms and terrain heterosexuality where it does not entirely belong. The following explication of Finley's work in the historical terms of hysteria may be marked, therefore, by Finley's heterosexuality, if not, as well, by my own. See Hart, "Identity and Seduction: Lesbians in the Mainstream," *Acting Out: Feminist Performances* (Ann Arbor: University of Michigan Press, 1993): 134.

23 See Ferdinand de Saussure on the complexities of the "arbitrary" relation between sign and signified, a relation arguably at the heart of the modernist thrall with alienation. Heralding the relation between sign and signified "arbitrary" has made room for the recognition of socio-political convention at the heart of symbolic systems, and for the mutability of such conventions. But privileging the concept of random or arbitrary relation potentially obscures the sensuous effects of the historical *arbitrations* of those relations which the seeming arbitrary has serviced. See de Saussure's *Course in General Linguistics* (New York: McGraw Hill, 1959 [1915]): 65–78.

24 The notion of re-performance here is complex. Performance is arguably, after Richard Schechner, always already twice-behaved behavior. Re-performance thus suggests a kind of Brechtian alienation on the twice-behaved, as if performing performance. Such thrice-behaved behavior implies critical attention to the dynamics of performativity. See Schechner, *Between Theatre and Anthropology* (Chicago: University of Chicago Press, 1985).

25 Irigaray's notion of hysterical mimicry is one in which woman, positioned as mirror to man, rejects "imposed mimesis" and instead of reflecting that which society tells her to mirror – male virility – mirrors her own patriarchal oppression by that dictate. See Irigaray, *Speculum of the Other Woman* (Ithaca, NY: Cornell University Press, 1985): 54.

26 The collapse of aesthetic distance between sign and signified, symbol and literal, threatens comprehensibility and rings not only of hysteria, but of psychosis. Because women have been "left out of the sociosymbolic contract, of language as the fundamental social bond," Julia Kristeva has noted that a "therefore difficult, if not impossible, identification with the sacrificial logic of separation and syntactical sequence at the foundation of language and the social code leads to the rejection of the symbolic – lived as the rejection of the paternal function and ultimately leading to psychosis" (Kristeva, "Women's Time," *Signs* 7, no. 1 (1981): 24. The irony, here, is that according to dominant codes of gender, psychosis is always already the "normal" state of femininity. As Judith Bardwick notes, "The insitence that femininity evolves from necessarily frustrated masculinity makes femininity a sort of normal pathology" (Bardwick, *The Psychology of Women: A Bio-Cultural Conflict* (New York: Harper and Row, 1971)). Thus woman herself, to the degree that she stands as "woman," either accepting *or* rejecting the paternal function, is always already pathological, she automatically "threatens comprehensibility." Her "normal" threat to comprehensibility is scripted onto her literal body as she is marked with codes of gender. Her psychosis is thus linked to her bodily markings – the literal site of her symbolic engenderment as woman. Rendering the symbolic literal is, then, rendering the impact of the symbolic on bodies.

27 This notion of not taking makeup seriously is strangely countered by MAC's declaration across the bottom of a recent Viva Glam lipstick ad that "Every cent of the retail selling price of MAC Viva Glam lipstick is donated to the fight against AIDS."

5 AFTER US THE SAVAGE GODDESS

1 Simone de Beauvoir put the issue succinctly: "Woman has a double and deceptive visage: she is all that man desires and all that he does not attain . . . She is all, that is, on the plane of the inessential; she is all the Other. And, as the other, is other than herself, other than what is expected of her" (*The Second Sex* (New York: Vintage Books, 1989)).

2 See Irigaray 1985a. See Monique Wittig on the ways this splitting is inherently structured in language, constructing the real (for her figured in terms of the "literal" mark of the letter), in "The Mark of Gender," *Feminist Issues* 5, no. 2 (1985): 5–6.

3 For a similar analysis of the problematics of reading as a woman see Tania Modleski, "Some Functions of Feminist Criticism, or, The Scandal of the Mute Body," *Feminism Without Women* (New York: Routledge, 1991): 35–58. For an example of the trope of woman as endlessly inhabitable space see an instructive example in Derrida's reading of Nietzsche in *Spurs: Nietzsche's Style* (Chicago: University of Chicago Press, 1979). In this text, Derrida finds that Nietzsche is himself of the women he posits ambiguously (with attraction and revultion) throughout his texts. Derrida finds Nietzsche splitting woman into three variables: the castrated, the castrating, and beyond that "double negation," the affirmative woman who does not recognize castration, or, conversely, recognizes that it has not taken place. In all three cases woman becomes a textual space relative to the apprehension (in the double sense of either to get or to project fearfully) of castration. The ultimate end of these parsings is to find, without much alarm, that Nietzsche like other modernists has himself become all these women: "Nietzsche is a bit lost in the web of his text, like a spider, unequal to what he has produced – like a spider, I say, or like many spiders, those of Nietzsche, those of Lautreamont, of Mallarme, of Freud and Abraham. He was, and he dreaded, such a castrating woman. He was, and he loved, such an affirmative woman" (1979: 101).

   To be fair, Derrida writes of this as the "question of woman" rather than women per se, but the line between the question and the women who find themselves embodying that question is necessarily ambiguous, for Derrida as for Nietzsche. And to write that these modernist forefathers of his own thought couldn't control their own webs (like the German *Weib*) is to suggest that Derrida, the son, has a better understanding of the "question" than the father(s) – claiming the pen *à la* Oedipus simply to dot the final mark again on the self-same "question" across the body of woman.

4 Interestingly, the word *science* derives from the Latin *scienta*, from *scire*, "to separate one thing from another," which is related to the Indo-European root *skei*, "to cut, split." *Science* is thus related to another group of Indo-European words, including the Old Irish *scian*, "knife," the Germanic *scitan*, "to separate," and the Greek *skhigein*, "to split." See Mary Ellen Pitts, "The Holographic Paradigm: A New Model for the Study of Literature and Science," *Modern Language Studies* 20, no. 4 (1990): 80.

5 It is imperative to note that "Primitivism" – a Western obsession with, nostalgia for, and mimesis of forms and practices of racial/cultural Others (and particularly African Others) deemed less evolved or under-developed or closer to the wild than the civilized – is an aspect of the history of Western patriarchal thought, art, and deed, not an aspect of an actual Other, the so-labeled primitive. The word "primitivism" carries with it ethnocentric and pejorative connotations. William Rubin, editor of the Museum of Modern Art's two volume survey of *'Primitivism' in 20th-Century Art*, justifies his use of the term by pointing out that "no other generic term proposed as a replacement of 'primitive' has been found acceptable to its critics; none has been proposed for 'primitivism.'" As Rubin rightly states, "That the derived term primitivism is ethnocentric is surely true – and logically so, for it refers

not to the tribal arts in themselves, but to the Western interest in and reaction to them. Primitivism is thus an aspect of the history of modern art, not of tribal art." (Rubin, ed. 1984:5). Despite Rubin's acknowledgment of ethnocentrism, however, his exhibition ignored the historical implications and political consequences of modernism's incorporation of "primitive" art. See James Clifford, *Predicament of Culture* (Cambridge, MA: Harvard University Press, 1988): Chapter 9, and Marianna Torgovnick, *Gone Primitive* (Chicago: University of Chicago Press, 1990): Chapter 6.

6   I take the word "danger" from Artaud, writing in the 1930s of the modern West's loss of the "danger" of ritual he found exemplified in Balinese trance dance (*Antonin Artaud: Selected Writings*, ed. Susan Sontag (Berkeley: University of California Press, 1988): 235, 236, 242). Like Surrealism generally, Artaud linked the primitive with the sexual and the unconscious, arguing that the primitive bypassed the mind to access the body, feeding the spectator's "taste for crime, his erotic obsessions, his savagery, his fantasies" (1988:244). I take the word "uncivilized" from Hugo Ball, one of the founders of Dada in 1916, cited in Hans Richter, *Dada: Art and Anti-Art* (New York: Oxford University Press, 1965): 37. Early Dada use of "negro rhythms" and "tom tom" drums as well as pseudo African masks were intended as a confrontation of the primitive in the space of the civilized, the "low" and viscerally connected savage in the (war-torn) space of the "high" and alienated bourgeois.

7   It was not until the turn of the century that the phrase "primitive art" ceased to include Japanese, Egyptian, Persian, and most other non-Western styles and came to mean specifically tribal arts. See William Rubin, ed., *"Primitivism" in 20th-Century Art* (New York: The Museum of Modern Art, 1984): 3. When the distinction did evolve between "archaic" and "primitive" arts, the single most important difference was that ancient Egyptian, Persian, and Asian (archaic) expression was considered noble, or artistic, while African and Oceanic arts retained an ignoble connotation, an ignobility inseparable from contemporary racisms.

8   Raymond Williams has defined modernism as intent on a "violent break with tradition: the insistence on a clean break with the past." But that "past" was the Western past. Primitivism offered modernists a pre-historical past – a past outside of Western habits of understanding, offering, instead of tradition, the "innately creative, the unformed and untamed realm of the pre-rational and the unconscious" (*The Politics of Modernism* (New York: Verso, 1989):52, 58). Of course, such a consideration of the primitive was rife with racisms of the day which read tribal societies as antithetical to "progress," stuck in prehistory. See Williams (1989: 49–63), on the concomitance of primitivism and futurism in the combustive generation of modernism, and Daniel Miller, "Primitive Art and the Necessity of Primitivism to Art," *The Myth of Primitivism* (New York: Routledge, 1991): 55–6.

9   See Paul Ricoeur on the hermeneutics of suspicion in *Freud and Philosophy: An Essay on Interpretation* (New Haven: Yale University Press, 1970): 28f. For psychoanalysis, of course, the literal dream became the key to interpreting the experience of the modern in the dreamscape of the modern world, and repressed sexuality became its "primitive" driving function – that which the modern has colonized and repressed. "Civilization behaves towards sexuality as a people or a stratum of its population does which has subjected another one to its exploitation" (Freud, *Civilization and Its Discontents* (New York: Norton, 1961): 57).

10   This effort to inhabit the condition of vision was by no means limited to visual media. Imagism, for example, sought to capture the condition of vision in text. In performing arts, the drive for "unifying vision" saw the development of the novel role of director – he who orchestrates the gaze and conditions the viewer toward the "mind's eye" of the artist himself. The New Vision movement, a formalist take on futurist ideology of the body-as-machine and Dadaist photomontage, went so far as

to imagine the camera as a new body, a kind of prosthesis, "optimistically believed to extend the powers of the body." See Maud Lavin, "Androgyny, Spectatorship, and the Weimar Photomontages of Hannah Höch," *New German Critique* 51 (Fall 1990): 68.

11 In Judy Chicago, Suzanne Lacy, Sandra Orgel, and Aviva Rahmani's 1972 performance piece *Ablutions*, a tape of women's oral testimonies of rape was played as a naked woman was bound with white gauze, another woman nailed beef kidneys to the wall, and two others bathed themselves in a tub containing eggs, blood and clay. See Moira Roth, *The Amazing Decade* (Los Angeles: Astro Artz, 1983): 86; and Judy Chicago, *Through the Flower: My Struggles as a Woman Artist* (New York: Penguin, 1993 [1975]): 217–19. Mary Beth Edelson's work is perhaps most representative of feminist ritual-based work, using symbol and myth of women's "lost" history in order to recuperate a sense of female heritage. For Edelson, "the concept of ritual is used to bind contemporary women to their history [and] a collective community of women" (Roth 1983:92). The use of ritual is not unique to feminist performance, and is indeed a fascination point of modernism in general. Antonin Artaud looked to primitive ritual as inherently opposed to theatre, and, arguably, the alienated perspectivalism of "spectacle," in his search to "heal the split between language and flesh." Yet, Susan Sontag argues that Artaud does not present a clear political underpinning to his invocation of ritual, arguing that his "nostalgia . . . is deliberately not political – however frequently it brandishes the word 'revolution'" (Sontag, "Artaud," *Antonin Artaud: Selected Writings* (Berkeley: University of California Press, 1988): xxxv, xli). But if Artaud did not present his primitivism as blatantly political (though Sontag's statement that it was *deliberately* apolitical is debatable), cultural feminist invocations of ritual were adamantly presented as political. Still, the nostalgic (versus critical) articulation of the primitive in cultural feminism shares much with Western modernism and is thus arguably complicit in many modernist tenets it would perhaps have preferred to disavow.

12 Carolee Schneemann, *More Than Meat Joy* (New Paltz, NY: Documentext, 1979): 234–9. The text Schneemann extracted from her vagina claimed to quote "a happy man/a structuralist filmmaker" – she does not give his name. Interestingly, she has told me that the text was actually "based on a letter I wrote but never sent to a well-known female structuralist critic, placed in the guise of a male structuralist filmmaker" because Schneemann felt the critic's structuralism recapitulated misogynist views.

13 Helene Cixous and Catherine Clement, *The Newly Born Woman*, (Minneapolis: University of Minnesota Press, 1986 [1975]). I cite this book as exemplary of essentialist cultural feminism in its attempt to mend the wrongs of culture through a celebration of the "rights of nature." However, it should be noted that Cixous's is not a naive essentialism. On close reading one finds that she is advocating essentialism as primarily a political strategy, acknowledging that "One can no more speak of 'woman' than of 'man' without being trapped within an ideological theater where the proliferation of representations, images, reflections . . . invalidate in advance any conceptualization" (1986:83). Published in French in 1975, Cixous advocated "writing the body," or *écriture feminine*, a project some recent materialist theorists have read as linked to contemporary explicit body performance art. See Maria Pramaggiore, "Resisting/Performing/Femininity: Words, Flesh, and Feminism in Karen Finley's *Constant State of Desire*," *Theater Journal* 44 (1992): 269–90; and Jeanie Forte, "Focus on the Body: Pain, Praxis, and Pleaure in Feminist Performance," *Critical Theory and Performance*, (Ann Arbor: University of Michigan Press, 1992).

14 See Susan Rubin Suleiman, *Subversive Intent: Gender, Politics, and the Avant-Garde* (Cambridge MA,: Harvard University Press, 1989). Suleiman links contemporary feminist art practice to the historical avant-garde, though not specifically to modernist primitivism.

15 Christopher Innes, *Avant-Garde Theatre: 1892–1992* (New York: Routledge, 1993): 3. Innes sees primitivism as the defining characteristic of the modernist avant-garde in general, however, he is only concerned with a nostalgic primitivism and can be criticized for underemphasizing the confrontative potential in primitivism – the potential for anti-art/anti-civilization critique. Many recent cultural theorists, building on historical materialism, have explicated ways that modernist "primitivism" functioned as an underground mainstream against which "civilization" defined itself – the primitive has supported modernity even as she threatened, or stood in distinction to, that very erection. The work of James Clifford is exemplary in this regard. See *The Predicament of Culture* (Cambridge, MA: Harvard University Press, 1988): Chapters 4 and 9.

16 I refer here to the split within the modernist avant-garde between (1) "high" modernist aesthetics which incorporated primitive as well as "new" or experimental forms in the effort to expand the domain of Western aesthetics and (2) anti-art movements which confronted the institution of art itself. See Andreas Huyssen, *After the Great Divide: Modernism, Mass Culture, Post-modernism* (Bloomington: Indiana University Press, 1986); Rosalind Krauss, *The Originality of the Avant-Garde*, (Cambridge MA,: MIT Press, 1988); Peter Burger *Theory of the Avant-Garde* (Minneapolis: University of Minnesota Press, 1984). This distinction between incorporative high modernism and transgressive or confrontative modernism becomes slippery, however, since the historical trajectory of modernism has been to *incorporate* anti-art transgression *as* an aesthetic versus a politic. The slippery distinction between incorporative and transgressive modernism is arguably linked to the distinction between "reactionary" and "resistant" postmodernism as outlined by Hal Foster, "Postmodernism: A Preface," *The Anti-Aesthetic* (Port Townsend, WA: Bay Press, 1983), again raising questions about the extent of the so-called "break" between the modern and the postmodern.

17 In Kandinsky's expressionism, primitivism was linked to a celebration of naiveté, innocence, and "pure" creativity – a "chastity" which nevertheless must be overcome, colonized, at the same time that it is emulated. Kandinsky, a member of the German Jugendstil movement, admired the art of the "youth" for what he saw as its "direct, intuitive expression of the interior essence of things" – an "indigenous source of primitive inspiration" (Goldwater, *Primitivism in Modern Art* (Cambridge MA,: Harvard University Press, 1938): 192). That the primitive was linked to the childish reflects the common notion, upheld by Darwinian science, that the "lower" races are less evolved than the European. Though Kandinsky was not an anti-artist, his explorations of inspiration and spiritualism influenced artists who worked to contradict "high" traditions, such as Dadaist Hugo Ball who was inspired by Kandinsky's *Concerning the Spiritual in Art* (New York: Dover, 1977). These artists looked to the "savage" and "uncivilized" as a source of social and political confrontation as well as inspiration. The word "dada" is itself a combination of reference to the childish, the primitive, and the pathological. It means "hobby horse" in French, it is a Kru African word for a sacred cow's tail, and in German it indicates "idiot naiveté." See Tristan Tzara's "Dada Manifesto" in Mel Gordon, *Dada Performance* (New York: Performing Arts Journal Press, 1987): 45–6; and Richter, *Dada: Art and Anti-Art* (New York: Oxford University Press, 1965): 32. See Carl Schorske on modernist preoccupation with the primitive "art of the child" in *Fin-de-Siècle Vienna: Politics and Culture* (New York: Vintage Books, 1981): 327–9.

18 Darwin spells out his hierarchy of natural selection in "Secondary Sexual Characteristics," *On the Origin of the Species* (Chicago: Encyclopaedia Britannica Series, Great Books of the Western World, vol. 49, 1955). Having made it clear that differentiation or modification is the mode of evolution, Darwin points out that males are more evolved than females: "Males differ much more from one another than do the females. This fact indicates that . . . it has been the male which has been

chiefly modified since the several races diverged from their common stock" (1955:564). He goes on to link women to primitive races, saying "It is generally admitted that with woman the powers of intuition, of rapid perception, and perhaps of imitation, are more strongly marked than in man; but some, at least, of these faculties are characteristic of the lower races, and therefore of a past and lower state of civilization" (1955:566).

19 That women's lack of differentiation is marked by shame is a Freudian interpretation of Darwin's theories. Freud, who saw the clitoris as an atrophied "penis-equivalent" wrote in "Femininity" that women's only contribution to "the history of civilization" has been the discovery of plaiting and weaving. The reason for women's initiative in this area was, according to Freud, shame – the effort to conceal the insufficiency of their genitals in a mimetic extension of pubic hair (*New Introductory Lectures on Psychoanalysis* (New York: W.W. Norton, 1965): 104, 117).

20 Freud's theories altered the child/woman analogy somewhat, building on Krafft-Ebing's notion of children's bisexuality. While Darwin had males differentiating out of primordial femaleness, Freud has little girls and little boys all starting out with "masculine sexuality" (*Three Essays on the Theory of Sexuality* (New York: Basic Books, 1962): 87). See also Freud 1965:104. At puberty male sexuality develops straighforwardly (read progressively) while the female must take a step backward (read digress). At puberty, a girl is "overtaken by repression" and she "holds herself back." "Sexual development now diverges greatly. That of males is the more straightforward and the more understandable, while that of females actually enters upon a kind of involution" (1962:73). At puberty it is as if girls take a step back into childhood – into primitivity. Women's sexuality is generally more polymorphously perverse (undifferentiated), remaining closer to children's (primitive's). The following two quotes from *Three Essays* exemplify the general conflation of children, "savages," and women as polymorphous or undifferentiated. The first quote equates children and primitive peoples: "Psychoanalysis considers that a choice of an object independently of its sex – freedom to range equally over male and female objects – as it is found in childhood, in primitive states of society and early periods of history, is the original basis from which, as a result of restriction in one direction or the other, both the normal and the inverted types develop" (1962:12). The second quote equates children, women, and *prostitutes* for their undifferentiated, polymorphous perversities. "In this respect children behave in the same kind of way as an average uncultivated woman in whom the same polymorphously perverse disposition persists. Under ordinary conditions she may remain normal sexually, but if she is led on by a clever seducer she will find every sort of perversion to her taste and will retain them as part of her own sexual activities. Prostitutes exploit the same polymorphous, that is, infantile, disposition for the purposes of their profession; and, considering the immense number of women who are prostitutes or who must be supposed to have an aptitude for prostitution without becoming engaged in it, it becomes impossible not to recognize that this same disposition to perversions of every kind is a general and fundamental human characteristic" (1962:57). It is this fundamental "human" characteristic exhibited by women, children, whores and primitives from which men most successfully differentiate through "mastery." See Freud also for the masculine "instinct for mastery" (1962:54)

21 The body of work addressing this issue is enormous, from Roland Barthes to Edward Said to James Clifford. For delineations of various contemporary ethnographic methods see George E. Marcus and Michael M. J. Fischer, *Anthropology as Cultural Critique* (Chicago: University of Chicago Press, 1986) and Marcus's more recent "The Modernist Sensibility in Recent Ethnographic Writing and the Cinematic Metaphor of Montage," *Visualizing Theory: Selected Essays for V.A.R, 1990–1994* (New York: Routledge, 1994).

22 In an interesting quote from *Three Essays*, Freud intimates that civilization has

stunted women's sexuality (the logic being that women, as primitive, cannot thrive in civilization). Men's "erotic life alone has become accessible to research. That of women – partly owing to the stunting effect of civilized conditions and partly owing to their conventional *secretiveness* and insincerity – is still veiled in an impenetrable obscurity" (1962:17).

23 See Chapter 4 on the "hit" of commodities.

24 Interestingly, Picasso regularly gathered around Jarry in Paris in the 1890s and even adopted some of Jarry's personal eccentricities as well as a valuable collection of his manuscripts. See Michael Benedikt, "Introduction" to *Modern French Theater* (New York: E.P. Dutton, 1964): xiv; and Roger Shattuck, *The Banquet Years: The Origins of the Avant-Garde in France* (New York: Vintage Press, 1955): 218–19.

25 Maurice Maeterlinck, one of the leading dramatists of the symbolist movement, wrote in 1890: "every masterpiece is a symbol and the symbol can never support the active presence of man" (Marvin Carlson, *Theories of Theater* (Ithaca, NY: Cornell, 1984): 296). Because the literality, the physicality of the live body threatened the aesthetic distance afforded symbolic reading, symbolists often sought to replace living actors with shadows, masks and marionettes – an effort best illustrated in Edward Gordon Craig's "The Actor and the Uber-Marionette" in his *On the Art of the Theater*, (New York: Theater Art Books, 1907). Maeterlinck and Craig desired a theater of internal reflection, invoking, in Maeterlinck's words, "an old man sitting in his armchair, simply waiting by his lamp, listening unconsciously to all the eternal laws which reign around his house" (1907:296). At the turn of the century, tribal artifact was associated with the collapse of aesthetic distance, linked to tribal life and base physicality, not to armchair enlightenment. Interestingly however, after the first decade of the twentieth century, tribal artifacts increasingly became staple accouterment in the studios and at the desks of artists and intellectuals – arguably bringing those artifacts under the "eternal laws" of the symbol, under the lamp by the old man's armchair, even as they became "art." See Marianna Torgovnick, "Entering Freud's Study," *Gone Primitive* (Chicago: University of Chicago Press, 1990): 194–209.

26 Jarry, "Preliminary Address at the First Performance of *Ubu Roi*, December 10, 1896," *Selected Works of Alfred Jarry* (New York: Grove Press, 1965): 78; and *Ubu Roi*, program notes (1965:79). In an essay entitled "Theater Questions," Jarry addressed his audience's reaction. "It is not surprising that the public should have been aghast at the sight of its ignoble other self, which it had never before been shown completely. This other self . . . is composed of eternal human imbecility, eternal lust, eternal gluttony, the vileness of instinct magnified into tyranny . . . Ubu's speeches were not meant to be full of witticisms . . . but of stupid remarks, uttered with all the authority of the Ape." The primitive and the bodily were thus invoked as the vile "other," not however in distinction to the self but as part and parcel of that self (1965:83).

27 Arthur Symons, cited in Roger Shattuck, *The Banquet Years* (New York: Vintage Press, 1955): 207. The mimesis of child conventions was linked to primitivism. The concurrently developing Jungendstil painters in Germany, turn of the century precursors to Expressionism, were evolving childlike forms which, as Ernst Michalski put it, exhibited "a search in these primitive forms, for the 'ornamental fearfulness' of nature. One wanted to seize life at its lowest levels, at its origins." Jugendstil was a method of conscious reaction to high art, the "overrefinement" of Impressionism, and an effort to undo the effects of alienation and access some primal connection (Michalski in Goldwater, *Primitivism in Modern Art* (Cambridge, MA: Harvard University Press, 1938): 56).

28 The short play *Ubu Colonialist* makes the collapse of civilized and primitive, and even the racism underscoring that distinction, quite clear as Ubu is presented as a successful French colonist (*Selected Works of Alfred Jarry* (New York: Grove Press, 1965): 53–60).

29 Emile Durkheim, *Suicide* (New York: Free Press, 1951 [1897]). By 1912 Durkheim had taken this impulse further, cataloging primitive practice in *Elementary Forms of Religious Life* (New York: Free Press, 1915).

30 Performance art is a term that first appeared around 1970 and was applied retro-actively to describe artists' performative expressions post-abstract expressionism from the late 1950s. However, the roots of performance art are clearly in the modernist avant-garde, especially Futurism and Dadaism. See Roselee Goldberg, *Performance Art: From Futurism to the Present* (New York: Harry N. Abrams, 1988). Performance has actually become a marker for the break between modernism and postmodernism, supported by the argument that performance replaced modernist notions of a work of art as a formal, framed, material object with the notion of art as an event, a transaction. See Philip Auslander, *Presence and Resistance: Postmodernism and Cultural Politics in Contemporary American Performance* (Ann Arbor: University of Michigan Press, 1992); Johannes H. Birringer, *Theater, Theory, and Postmodernism* (Bloomington: Indiana University Press, 1991); and Henry Sayre, *The Object of Performance: The American Avant-Garde since 1970* (Chicago: University of Chicago Press, 1989). This notion of a "break" between modernism and postmodernism hinged on performance is obviously problematic, especially since, as Robyn Brentano has pointed out, "many of the characteristics of performance that scholars have cited to qualify it as a postmodern phenomenon – its interdisciplinary, collaborative, antihierarchical, contingent, and indeterminate qualities – are all aspects of performance that were evident in the modernist setting (in Dada, Futurism, and Surrealism)" (Brentano, "Outside the Frame: Performance, Art, and Life," *Outside the Frame: Performance and the Object* (Cleveland, OH: Cleveland Center for Contemporary Art, 1994)). See also Susan Rubin Suleiman's suspicions of this "break" in *Subversive Intent* (Cambridge, MA: Harvard University Press, 1989).

31 Annabelle Melzer uses the term "pseudo-Africanisms" to refer to particular phrases, such as Tristan Tzara's "zdranga zdranga; zoumbye zoumbye; cro cro cro" in his *La Premiere Adventure celeste de M'Antipyrine*, the first Dadaist play (Annabelle Melzer, *Latest Rage The Big Drum: Dada and Surrealist Performance* (Ann Arbor, MI: UMI Research Press, 1980): 70). For Tzara's play see Mel Gordon, *Dada Performance*, (New York: PAJ Press, 1987): 53–62. Such gibberish with an African twang was common in Huelsenbeck's and Ball's poetry as well. Tzara himself collected primitive art, had written numerous articles comparing primitive and Western art in periodicals such as *Nor-Sud* and *Sic,* and translated/invented some forty-two "African poems." See Tristan Tzara, "Poemes Negres," *Alcheringa/ethnopoetics* 2, no. 1 (1976). For an analysis of the primitivism of Janco's masks and Tzara's poetry as a search for a purer, "more integrated view of life," see Evan Maurer's essay "Dada and Surrealism" in William Rubin, ed., *'Primitivism' in 20th-Century Art* (New York: Museum of Modern Art, 1984): 535–40.

32 The intellectual center for this group was the journal *Documents*, in which ethnography was a core issue. See James Clifford "On Ethnographic Surrealism," *Comparative Studies in Society and History* 23, no. 4 (October 1981), for a discussion of the way Bataille's thought was shaped by ethnography, particularly Marcel Mauss. See also Denis Hollier, "Forward," *The College of Sociology* (Minneapolis: University of Minnesota Press, 1988). It is important to note that Leiris remained close to Surrealism and to Breton, despite Breton's hostility to the Collège.

33 Bataille, "The Solar Anus," *Visions of Excess* (Minneapolis: University of Minnesota Press, 1985): 5–9. Leiris, *Manhood* (San Francisco: North Point Press, 1984 [1946]): 63–5, 145.

34 *Ibid.*: 164; Bataille, "The Labyrinth," *Visions of Excess:* 177. Benjamin, "Theses on the Philosophy of History," *Illuminations* (New York: Schocken Books, 1969): 255. Of course Benjamin was a member of the German Frankfurt School, not the French

Collège de Sociologie, but his thinking, especially as concerns literality, occasionally converges with Bataille's in interesting ways.

35 Bataille writes with passion on the eye as the prime "cannibal delicacy" and juxtaposes the "inexplicable acuity of horror" that characterizes "civilized man," of which the most developed of these horrors is "the fear of the eye" ("Eye," *Visions of Excess*: 17). On the "passage" from "bloody sacrifice" that unites "gatherings of blacks" to the removed "symbolic sacrifice" of whites, see Hollier, "Attraction and Repulsion II," *The College of Sociology* (Minneapolis: University of Minnesota Press, 1988): 118–20. Again, that which punctures the alienating distance accorded the symbol is linked both to the explicit, bloody body and "black" cultural practice.

36 See Georges Bataille, "Sexual Plethora and Death" *Erotism* (San Francisco: City Lights Books, 1986): 105, for his use of "crack in the system." As Rosalind Krauss points out, Bataille equates the Marquis de Sade with pre-Columbian Aztec priests (Krauss, *The Originality of the Avant-Garde and Other Modernist Myths* (Cambridge, MA: MIT Press, 1988): 55).

37 Rosalind Krauss upholds Barthes's reading in "No More Play," but for two important feminist readings which take issue with Barthes's reading of the detail, see Naomi Schor, *Reading in Detail* (New York: Methuen, 1987): 79–97; and Jane Gallop, "The Bodily Enigma," *Thinking Through the Body*, (New York: Columbia University Press, 1988): 11–20.

38 See Benjamin, "On Language as Such and on the Language of Man" and "On the Mimetic Faculty," *Reflections* (New York: Schocken Books, 1986): 314–36. See also Susan Buck-Morss, "A Logic of Disintegration: The Role of the Subject," *The Origin of Negative Dialectics* (New York: Free Press, 1977): 82–95.

39 For Michele H. Richman, Bataille's repeated reference to castrated eyes provide a "metaphor for the inability or unwillingness of humans to recognize the repressed reality of being, given that the collective forms of sacrifice serving such a function in primitive societies have practically disappeared" (Richman, *Reading Georges Bataille* (Baltimore: Johns Hopkins Press, 1982): 91).

6 SEEING THE BIG SHOW

1 This passage was taken from a March 1990 performance of *Reverb-ber-ber-rations* in a section called "Trail Song" which does not appear in the printed text of the show in *Women and Performance* 5, no. 2 (1992). Unless otherwise indicated, all other quotes from *Reverb-ber-ber-rations* appearing in this article do appear in the printed text.

2 A version of this chapter has been published as "See the Big Show: Spiderwoman Theater Doubling Back," *Acting Out: Feminist Performances*, ed. Lynda Hart and Peggy Phelan (New York: Routledge, 1993).

3 Of course, all work is racially marked, as all bodies bear race. "White," however, has historically born the privilege of being "unmarked." See Peggy Phelan, *Unmarked: The Politics of Performance* (New York: Routledge, 1993): 93–111. See Kate Davy, "Outing Whiteness: A Feminist/Lesbian Project," *Theater Journal* 47, no. 2 (May 1995): 189–208; and Lauren Berlant, "National Brands/National Body," *Comparative American Identities: Race, Sex, and Nationality in the Modern Text* (New York: Routledge, 1991).

4 A fragment of Benjamin's "Theses on the Philosophy of History" resonates interestingly with the project of this chapter and bears repeating: "To articulate the past historically does not mean to recognize it 'the way it really was' (Ranke). It means to seize hold of a memory as it flashes up at a moment of danger. Historical materialism wishes to retain that image of the past which unexpectedly appears to man [sic] singled out by history at a moment of danger. The danger affects both the

content of the tradition and its receivers. The same threat hangs over both: that of becoming a tool of the ruling classes. In every era the attempt must be made anew to wrest tradition away from a conformism that is about to overpower it . . . Only that historian will have the gift of fanning the spark of hope in the past who is firmly convinced that even the dead will not be safe from the enemy if he wins. And this enemy has not ceased to be victorious" (1969:255).

5 From *Winnetou's Snake Oil Show from Wigwam City*. All quotes from this play are taken from a videotaped performance of the show.

6 Hortensia Colorado appears with Spiderwoman in *Winnetou's Snake Oil Show*. Together with her sister Vira Colorado, Hortensia Colorado also performs in her own company, The Colorado Sisters, based at Theater for the New City.

7 An article by Dirk Johnson on the front page of the *New York Times* on March 5, 1991, carried the headline: "Census Finds Many Claiming New Identity: Indian," a shift not always motivated by altruistic reasons but by the growing realization that an Indian heritage can mean special benefits. Other whites simply believe it is fashionable to be Indian and "stretch the truth about ancestry." Indians call such people "wanna-bees." The usual story from these people is: "My grandmother was a Cherokee princess."

8 The quotes in the following section are, unless otherwise specified, from an interview with Muriel Miguel, June 1990.

9 Spiderwoman press flyer, circa 1981

10 Interview with Lisa Mayo, Gloria Miguel, Muriel Miguel, and Hortensia Colorado, December 1989.

11 The problems of identity politics in terms of theater affiliations are complicated. Split Britches is widely heralded as "lesbian theater" but, as Deborah Margolin pointed out to me in a May 1991 interview, it is important to note that one of the founding members of the company, Margolin herself, is heterosexual. On Deb Margolin as "queer" see Lynda Hart and Peggy Phelan, "Queerer Than Thou: Being and Deb Margolin," *Theater Journal* 47, no. 2 (1995): 260–82.

12 Excerpted from an interview with Lisa Mayo, Gloria Miguel, and Muriel Miguel, December 1989.

13 Theater for the New City (TNC) is the country's leading presenter of new professional theater productions by Native American artists and playwrights. TNC presents an annual Pow-Wow by the Thunderbird American Indian Dancers and has been the dramatic home for Native American performance groups including Spiderwoman Theater, Off the Beaten Path, and Vira and Hortensia Colorado.

14 From the text of *Reverb-ber-ber-rations*. The inclusion of "Hey, hey, dooten day dooten day" at the end of the monolog does not appear in the text, but was included in the performance I saw both at Theater for the New City in March 1990 and in a solo performance of this section by Lisa Mayo at a rally against the War in the Gulf also at Theater for the New City in February 1991. See also Mayo's discussion of this section of the play in Burns and Hurlbutt, "Secrets."

15 "In this comic turn from the high ideals of the colonial imagination to its low mimetic literary effect, mimicry emerges as one of the most elusive and effective strategies of colonial power and knowledge" (Homi Bhabha, "Of Mimicry and Man: The Ambivalence of Colonial Discourse," *October* 28 (1984): 126).

16 The performance technique I'm trying to articulate here under the rubric "doubling back," or counter-mimicry, can be placed in relation to French ethnographer and dissident surrealist Michel Leiris's notion of "writing back," first articulated in the early 1950s in relation of the work of Aime Cesaire. See James Clifford, *The Predicament of Culture: Twentieth-Century Ethnography, Literature, and Art* (Cambridge, MA: Harvard University Press, 1988): 255–56.

17 From the text of *Reverb-ber-ber-rations*.

18 In *Winnetou's Snake Oil Show* this interruptive quality of the sacred is certainly true.

In *Reverb-ber-ber-rations*, on the other hand, the moments of serious invocation are more broadly interwoven into the fabric of the piece, balancing the parodic and the sincere to the degree that it is sometimes difficult to determine where the sacred and parodic begin and end.

EPILOG: RETURNING FROM THE DEAD

1 Simone de Beauvoir, *The Second Sex* (New York: Vintage Books, 1989): xxix. The passage is worth quoting at length: "[If], following Hegel, we find in consciousness itself a fundamental hostility toward every other consciousness; the subject can be posed only in being opposed – he set himself up as the essential, as opposed to the other, the inessential, the object. But the other consciousness, the other ego, sets up a *reciprocal* claim. . . . How is it then that this reciprocity has not been recognized between the sexes, that one of the contrasting terms is set up as the sole essential, denying any relativity in regard to its correlative and defining the latter as pure otherness?" Prior to this, de Beauvoir accuses Levinas of "disregarding the reciprocity of subject and object" and claims that the disregard of reciprocity, "which is intended to be objective, is in fact an assertion of masculine privilege" (1989:xxvii).
2 Many feminist works are particularly suggestive of reciprocity, even where that particular word is not invoked. Gloria Anzaldua uses the term "crossing" in *Borderlands/La Frontera* (San Francisco: Spinsters/Aunt Lute, 1987).
3 " . . . And the end of all our exploring / Will be to arrive where we started / And know the place for the first time . . . " (T.S. Eliot, "Little Gidding," *Norton Anthology of English Literature*, vol. 2 (New York: Norton, 1974): 2197.
4 The "subject" returns as *subjected* to its socio-historical-political constitution, and in such subjugation, looses its "disinterested" transcendency. As discussed in Chapter 6, this is Foucault's genealogical methodology: "I don't believe the problem can be solved by historicizing the subject as posited by the phenomenologists, fabricating a subject that evolves through the course of history. One has to dispense with the constituent subject, to get rid of the subject itself, that is to say, to arrive at an analysis which can account for the constitution of the subject within a historical framework. And this is what I would call genealogy, that is, a form of history which can account for the constitution of knowledges, discourses, domains of objects, and so on, without having to make reference to a subject which is either transcendental in relation to a field of events or runs in its empty sameness throughout the course of history" (*Power/Knowledge* (New York: Pantheon Books, 1980): 117).

Works Cited

Adams, Parveen (1989) "Of Female Bondage." In *Between Feminism and Psychoanalysis*, edited by Teresa Brennan. New York: Routledge.

Adorno, Theodor (1967) *Prisms*. Translated by Samuel and Shierry Wever. London: Neville Spearman.

—— (1984) *Aesthetic Theory*. Translated by C. Lenhardt. New York: Routledge and Kegan Paul.

Alpers, Svetlana (1983) *The Art of Describing*. Chicago: University of Chicago Press.

Anzaldua, Gloria (1987) *Borderlands/La Frontera*. San Francisco: Spinsters/Aunt Lute.

Argyle, Michael, and Mark Cook (1976) *Gaze and Mutual Gaze*. Cambridge: Cambridge University Press.

Artaud, Antonin (1988) *Antonin Artaud, Selected Writings*, edited by Susan Sontag, translated by Helen Weaver. Berkeley: University of California Press.

Auslander, Philip (1987) "Toward a Concept of the Political in Postmodern Theatre." *Theatre Journal* 38, no. 1: 20–34.

—— (1992) *Presence and Resistance: Postmodernism and Cultural Politics in Contemporary American Performance*. Ann Arbor: University of Michigan Press.

Ball, Hugo (1974) *Flight Out of Time: A Dada Diary*. Translated by Ann Raimes. New York: The Viking Press.

Banes, Sally (1983) *Democracy's Body: Judson Dance Theater, 1962–1964*. Ann Arbor: UMI Research Press.

—— (1987) *Terpsichore in Sneakers: Postmodern Dance*. Middletown, CT: Wesleyan University Press.

—— (1993) *Greenwich Village, 1963: Avant-Garde Performance and the Effervescent Body*. Durham, NC: Duke University Press.

Bardwick, Judith (1971) *The Psychology of Women: A Bio-Cultural Conflict*. New York: Harper and Row.

Barreras del Rio, Petra (1987) "Ana Mendieta: A Historical Overview." In *Ana Mendieta: A Retrospective*, edited by Petra Barreras del Rio, and John Perreault. New York: The New Museum of Contemporary Art.

Barreras del Rio, Petra, and John Perreault, eds. (1987) *Ana Mendieta: A Retrospective*. New York: The New Museum of Contemporary Art.

Barthes, Roland (1963) "La Metaphore de l'oeil." *Critique*, no. 195–6.

—— 1989 "The Reality Effect." In *The Rustle of Language*. Translated by Richard Howard. Berkeley: University of California Press.

Bataille, Georges (1967) *Story of the Eye*. Translated by Joachim Neugroschel. San Francisco: City Lights Books.

—— (1983) *Manet*. Paris: Editions Skira.

—— (1985) *Visions of Excess: Selected Writings, 1927–1939*. Translated by Allan Stoekl. Minneapolis: University of Minnesota Press.

—— (1986) *Erotism: Death and Sensuality*. San Francisco: City Lights Books.

—— (1988) "Attraction and Repulsion II: Social Structure." In *The College of Sociology: 1937–39*, edited by Denis Hollier. Minneapolis: University of Minnesota Press.

Baudelaire, Charles (1945) *Fusees.* Mexico, D.F.: Editions Quetzal.

Baudrillard, Jean (1981) (1994) *Simulacra and Simulation.* Translated by Shiela Faria Glaser. Ann Arbor: University of Michigan Press.

Becker, George J., ed. (1963) *Documents of Modern Literary Realism.* Princeton: Princeton University Press.

Benedikt, Michael, ed. (1964) *Modern French Theater: The Avant-Garde, Dada, and Surrealism.* New York: Dutton.

Benhabib, Seyla (1987) "The Generalized and the Concrete Other." In *Feminism as Critique,* edited by Seyla Benhabib and Drucilla Cornell. Minneapolis: University of Minnesota Press.

Benjamin, Jessica (1988) *Bonds of Love: Psychoanalysis, Feminism, and the Problem of Domination.* New York: Pantheon Books.

Benjamin, Walter (1969) *Illuminations,* edited by Hannah Arendt. New York: Schocken Books.

—— (1973) *Charles Baudelaire: A Lyric Poet in the Era of High Capitalism.* Translated by Harry Zohn. London: New Left Books.

—— (1979) "A Small History of Photography." In *One Way Street.* Translated by Edmund Jephcott and Kinglsey Shorter. London: New Left Books.

—— (1986) *Reflections,* edited by Peter Demetz. New York: Schocken Books.

Ben-Levi, Jack, Craig Houser, Leslie C. Jones, Simon Taylor (1992/93) "Introduction." In *Abject Art: Repulsion and Desire in American Art.* Exhibit Catalog, Whitney Museum, New York.

Berger, John (1972) *Ways of Seeing.* New York: Penguin Books.

Berlant, Lauren (1991) "National Brands/National Body." In *Comparative American Identities: Race, Sex, and Nationality in the Modern Text,* edited by Hortense J. Spillers. New York: Routledge.

Berman, Marshall (1982) *All That is Solid Melts into Air: The Experience of Modernity.* New York: Simon and Schuster.

Bernhard, Sandra (1992) "Bunny Wanna-Be." *Playboy,* September.

Bhabha, Homi (1984) "Of Mimicry and Man: The Ambivalence of Colonial Discourse." *October* 28: 125–33.

Birringer, Johannes H. (1991) *Theater, Theory, and Postmodernism.* Bloomington: Indiana University Press.

Blanchot, Maurice (1986) *The Writing of the Disaster.* Translated by Ann Smock. Lincoln: University of Nebraska Press.

—— (1992) "Glances from Beyond the Grave." *Yale French Studies* 81: 151–61.

Blau, Herbert (1990) *The Audience.* Baltimore: Johns Hopkins University Press.

Bloom, Pamela (1990) "Keeping the Faith: Native Americans Transform Tradition on Stage." *Taxi* January: 104–9.

Bordo, Susan (1993) *Unbearable Weight: Feminism, Western Culture, and the Body.* Berkeley: University of California Press.

Bovenschen, Sylvia (1978) "The Contemporary Witch, the Historical Witch and the Witch Myth: The Witch, Subject of the Appropriation of Nature and Object of the Domination of Nature." *New German Critique* 15 (Fall): 83–119.

Brennan, Teresa (1993) *History After Lacan.* New York: Routledge.

Brentano, Robyn (1994) "Outside the Frame: Performance, Art, and Life." In *Outside the Frame: Performance and the Object.* Cleveland, OH: Cleveland Center for Contemporary Art.

Breton, Andre (1969) *Manifestos of Surrealism.* Translated by R. Seaver and H.R. Lane. Ann Arbor: University of Michigan Press.

—— (1972) *Surrealism and Painting.* Translated by Simon Watson Taylor. London: MacDonald and Co.

Bright, Susie (1992) *Susie Bright's Sexual Reality: A Virtual Sex World Reader.* San Francisco: Cleis Press.

Bronfen, Elisabeth (1992) *Over Her Dead Body: Death, Femininity and the Aesthetic.* New York: Routledge.

Bronski, Michael (1984) *Culture Clash: The Making of a Gay Sensibility.* Boston: South End Press.

Brown, Norman O. (1966) *Love's Body.* New York: Random House.

Bryson, Norman (1988) "The Gaze in the Expanded Field." In *Vision and Visuality*, edited by Hal Foster. Seattle: Bay Press.

Buci-Glucksmann, Christine (1987) "Catastrophic Utopia: The Feminine as Allegory of the Modern." In *The Making of the Modern Body: Sexuality and Society in the Nineteenth Century*, edited by Catherine Gallagher and Thomas Laqueur. Berkeley: University of California Press.

Buck-Morss, Susan (1977) *The Origin of Negative Dialectics.* New York: Free Press.

—— (1989) *The Dialectics of Seeing: Walter Benjamin and the Arcades Project.* Cambridge, MA: MIT Press.

Burger, Peter (1984) *Theory of the Avant-Garde.* Translated by Michael Shaw. Minneapolis: University of Minnesota Press.

Burns, Judy, and Jerry Hurlbutt (1992) "Secrets: A Conversation with Lisa Mayo of Spiderwoman Theater." *Women and Performance.*

Burstyn, Varda, ed. (1985) *Women Against Censorship.* Vancouver: Douglas and McIntyre.

Butler, Judith (1990a) "Performative Acts and Gender Constitution: An Essay in Phenomenology and Feminist Theory." In *Performing Feminisms: Feminist Critical Theory and Theatre*, edited by Sue-Ellen Case. Baltimore: Johns Hopkins University Press.

—— (1990b) *Gender Trouble.* New York: Routledge.

—— (1991) "Contingent Foundations: Feminism and the Question of 'Post-modernism.'" *Praxis International* 11, no. 2 (July): 150–7.

—— (1993) *Bodies that Matter.* New York: Routledge.

Carby, Hazel V. (1987) *Reconstructing Womanhood: The Emergence of the African-American Woman Novelist.* New York: Oxford University Press.

Carlson, Marvin (1984) *Theories of the Theater.* Ithaca, NY: Cornell University Press.

Carr, C. (1986) "Unspeakable Practice, Unnatural Acts." *Village Voice*, June 24. Reprinted in *Acting Out: Feminist Performances*, edited by Lynda Hart and Peggy Phelan. New York: Routledge, 1993.

—— (1990) "War on Art," *Village Voice*, June 5: 25–8.

1992 "Guerrilla Girls: Combat in the Art Zone." *Mirabella* July: 32–5.

—— (1993) "A Public Cervix Announcement." In *On Edge: Performance at the End of the Twentieth Century.* Hanover, NH: University Press of New England. First published in *Village Voice* May 1989.

—— (1993) *On Edge: Performance at the End of the Twentieth Century.* Hanover, NH: University Press of New England. First published in *Art Vu Magazine* Fall 1991.

Case, Sue-Ellen (1990) "Introduction." In *Performing Feminisms: Feminist Critical Theory and Theater*, edited by Sue-Ellen Case.

Chicago, Judy (1993) [1975] *Through the Flower: My Struggles as a Woman Artist.* New York: Penguin Books. First published New York: Doubleday.

Chua, Lawrence (1990) "Out and About with Sandra Bernhard." *Village Voice* February 6: 37–9.

Cixous, Helene, and Catherine Clement (1986) (1975) *The Newly Born Woman.* Translated by Betsy Wing. Minneapolis: University of Minnesota Press.

Clark, T.J. (1985) *The Painting of Modern Life: Paris in the Art of Manet and His Followers.* New York: Knopf.

Clifford, James (1981) "On Ethnographic Surrealism." *Comparative Studies in Society and History* 23 (October): 543–64.

—— (1988) *The Predicament of Culture: Twentieth-Century Ethnography, Literature, and Art.* Cambridge, MA: Harvard University Press.

Collins, Patricia Hill (1990) *Black Feminist Thought: Knowledge, Consciousness, and the Politics of Empowerment.* New York: Routledge.

Copjec, Joan (1981) "Flavit et Dissipati Sunt." *October* 18: 20–40.

Coutts-Smith, Kevin (1991) "Some General Observations of the Problem of Cultural Colonialism." In *The Myth of Primitivism: Perspectives on Art,* edited by Susan Hiller. New York: Routledge.

Craig, Edward Gordon (1907) *On the Art of the Theater.* New York: Theater Art Books.

Crane, Diana (1987) *The Transformation of the Avant-Garde: The New York Art World, 1940–1985.* Chicago: University of Chicago Press.

Crary, Jonathan (1991) *Techniques of the Observer: On Vision and Modernity in the Nineteenth Century.* Cambridge, MA: MIT Press.

Culler, Jonathan (1982) *On Deconstruction: Theory and Criticism after Structuralism.* Ithaca: Cornell University Press.

Darwin, Charles (1955) *On the Origin of the Species.* Chicago: Encyclopedia Britannica Series, Great Books of the Western World, vol. 49.

Davis, Natalie Zemon, and Peter Starn (1989) "Introduction." Special Issue on Memory and Counter-Memory. *Representations* no. 26 (Spring): 1–6.

Davy, Kate (1995) "Outing Whiteness: A Feminist/Lesbian Project." *Theater Journal* 47, no. 2 (May): 189–208.

Dayan, Joan (1991) "Vodoun: Or, The Voice of the Gods." *Raritan* 10, no. 3: 32–57.

de Beauvoir, Simone (1989) (1952) *The Second Sex.* Translated by H.M. Parshley. New York: Vintage Books.

Delacoste, Frederique, and Priscilla Alexander, eds (1987) *Sex Work: Writings By Women in the Sex Industry.* San Francisco: Cleis Press.

de Lauretis, Teresa (1985) *Alice Doesn't: Feminism, Semiotics, Cinema.* Bloomington: Indiana University Press.

—— (1987) *Technologies of Gender.* Bloomington: Indiana University Press.

—— (1990) "Sexual Difference and Lesbian Representation." In *Performing Feminisms,* edited by Sue-Ellen Case. Baltimore: Johns Hopkins University Press.

Deleuze, Gilles, and Felix Guattari (1983) *Anti-Oedipus: Capitalism and Schizophrenia.* Translated by Robert Hurley, Mark Seem and Helen R. Lane. Minneapolis: University of Minnesota Press.

Derrida, Jacques (1979) *Spurs: Nietzsche's Style.* Translated by Barbara Harlow. Chicago: University of Chicago Press.

Derrida, Jacques, and Christie V. McDonald (1982) "Choreographies." *Diacritics* 12, no. 2.

de Saussure, Ferdinand (1959) [1915] *Course in General Linguistics.* New York: McGraw-Hill.

Diamond, Elin (1988) Brechtian Theory/Feminist Theory: Toward a Gestic Feminist Criticism." *The Drama Review* 32, no. 1: 82–94.

—— (1989) "Mimesis, Mimicry, and the True-Real." *Modern Drama* 32, no. 1: 58–72.

—— (1990/91) "Realism and Hysteria: Toward a Feminist Mimesis." *Discourse* 13, no. 1 (Fall–Winter): 59–92.

Doane, Mary Ann (1984) "The 'Woman's Film': Possession and Address." In *Revision: Essays in Feminist Film Criticism,* edited by Mary Ann Doane, Patricia Mellencamp, and Linda Williams. Los Angeles: The American Film Institute.

—— (1987) *Desire to Desire: The Woman's Film of the 1940s.* Bloomington: Indiana University Press.

Dolan, Jill (1988) *The Feminist Spectator as Critic.* Ann Arbor: UMI Research Press.

Duberman, Martin (1972) *Black Mountain: An Exploration in Community.* New York: E.P. Dutton.

Dubin, Steven C. (1992) *Arresting Images: Impolitic Art and Uncivil Actions.* New York: Routledge.

Duncan, Carol (1988) "The Aesthetics of Power in Modern Erotic Art." In *Feminist Art Criticism*, edited by Arlene Raven, Cassandra Langer, Joanna Frueh. New York: Icon Editions.

Durkheim, Emile (1915) *Elementary Forms of Religious Life*. Translated by Joseph Ward Swain. New York: Free Press.

—— (1951) [1897] *Suicide*. Translated by John A. Spaulding. New York: Free Press.

Dyer, Richard (1988) "White." *Screen* 29, no. 4: 44–64.

Eliot, T.S. (1974) (1942) "Little Gidding." In *Norton Anthology of English Literature*, vol. 2. New York: Norton.

Ellis, John (1980) "On Pornography." *Screen* 21, no. 1 (Spring).

Fabian, Johannes (1983) *Time and the Other: How Anthropology Makes Its Object*. New York: Columbia University Press.

Faunce, Sarah, and Linda Nochlin (1988) *Courbet Reconsidered*. Brooklyn, NY: The Brooklyn Museum.

Finch, Casey (1992) "Two of a Kind." *Artforum* February: 91–4.

Finke, Laurie A. (1990) "Painting Women: Images of Femininity in Jacobean Tragedy." In *Performing Feminisms*, edited by Sue-Ellen Case. Baltimore: Johns Hopkins University Press.

Finley, Karen (1988) *"The Constant State of Desire"*. *The Drama Review* 32, no. 1: 139–51.

Forte, Jeanie (1988) "Women's Performance Art: Feminism and Postmodernism." *Theater Journal* 40 (May).

—— (1992) "Focus on the Body: Pain, Praxis, and Pleasure in Feminist Performance." In *Critical Theory and Performance*, edited by Janelle G. Reinelt and Joseph R. Roach. Ann Arbor: University of Michigan Press.

Foster, Hal (1982) "Subversive Signs." *Art in America* 70, no. 10 (November).

—— (1985a) "For a Concept of the Political in Contemporary Art." In *Recodings: Art, Spectacle, Cultural Politics*. Port Townsend, WA: Bay Press.

—— (1985b) "The 'Primitive' Unconscious in Modern Art." *October* 34: 45–70.

—— (1993) "Postmodernism in Parallax." *October* 63 (Winter): 3–20.

Foster, Hal, ed. (1983) *The Anti-Aesthetic: Essays on Postmodern Culture*. Port Townsend, WA: Bay Press.

—— (1988) *Vision and Visuality*. Dia Art Foundation Discussions in Contemporary Culture, no. 2. Seattle: Bay Press.

Foucault, Michel (1976) *The Archaeology of Knowledge and the Discourse on Language*. New York: Harper.

—— (1977) *Language, Counter-Memory, Practice*. Ithaca, NY: Cornell University Press.

—— (1980a) *The History of Sexuality*. New York: Vintage Books.

—— (1980b) *Power/Knowledge*. New York: Pantheon Books.

Freud, Sigmund (1953–74) "The Question of Lay Analysis." In *Standard Edition of the Complete Psychoanalytic Works of Sigmund Freud*, vol. 20. London: Hogarth.

—— (1958) "The Uncanny." In *On Creativity and the Unconscious*, edited by Benjamin Nelson. New York: Harper and Row..

—— (1961) *Civilization and Its Discontents*. Translated by James Strachey. New York: Norton.

—— (1962) *Three Essays on the Theory of Sexuality*. Translated by James Strachey. New York: Basic Books.

—— (1965) "Femininity." In *New Introductory Lectures on Psychoanalysis*, edited and translated by James Strachey. New York: W.W. Norton.

Friedan, Betty (1963) *The Feminine Mystique*. New York: Dell.

Frye, Marilyn (1983) "To Be and Be Seen: The Politics of Reality." In *The Politics of Reality: Essays in Feminist Theory*. Trumansburg, NY: The Crossing Press.

Fuchs, Elinor (1989) "Staging the Obscene Body." *The Drama Review* 33, no. 1: 33–58.

Fuss, Diana (1989) *Essentially Speaking: Feminism, Nature, and Difference*. New York: Routledge.

Gallop, Jane (1988) *Thinking through the Body.* New York: Columbia University Press.
—— (1989) "French Theory and the Seduction of Feminism." In *Men in Feminism*, edited by A Jardine and P. Smith. New York: Routledge.
Gilbert, Sandra M., and Susan Gubar (1979) *The Madwoman in the Attic: The Woman Writer and the Nineteenth-Century Literary Imagination.* New Haven: Yale University Press.
Gilman, Sander L. (1985) "Black Bodies, White Bodies: Toward an Iconography of Female Sexuality in Late Nineteenth-Century Art, Medicine, and Literature." In *"Race," Writing, and Difference*, edited by Henry Louis Gates, Jr.. Chicago: University of Chicago Press.
Goldberg, Roselee (1988) *Performance Art: From Futurism to the Present.* New York: Harry N. Abrams.
Goldman, Robert (1992) *Reading Ads Socially.* New York: Routledge.
Goldwater, Robert (1938) *Primitivism in Modern Art.* Cambridge, MA: Harvard University Press.
Gordon, Mel (1987) *Dada Performance.* New York: Performing Arts Journal Press.
Gray, Paul (1964) "Stanislavski and America: A Critical Chronology." *The Drama Review* 9, no. 2: 21–60.
Greenberg, Clement (1966) "Modernist Painting." In *The New Art*, edited by Gregory Battcock. New York: Dutton.
Haraway, Donna (1989) *Primate Visions: Gender, Race, and Nature in the World of Modern Science.* New York: Routledge.
Hart, Lynda (1992) "Motherhood According to Finley: The Theory of Total Blame." *The Drama Review* 36, no. 1: 124–34.
—— (1993a) "Introduction." In *Acting Out: Feminist Performances*, edited by Lynda Hart and Peggy Phelan. Ann Arbor: University of Michigan Press.
—— (1993b) "Identity and Seduction: Lesbians in the Mainstream." In *Acting Out: Feminist Performances*, edited by Lynda Hart and Peggy Phelan. Ann Arbor: University of Michigan Press.
—— (1994) *Fatal Women: Lesbian Sexuality and the Mark of Aggression.* New York: Routledge.
Hart, Lynda, and Peggy Phelan (1995) "Queerer Than Thou: Being and Deb Margolin." *Theater Journal* 47, no. 2: 260–82.
Henderson, John A. (1971) *The First Avant-Garde, 1887–1894.* London: George G. Harrap.
Hess, Elizabeth (1991) "Backing Down: Behind Closed Doors at the NEA." *Village Voice* September 25: 37.
Hiller, Susan, ed. (1991) *The Myth of Primitivism: Perspectives on Art.* New York: Routledge.
Holder, Maryse (1973) "Another Cuntree: At Last, a Mainstream Female Art Movement." *Off Our Backs* (September). Reprinted in *Feminist Art Criticism*, edited by Arlene Raven, Cassandra Langer, Joanna Frueh. New York: Icon Editions, 1988.
Hollier, Denis, ed. (1988) *The College of Sociology.* Minneapolis: University of Minnesota Press.
hooks, bell (1992) *Black Looks: Race and Representation.* Boston: South End Press.
Hughes, Holly, Peggy Shaw, and Lois Weaver (1989) "Dress Suits to Hire." *The Drama Review* 33, no. 1: 132–52.
Hunt, Lynn, ed. (1993) *The Invention of Pornography: Obscenity and the Origins of Modernity, 1500–1800.* New York: Zone Books.
Hurston, Zora Neale (1969) [1942] *Dust Tracks on a Road.* Urbana: University of Illinois Press.
Huyssen, Andreas (1986) *After the Great Divide: Modernism, Mass Culture, Post-Modernism.* Bloomington: Indiana University Press.
—— (1990) "Mapping the Postmodern." In *Feminism/Postmodernism*, edited by Linda J. Nicholson. New York: Routledge.

Innes, Christopher (1993) *Avant Garde Theatre: 1892–1992*. New York: Routledge.

Irigaray, Luce (1985a) *This Sex Which Is Not One*. Translated by Catherine Porter with Carolyn Burke. Ithaca: Cornell University Press.

—— (1985b) *Speculum of the Other Woman*. Translated by Gillian C. Gill. Ithaca: Cornell University Press.

Jackson, Shannon (1996) "White Noises." In *More Monologues by Women for Women*, edited by Tori Haring-Smith. New York: Heinemann Press.

James, David E. (1989) *Allegories of Cinema: American Film in the Sixties*. Princeton, NJ: Princeton University Press.

Jarry, Alfred (1965) *The Selected Works of Alfred Jarry*, edited by Roger Shattuck. New York: Grove Press.

Jay, Martin (1973) *The Dialectical Imagination*. Boston: Little, Brown, and Company.

—— (1993) *Downcast Eyes: The Denigration of Vision in Twentieth-Century Thought*. Berkeley: University of California Press.

—— (1994) "The Disenchantment of the Eye: Surrealism and the Crisis of Ocularcentrism." In *Visualizing Theory*, edited by Lucien Taylor. New York: Routledge.

Johnson, Dirk (1991) "Census Finds Many Claiming New Identity." *New York Times* March 5: A1, 16.

Jones, Amelia G. (1993) "The Ambivalence of Male Masquerade: Duchamp as Rrose Selavy." In *The Body Imaged: The Human Form and Visual Culture since the Renaissance*, edited by Kathleen Adler and Marcia Pointon. London: Cambridge University Press.

Jones, Leslie (1992/93) "Transgressive Femininity." In *Abject Art: Repulsion and Desire in American Art*, edited by Jack Ben-Levi, Craig Houser, Leslie C. Jones, Simon Taylor. Exhibit Catalog, Whitney Museum, New York.

Jordanova, Ludmilla (1989) *Sexual Visions*. London: Harvester Wheatsheaf.

Juno, A., and V. Vale, eds. (1991) *Angry Women*. Hong Kong: Re-Search Publications.

Kandinsky, Wassily (1977) *Concerning the Spiritual in Art*. Translated by M.T.H. Sadler. New York: Dover.

Kappeler, Suzanne (1986) *The Pornography of Representation*. Cambridge: Polity Press.

Kaprow, Allan (1966) *Assemblage, Environments, and Happenings*. New York: Abrams.

Keller, Evelyn Fox, and Christine Grontkowski (1983) "The Mind's Eye." In *Discovering Reality: Feminist Perspectives on Epistemology, Metaphysics, Methodology, and Philosophy of Science*, edited by Sandra Harding and Merrill B. Hintikka. Dordrecht: D. Reidel.

Kendrick, Walter (1987) *The Secret Museum: Pornography in Modern Culture*. New York: Penguin.

Kern-Foxworth, Marilyn (1994) *Aunt Jemima, Uncle Ben, and Rastus: Blacks in Advertising, Yesterday, Today, and Tomorrow*. Westport, CT: Greenwood Press.

Kilkelly, Ann (1994) "Ghost Notes, Rhythms, and Lamentations." *Women and Performance* 7, no. 1: 65–81.

Kirby, Michael (1965) *Happenings*. New York: Dutton.

Koch, Gertrude (1989) "The Body's Shadow Realm." Translated by Jan-Christopher Horak and Joyce Rheuban. *October* 50 (Fall): 3–29.

Kojève, Alexandre (1969) *Introduction to the Reading of Hegel*. Ithaca: Cornell University Press.

Kotz, Liz (1992) "The Body You Want: An Interview with Judith Butler." *Artforum* November: 82–9.

Koyre, Alexandre (1957) *From the Closed World to the Infinite Universe*. Baltimore: Johns Hopkins University Press.

Krauss, Rosalind E. (1985) "Corpus Delicti." In *L'Amour Fou: Photography and Surrealism*, edited by R. Krauss and J. Livingston. New York: Abbeville Press.

—— (1988) *The Originality of the Avant-Garde and Other Modernist Myths*. Cambridge, MA: MIT Press.

—— (1993a) *The Optical Unconscious.* Cambridge, MA: MIT Press.
—— (1993b) "Gleams and Reflections." In *Cindy Sherman: 1975–1993.* New York: Rizzoli.
Kristeva, Julia (1981) "Women's Time." *Signs* 7, no. 1: 13–35.
—— (1986) "The True-Real." In *The Kristeva Reader*, edited by Toril Moi. New York: Columbia University Press.
Kroker, Arthur and Marilouise, eds (1991) *The Hysterical Male: New Feminist Theory.* New York: St. Martins Press.
Lacan, Jacques (1977) "The Signification of the Phallus." In *Ecrits.* Translated by Alan Sheridan. New York: W.W. Norton and Company.
—— (1981) *Four Fundamental Concepts of Psychoanalysis.* Translated by Alan Sheridan. New York: W.W. Norton and Company.
—— (1982) *Feminine Sexuality*, edited by Jacqueline Rose and Juliet Mitchell, translated by Jacqueline Rose, New York: W.W. Norton and Company.
Langer, Cassandra (1988) "Against the Grain." In *Feminist Art Criticism*, edited by Arlene Raven, Cassandra Langer, and Joanna Frueh. New York: Icon Editions.
Lavin, Maud (1990) "Androgyny, Spectatorship, and the Weimar Photomontages of Hannah Höch." *New German Critique* 51 (Fall).
—— (1993) *Cut With The Kitchen Knife: The Weimar Photomontages of Hannah Höch.* New Haven: Yale University Press.
Lears, Jackson (1994) *Fables of Abundance: A Cultural History of Advertising in America.* New York: Basic Books.
Lederer, Laura, ed. (1980) *Take Back the Night: Women On Pornography.* New York: Morrow.
Leiris, Michel (1984) (1946) *Manhood: A Journey from Childhood into the Fierce Order of Virility.* Translated by Richard Howard. San Francisco: North Point Press.
Leiris, Michel, and Jacqueline Delange (1968) *African Art.* London: Thames and Hudson.
Levin, David Michael (1993) *Modernity and the Hegemony of Vision.* Berkeley: University of California Press.
Lippard, Lucy (1976) *From the Center: Feminist Essays on Women's Art.* New York: E.P. Dutton.
Lipton, Eunice (1992) *Alias Olympia.* New York: Charles Scribner's Sons.
Lorde, Audre (1981a) "An Open Letter to Mary Daly." In *This Bridge Called My Back*, edited by Cherrie Moraga and Gloria Anzaldua. New York: Kitchen Table: Women of Color Press.
—— (1981b) "The Master's Tools Will Never Dismantle the Master's House." In *This Bridge Called My Back*, edited by Cherrie Moraga and Gloria Anzaldua. New York: Kitchen Table: Women of Color Press.
McClintock, Anne (1993) "Sex Workers and Sex Work." *Social Text* 37 (Winter): 1–10.
—— (1995) *Imperial Leather: Race, Gender and Sexuality in the Colonial Conquest.* New York: Routledge.
MacDonald, Scott (1988) "Carolee Schneemann." In *Critical Cinema: Interviews with Independent Filmmakers.* Berkeley: University of California Press.
Madonna (1993) Interview with Mike Meyers in *Interview*, June 1993: 102.
Magnuson, Ann (1992) "I Have a Sex Book, Too." *Paper Magazine* October: 20–5.
Marchand, Roland (1985) *Advertising and the American Dream.* Berkeley: University of California Press.
Marcus, George E. (1994) "The Modernist Sensibility in Recent Ethnographic Writing and the Cinematic Metaphor of Montage." In *Visualizing Theory: Selected Essays for V.A.R, 1990–1994*, edited by Lucien Taylor. New York: Routledge.
Marcus, George E., and Michael M. J. Fischer (1986) *Anthropology as Cultural Critique.* Chicago: University of Chicago Press
Marcus, Steven (1974) *The Other Victorians: A Study of Sexuality and Pornography in Mid-Nineteenth-Century England.* New York: Basic Books.

Margolin, Deborah (1991) Interview with author. April.

Martin, Emily (1990) "Science and Women's Bodies: Forms of Anthropological Knowledge." In *Body/Politics*, edited by Mary Jacobus, Evelyn Fox Keller, and Sally Shuttleworth. New York: Routledge.

Marx, Karl (1977) *Capital* I. Translated by Ben Fawkes. New York: Vintage Books.

Mayne, Judith (1990) *The Woman at the Keyhole: Feminism and Women's Cinema.* Bloomington: Indiana University Press.

Melzer, Annabelle (1980) *Latest Rage The Big Drum: Dada and Surrealist Performance.* Ann Arbor, MI: UMI Research Press.

Mercer, Kobena (1991) "Looking for Trouble." *Transition* 51: 184–97.

—— (1993) "Reading Racial Fetishism: The Photographs of Robert Mapplethorpe." In *Fetishism as Cultural Discourse*. Ithaca: Cornell University Press.

Miller, Daniel (1991) "Primitive Art and the Necessity of Primitivism to Art." In *The Myth of Primitivism: Perspectives on Art*, edited by Susan Hiller. New York: Routledge.

Minh-Ha, Trinh T. (1986/87) "Difference: 'A Special Third World Women Issue.'" *Discourse* 8 (Fall/Winter): 11–38.

Mitchell, Timothy (1988) *Colonising Egypt.* New York: Cambridge University Press.

Modleski, Tania (1991) *Feminism Without Women: Culture and Criticism in a "Postfeminist" Age.* New York: Routledge.

Montano, Linda (1981) *Art in Everyday Life.* Los Angeles: Astro Artz.

—— (1989) "Summer Saint Camp 1987." *The Drama Review* 33, no. 1.

Morris, Robert (1965) "Notes on Dance." *The Drama Review* 10, no. 2. Reprinted in *Happenings and Other Acts*, edited by Mariellen Sandford. New York: Routledge, 1995.

Motherwell, Robert, ed. (1951) *The Dada Painters and Poets: An Anthology.* Boston: G.K. Hall.

Mulvey, Laura (1975) "Visual Pleasure and Narrative Cinema." *Screen* 16, no. 3.

—— (1992) "Pandora: Topographies of the Mask and Curiosity." In *Sexuality and Space*, edited by Beatriz Colomina. New York: Princeton Architectural Press.

Mussmann, Linda (1987) *If Kansas Goes.* Unpublished playscript. Produced by Time and Space Limited Theater at Marymount Manhattan College in New York City in 1987.

Nicholson, Linda J., ed. (1990) *Feminism/Postmodernism.* New York: Routledge Press.

Nochlin, Linda (1971) *Realism.* New York: Penguin.

Nye, Robert A. (1993) "The Medical Origins of Sexual Fetishism." In *Fetishism as Cultural Discourse*, edited by Emily Apter and William Pietz. Ithaca: Cornell University Press.

Ono, Yoko (1970) *Grapefruit*, 2nd ed. New York: Simon and Schuster.

Owens, Craig (1983) "The Discourse of Others: Feminists and Postmodernism." In *The Anti-Aesthetic*, edited by Hal Foster. Port Townsend, WA: Bay Press.

Panovsky, Dora and Erwin (1956) *Pandora's Box: The Changing Aspects of a Mythical Symbol.* New York: Pantheon.

Panovsky, Erwin (1991) *Perspective as Symbolic Form.* Translated by Christopher S. Wood. New York: Zone Books.

Patraka, Vivian M. (1992) "Binary Terror and Feminist Performance: Reading Both Ways." *Discourse* 14, no. 2 (Spring): 163–85.

Phelan, Peggy (1990) "Money Talks," *The Drama Review* (Spring): 4–15.

—— (1991) "Money Talks, Again." *The Drama Review* (Fall): 131–42.

—— (1993) *Unmarked: The Politics of Performance.* New York: Routledge.

Pheterson, Gail, ed. (1989) *A Vindication of the Rights of Whores.* Seattle: Seal Press.

Pitts, Mary Ellen (1990) "The Holographic Paradigm: A New Model for the Study of Literature and Science." *Modern Language Studies* 20, no. 4: 80–9.

Pontalis, J.B. (1992) "Michel Leiris, or Psychoanalysis Without End." *Yale French Studies* 81: 128.

Pramaggiore, Maria (1992) "Resisting/Performing/Femininity: Words, Flesh, and Feminism in Karen Finley's *Constant State of Desire*." *Theater Journal* 44: 269–90.

Press, Joy and Simon Reynolds (1995) *The Sex Revolts.* Cambridge, MA: Harvard University Press.

Rabkin, Gerald, *et al.* (1986) "The Controversial 1985–6 Theater Season: A Politics of Reception." *Performing Arts Journal* 10, no. 1: 7–33,

Rainer, Yvonne (1974) *Work: 1961–1973.* Halifax: Press of the Nova Scotia College of Art and Design.

Rich, Adrienne (1979) "When We Dead Awaken: Writing as Re-vision." In *On Lies, Secrets, and Silence.* New York: W. W. Norton.

Richman, Michele H. (1982) *Reading Georges Bataille: Beyond the Gift.* Baltimore: Johns Hopkins University Press.

Richter, Hans (1965) *Dada: Art and Anti-Art.* New York: Oxford University Press.

Ricoeur, Paul (1970) *Freud and Philosophy: An Essay on Interpretation.* Translated by Denis Savage. New Haven: Yale University Press.

Robinson, Amy (1996) "Forms of Appearance of Value: Homer Plessy and the Politics of Privacy." In *Performance and Cultural Politics*, edited by Elin Diamond. New York: Routledge.

Rosaldo, Michelle (1977) "Women, Culture, and Society." In *The Bonds of Womanhood*, edited by Nancy Cott. New Haven: Yale University Press.

Rose, Barbara (1993) "Is it Art? Orlan and the Transgressive Act." *Art in America* 81, no. 2 (February): 76–81.

Rose, Jacqueline (1982) "Introduction II." In Jacques Lacan, *Feminine Sexuality: Jacques Lacan and the École Freudienne.* New York: W. W. Norton.

Roth, Moira (1983) *The Amazing Decade: Women and Performance Art in America, 1970–1980.* Los Angeles: Astro Artz.

—— (1988) "Suzanne Lacy: Social Reformer and Witch." *The Drama Review* 32, no. 1: 50–1.

Rubin, Gayle (1975) "The Traffic in Women: Notes on the 'Political Economy' of Sex." In *Toward an Anthropology of Women*, edited by Rayna R. Reiter. New York: Monthly Review Press.

Rubin, William, ed. (1984) *"Primitivism" in 20th-Century Art.* New York: The Museum of Modern Art.

Sandford, Mariellen, ed. (1995) *Happenings and Other Acts.* New York: Routledge.

Sartre, Jean Paul (1966) *Being and Nothingness.* Translated by Hazel E. Barnes. New York: Pocket Books.

Sayre, Henry (1989) *The Object of Performance: The American Avant-Garde since 1970.* Chicago: University of Chicago Press.

Schechner, Richard (1986) *Between Theatre and Anthropology.* Philadelphia: University of Pennsylvania Press.

—— (1988) "Karen Finley: A Constant State of Becoming." *The Drama Review* 32, no. 1: 152–8.

Schneemann, Carolee (1975) *Cezanne, She Was a Great Painter.* New Paltz, NY: Tresspuss Press.

—— (1979) *More Than Meat Joy.* New Paltz, NY: Documentext.

—— (1989) "Fresh Blood: A Dream Morphology." Unpublished performance text.

—— (1990) Interview. "On the Body as Material." *Artweek* October 4: 24–5.

—— (1992) Interview with author. Unpublished.

Schneider, Rebecca (1988/89) "Narrative History, Female Subjectivity, and the Theater of Linda Mussmann: Going Forward by Going Back." *Women and Performance* 4, no. 1: 64–82.

—— (1989a) "Holly Hughes: Polymorphous Perversity and the Lesbian Scientist, an Interview." *The Drama Review* 33, no. 1: 171–83.

—— (1989b) Interview with Lisa Mayo, Gloria Miguel, Muriel Miguel, Hortensia Colorado. December.

—— (1990) Interview with Muriel Miguel. June.

—— (1991) Interview with Deborah Margolin. April.

—— (1993) "See the Big Show: Spiderwoman Theater Doubling Back." In *Acting Out: Feminist Performances*, edited by Lynda Hart and Peggy Phelan. Ann Arbor: University of Michigan Press.

Schor, Naomi (1987) *Reading in Detail: Aesthetics and the Feminine*. New York: Methuen.

—— (1993) "Fetishism and Its Ironies." In *Fetishism as Cultural Discourse*, edited by Emily Apter and William Pietz. Ithaca: Cornell University Press.

Schorske, Carl (1981) *Fin-de-Siècle Vienna: Politics and Culture*. New York: Vintage Books.

Schuler, Catherine (1990) "Spectator Response and Comprehension: The Problem of Karen Finley's *Constant State of Desire.*" *The Drama Review* 34, no. 1: 131–45.

Schutzman, Mady (1994) "The Aesthetics of Hysteria: Performance, Pathology, and Advertising." Ph.D. dissertation, New York University.

Seigel, Jerrold (1986) *Bohemian Paris: Culture, Politics, and the Boundaries of Bourgeois Life, 1830–1930*. New York: Viking.

Shattuck, Roger (1955) *The Banquet Years: The Origins of the Avant-Garde in France, 1885 to World War I*. New York: Vintage Press.

Sherman, Cindy (1993) *Cindy Sherman, 1975–1993*, text by Rosalind Krauss. New York: Rizzoli.

Showalter, Elaine 1985 *The Female Malady*. New York: Penguin Books.

Solomon, Alisa (forthcoming) *Re-Dressing the Canon: Essays on Theater and Gender*. New York: Routledge.

Solomon-Godeau, Abigail (1991) "Suitable for Framing: The Critical Recasting of Cindy Sherman." *Parkett* no. 29.

Sonnega, William (1995) "Morphing Borders: The Remanence of MTV." *The Drama Review* 39, no. 1: 45–61.

Sontag, Susan (1977) *On Photography*. New York: Farrar, Straus, and Giroux.

—— (1988) "Artaud." In *Antonin Artaud: Selected Writings*, edited by Susan Sontag. Berkeley: University of California Press.

Spiderwoman Theater (1981) "Our Source." Press release.

—— (1992) *Reverb-ber-ber-ations*. *Women and Performance* 5, no. 2: 185–212.

Sprinkle, Annie (1991) *Annie Sprinkle: Post Porn Modernist*. Amsterdam: Torch Books.

Stiles, Kristine (1992) "Survival Ethos and Destruction Art." *Discourse* 14, no. 2 (Spring): 74–102.

—— (1993) "Between Water and Stone: Fluxus Performance, A Metaphysics of Acts." In *In the Spirit of Fluxus*, exhibition publication edited by Elizabeth Armstrong and Joan Rothfuss. Minneapolis: Walker Art Center.

Stoekl, Allan (1985) "Introduction." In George Bataille, *Visions of Excess: Selected Writings, 1927–1939*. Minneapolis: University of Minnesota Press.

Stoianovich, Traian (1981) "Gender and Family: Myths, Models and Ideologies." *The History Teacher* 15, no. 1 (November).

Suleiman, Susan Rubin (1986) "(Re)Writing the Body: The Politics and Poetics of Female Eroticism." In *The Female Body in Western Culture*, edited by Susan Rubin Sulieman. Cambridge, MA: Harvard University Press.

—— (1990) *Subversive Intent: Gender, Politics, and the Avant-Garde*. Cambridge MA, Harvard University Press.

Tannen, Deborah (1993) "Markers: Wears Jump Suit, Sensible Shoes, Uses Husband's Last Name." *New York Times Magazine*, June 20: 18–19, 52–4.

Tannen, Mary (1996) "Counter Intelligence: The Subversive Message of the Small Makeup Companies." *New York Times Magazine*, February 11: 58–9.

Taussig, Michael (1989) "The Nervous System: Homesickness and Dada." *Stanford Humanities Review* 1, no. 1: 44–81.

—— (1992) *The Nervous System.* New York: Routledge.

—— (1993) *Mimesis and Alterity: A Particular History of the Senses.* New York: Routledge.

—— (1994) "Physiognomic Aspects of Visual Worlds." In *Visualizing Theory: Selected Essays from V.A.R.,* edited by Lucien Taylor. New York: Routledge.

Theweleit, Klaus (1987) *Male Fantasies,* vol. 1. Minneapolis: University of Minnesota Press.

Torgovnick, Marianna (1990) *Gone Primitive: Savage Intellects, Modern Lives.* Chicago: University of Chicago Press.

Tzara, Tristan (1976) "Poemes Negres." Translated by Pierre Joris. *Alcheringa/ ethnopoetics* 2, no. 1.

Vance, Carole S., ed. (1983) *Pleasure and Danger: Exploring Female Sexuality.* Boston: Routledge and Kegan Paul.

—— (1989) "The War on Culture." *Art in America* September: 39–45.

—— (1990) "Misunderstanding Obcenity." *Art in America* May: 49–55.

Vattimo, Gianni (1988) *The End of Modernity.* Translated by Jon R. Snyder. Baltimore: Johns Hopkins University Press.

Vitz, Paul C., and Arnold B. Glimcher (1984) *Modern Art and Modern Science: The Parallel Analysis of Vision.* New York: Praeger.

Wandor, Micheline (1986) *Carry On, Understudies.* New York: Routledge and Kegan Paul.

Weigel, Sigrid (1985) "Double Focus: On the History of Women's Writing." In *Feminist Aesthetics,* edited by Gisela Ecker, translated by Harriet Anderson. Boston: Beacon Press.

Whyte, Raewyn (1993) "Robbie McCauley: Speaking History Otherwise." In *Acting Out: Feminist Performance,* edited by Lynda Hart and Peggy Phelan. Ann Arbor: University of Michigan Press.

Williams, Linda (1989) *Hard Core: Power, Pleasure, and the "Frenzy of the Visible."* Berkeley: University of California Press.

Williams, Raymond (1973) *The Country and The City.* New York: Oxford University Press.

—— (1989) *The Politics of Modernism.* New York: Verso.

Williams, Rosalind (1982) *Dream Worlds: Mass Consumption in Late 19th-Century France.* Berkeley: University of California Press.

Williamson, Judith (1983) "Images of Woman," *Screen* 24 (November).

—— (1986a) *Consuming Passions: The Dynamics of Popular Culture.* London: Marion Boyars.

—— (1986b) "Woman is an Island: Femininity and Colonization." In *Studies in Entertainment: Critical Approaches to Mass Culture* edited by Tania Modleski. Bloomington: University of Indiana Press.

Wittig, Monique (1985) "The Mark of Gender," *Feminist Issues* 5, no. 2: 3–12.

Yeats, William Butler (1958) *The Autobiographies of W.B. Yeats.* New York: Macmillan.

Zizek, Slavoj (1989) *The Sublime Object of Ideology.* New York: Verso.

Index